AF375221

# Contents

# Preface

According to the NEP rules set by the Central Board, new syllabus has been offered for University and College students. In this regard, the absence of a proper all- encompassing book catering to the specific needs of students has been felt.

Hence, it is our sincere effort to present before the student, a book that includes both the text as well as possible questions in the exact pattern and syllabi of the semester examinations. The texts have been included for preliminary reading and is supplemented by a through study of an exhaustive complimentary notes. It should be remembered that answers to questions have to both brief and complete, concise and to the point and this book attempts to address such a need of students preparing for the examination.

We are indebted to all our near and dear ones, our teachers and our colleagues for motivating us to undertake such a task.

# CHAPTER ONE

# LITERARY TYPES

## Different types of Novels

### 1.Bildungsroman

The bildungsroman is a specific genre that focuses on the psychological and moral growth of a protagonist from their childhood into maturity, highlighting the personal evolution from youth to adulthood.

The Bildungsroman literary genre originated in Germany. The German word "bildung" means education" and the German word "roman" means "novel." Thus, "Bildungsroman" translates to "a novel of education" or "a novel of formation."

The German word bildungsroman originated in 18th century Germany, with Goethe's novel Wilhelm Meister's Apprenticeship often cited as the first major example of bildungsroman. From its early development in German literature, the bildungsroman spread internationally during the 19th century, shaping the coming-of-age novels genre as it expanded across Europe and beyond. Today, the typical bildungsroman remains a popular narrative form, capturing the universal experience of growing up through its symbolic depiction of the protagonist's search for identity and place in the world.

### Defining Features of Bildungsroman Novels

The bildungsroman definition refers to a literary genre that centers on the psychological and moral growth of a protagonist from youth to adulthood. There are several defining features and characteristics that exemplify the classic example of bildungsroman form.

**Key Supporting Characters in Bildungsroman:** The bildungsroman meaning involves a journey of self-discovery, and the protagonist is often assisted by supporting characters who act as guides or foils. Common archetypes include the wise mentor who provides guidance, close friends or peers who reflect societal pressures, and authority figures who create obstacles that test the protagonist's development. These relationships and interactions shape hvthe protagonist along their journey to maturity.

**Recurring Themes in Bildungsroman Literature:** Maturation, morality, identity, and social pressures are themes frequently explored in examples of Bildungsroman. The contrast between childhood innocence and adult experience is central. Other common themes include family dynamics, developing ideologies, and intellectual growth. The protagonist's inner transformation from youth to adulthood remains the primary focus rather than external events.

**Narrative Techniques in Bildungsroman:** These novels use techniques like frame narratives, intricate backstories, and detailed flashbacks to provide context about the protagonist's past and upbringing. Symbolism and recurring motifs are woven throughout the journey to represent key ideas. The structure follows the character's progression but may not adhere to chronological order.

**Archetypes of Protagonists in Bildungsroman:** The protagonist is typically a sensitive, naïve youth or young adult from the middle or lower classes on a quest for identity. Common types include orphans, students, artists, and other social outsiders. Their bildungsroman examples follow their adventures into unfamiliar realms where their worldview is challenged by new ideologies and experiences.

**Diverse Interpretations of Bildungsroman**

While early a bildungsroman example predominantly featured male protagonists on a stereotypical hero's journey, contemporary interpretations showcase more diverse perspectives. Postmodern and feminist bildungsromans may focus on minorities, women, or other marginalized groups with non-traditional coming-of-age stories. Variations like the kunstlerroman, or "artist's novel" concentrate specifically on an artist's growth to maturity. Bildungsromans have also expanded beyond novels to mediums like film, TV, and graphic novels.

The genre continues to evolve and reinvent itself in different cultural contexts. For example, post-colonial bildungsromans examine issues of race, language, and clashing cultures as protagonists search for identity. The protagonist's journey to adulthood may involve reconciling their heritage with new environments.

**Bildungsroman vs Coming-Of-Age**

The bildungsroman and coming-of-age genres share similarities, but have distinctions. While both focus on a character's transition into adulthood, bildungsromans emphasize the protagonist's inner development versus external events. Coming-of-age stories have a broader scope that may explore relationships or societal issues.

**Characteristics**

Common characteristics of the bildungsroman include a quest for identity, maturation themes, youthful protagonists, and symbolic/ metaphorical journeys. Protagonists are shaped by their relationships, environment, and societal institutions. The structure generally follows a protagonist from childhood into maturity in four main stages that mark their psychological and moral growth.

Bildungsroman novel examples range from 19th century classics like Great Expectations to more contemporary works like The Perks of Being a Wallflower, showcasing the genre's evolution. Bildungsroman book examples also include memoirs and semi-autobiographical novels depicting the author's own coming-of-age experiences.

**Bildungsroman Stages**

The 4 stages of bildungsroman are The Call, The Apprenticeship, Maturity, and Acceptance/Remedy. Each marks a pivotal point in the protagonist's development.

**Stage 1: The Call**

Much like "The Call" in the Heroic Journey, the call spurs the character on their journey towards spiritual or psychological growth. The character is often unhappy with something in their current life, and it pushes them to search for answers to their unhappiness elsewhere in the world.

The protagonist is usually from a small town or village, and they journey to a more complex realm, or to a large city.The protagonist must separate from their family in order to gain an identity that is separate and distinct.The protagonist searches for answers beyond their home.

**Stage 2: The Apprenticeship**

The Apprenticeship is the growth process that the character goes through in order to reach maturity and moral change. This stage is called the Apprenticeship because the character must undertake an education away from their origins in order to learn and to master his or her place in society.Education is crucial to the protagonist's progress into maturity.

The protagonist is often disappointed by this new world, as it does not live up to their expectations.The protagonist finds their education in the disappointment of the new world, and this allows them to successfully mature and gain their distinct identity.

**Stage 3: Maturity**

Maturity is not easily won; it is a long and arduous process, with many mistakes, tests, and internal obstacles that the character must face in order to finally gain maturity. They walk away with a newfound sense of themselves, and they know they are different people now.The protagonist achieves their maturity with difficulty, and it allows them a sense of pride in having obtained it through the tests and obstacles they've had to face.The protagonist experiences psychological, moral, and/or spiritual growth.The protagonist and the readers accept that they are not a superior character: they are flawed, but they are fundamentally good.

**Stage 4: Acceptance and Remedy**

In this stage, the character typically will return to their place of origins, and they will use their newfound knowledge to help others. In some cases, the character will not return home, but they will reach out and try to remedy a situation or a problem using the wisdom they've gained on their journey.The protagonist usually returns to the place they left originally.

The reader is able to see the contrast between the protagonist at the beginning of the novel and the person they've become once they return to the place they left.

The protagonist is able to help others with their newfound maturity and wisdom.

**2.Picaresque novel**

The picaresque novel (Spanish: "picaresco", from "pícaro", for "rogue" or "rascal") is a popular style of novel that originated in Spain and flourished in Europe in the 17th and 18th centuries and has continued to influence modern literature. The term denotes a subgenre of usually satiric prose fiction and depicts in realistic, often humorous detail the adventures of a roguish hero of low social degree living by his or her wits in a corrupt society.

Lazarillo de Tormes, published anonymously in Antwerp and Spain in 1554 is variously considered either the first picaresque novel or an antecedent to the genre. The title character Lazarillo is a pícaro who must live by his wits in an impoverished country full of hypocrisy. The autobiography of Benvenuto Cellini, written in Florence beginning in 1558, also has much in common with the picaresque. The first unquestioned picaresque novel was published in 1599: Mateo Alemán's Guzmán de Alfarache, characterized by religiosity. Francisco de Quevedo's El buscón (1626) is considered the masterpiece of the subgenre, because of his baroque style and the study of the delinquent psychology.

In other European countries, these Spanish novels were read and imitated. In Germany, Grimmelshausen wrote Simplicissimus (1669), the most important of non-Spanish picaresque novels. It describes the devastation caused by the Thirty Years' War. In France, this kind of novel declined into an aristocratic adventure: Le Sage's Gil Blas (1715). In England, the body of Tobias Smollett's work, and Daniel Defoe's Moll Flanders (1722) are considered picaresque, but they lack of the sense of religious redemption of delinquency that was very important in Spanish and German novels. The triumph of Moll Flanders is more economic than moral.

In the English-speaking world, the term "picaresque" has referred more to a literary technique or model than to the precise genre that the Spanish call picaresco. The English-language term can simply refer to an episodic recounting of the adventures of an antihero on the road. Henry Fielding proved his mastery of the form in Joseph Andrews (1742), The Life of Jonathan Wild the Great (1743) and The History of Tom Jones, a Foundling (1749), but, as Fielding himself wrote, these novels were written in imitation of the manner of Cervantes, author of Don Quixote, not in imitation of the picaresque novel.

Other novels with elements of the picaresque include the French Candide, and the later English The Luck of Barry Lyndon.

**3.Gothic Novel**

The term "Gothic" was first used in conjunction with a Medieval style of ornate and intricate architecture that originated in France around the 12th century. It wasn't until the Romantic era in the late 18th century that the word was applied to literature. The first mention of Gothic literature appeared in English writer Horace Walpole's The Castle of Otranto, published in 1764. Walpole applied the word in the subtitle, "A Gothic Story." The use was intended to be a sophisticated joke to suggest that the story was an antique relic even though it was mere fiction.

Walpole used the word "Gothic" in the sense of "barbarous" or "deriving from Middle Ages," and many were even fooled into believing his story actually held truth. His tale of love, death, and supernatural elements paved the way for a fictional genre that has been explored by prominent authors from the likes of Edgar Allan Poe, the Brontë sisters, and many more. Although the books from these prolific writers were published centuries ago, today they provide a strong connection to the past and an important resource for both contemporary fiction writers and avid literary collectors alike.

## What is Gothic Literature?

Gothic literature is a genre that emerged as one of the eeriest forms of Dark Romanticism in the late 1700s, a literary genre that emerged as a part of the larger Romanticism movement. Dark Romanticism is characterized by expressions of terror, gruesome narratives, supernatural elements, and dark, picturesque scenery. This fictional genre encompasses many different elements, and has undergone a series of revivals since its inception.

## Defining Elements of Gothic Literature

Many of the defining elements of Gothic literature parallel those of the Middle Ages, incorporating similar themes and settings. Readers' fascination with terror paved the way for a thrilling new ideal that helped popularize the movement. There are many aspects of Gothic literature that make it compelling to audiences both then and now, which include mystery and suspense, atmosphere and setting, and omens and curses.

### 1. Mystery and Fear

One of the crucial components of a captivating Gothic story evokes feelings of suspense and fear. Anything that is beyond scientific understanding lends way to mystery, and Gothic atmospheres leverage this principle. Many Gothic works contain scenes, events and objects such as burials, flickering candles, evil potions, and other frightful concepts.

We see this in Ann Radcliffe's 1794 novel, *The Mysteries of Udolpho*. The story centers around Emily St. Aubert, an orphaned girl who was subjected to cruelties by guardians and imprisoned in castles. The work included strange, fearful events and a haunting atmosphere that came to define the genre in the years to come.

### 2. Omens and Curses

Foreshadowing, a literary device used to hint at events to come, occurs in the form of visions, omens, and curses throughout many narratives in Gothic literature. Often, tragedies are preceded by bad luck, intended to derail the lives of main characters. For example, an object might fall and break or a shadowy figure might be lurking in the dark. Edgar Allan Poe uses this element in his short story, "The Black Cat," published in 1843. The superstitious nature of the title is ominous in itself, and Poe furthers the foreshadowing by naming one of the cats "Pluto," a reference to the god of the dead in Roman mythology.

### 3. Atmosphere and Setting

Gothic novelists set the tone by carefully choosing the physical location of a scene, as the atmosphere and environment of a Gothic novel directly contributed to the feeling of fear and uneasiness. Authors often used settings like dark forests, unnerving mountain regions, ominous climatic conditions, and threatening storms. Castles, romanticized in the Medieval period, played a large role in early Gothic writings. For example, Gothic writer Mary Shelley set her scenes amid creepy locations such as graveyards, gloomy castles, and even developed the persona of a grotesque monster to emphasize the eerie plot of her 1818 novel **Frankenstein**.

Many early writers had a fascination with exoticism and foreign, unexplored territory. This was explored in William Beckford's 1786 novel Vathek, an omniscient story about an Arabian caliph whose reign is marked by turbulence and unrest. It is set in the Middle East and helped spark interest in Arab and Asian culture.

**4. Supernatural and Paranormal Activity**

Much of Gothic literature's allure comes from the genre's suggestion of supernatural or inexplicable events, such as inanimate objects coming to life, ghosts, spirits, and vampires like that of Bram Stoker's 1897 Gothic fantasy, Dracula.

A more contemporary, and less conventional, example is Toni Morrison's Beloved, which was published in 1987 and is widely considered to be a modern take on the traditional Gothic novel. The story centers around a former slave named Sethe, and her daughter, whose home in Cincinnati is haunted by a revenant believed to the ghost of Sethe's eldest daughter. It follows the convention of fear and horror, calling upon supernatural elements like that of the ghost to drive the plot.

**5. Romance**

As it's widely believed Gothic literature stemmed from Romantic literature, the two genres share overlapping characteristics. Many Gothic novels are plagued by a passionate romance that often leads to sorrow and tragedy. The works of Charles Dickens centered on a Romantic-style love affair, but also featured horrific villains and Gothic settings. In the Victorian era, Gothic novels even provided an outlet for exploration of sexuality, as seen in Edgar Allan Poe's 1849 poem, "Annabel Lee."

**6. Villain**

Much like that of various literary genres, villains play a pivotal role in Gothic literature. In traditional Gothic novels, villains took the form of autocratic, male characters, often in authoritative positions like that of priests or kings. They're complex, and initially sympathetic as to fool the reader of their deceptive nature. Villains like Dracula and Mr. Hyde from

Robert Louis Stevenson's, The Strange Case of Dr. Jekyll and Mr. Hyde are examples of complex, villainous characters.

### 7. Emotional Distress

Often, Gothic writers use melodrama or "high emotion" to convey a thought. This exaggerated, impassioned language helps convey the panic and terror inherent in many characters. Themes of madness and emotional distress were seen in many of the 20th century Gothic novels that depicted the condition of psychosis. For example, Charlotte Perkins Gilman's short story, "The Yellow Wallpaper," is written from the perspective of a woman suffering from postpartum depression.

### 8. Nightmares

Nightmares serve as a particularly important omen within Gothic literature. Nightmares have an ancient association with the act of foretelling and were used to exacerbate the haunting aspects of a novel's plot. The dreams allow authors to better demonstrate the emotions of their characters in a more immediate and frightening state. Stephen King's Bag of Bones depicts that of Mike Noonan, a character plagued by nightmares of frightening visions including the death of his wife.

### 9. Anti-hero

More often than not, the protagonist takes the form of the anti-hero, a flawed protagonist with monstrous elements popularized by this genre of writing. Originally, protagonists were males as well, but as the feminist movement emerged, English novelists like Clara Reeve began introducing female protagonists into their works.

Protagonists tend to hold a high social rank and strong physical presence. Their doom is foreshadowed, and they are burdened by sorrow or a horrific tragedy. Often, they're easily influenced, driven much by passion. Classic protagonist examples include Cathy and Heathcliff from Emily Bronte's Wuthering Heights, and Dorian Gray from Oscar Wilde's **The Picture of Dorian Gray.**

### 10. Damsel in Distress

Gothic works often include a woman who suffers at the expense of a villain. They carry feelings of sadness, oppression, and loneliness, and many were depicted as virginal in early Gothic pieces. The damsel's character is often held captive in a castle, terrorized by a nobleman, and rendered powerless. This brooding woman appealed to the readers' pathos, particularly with the example of Horace Walpole's character Matilda, whose unwavering loyalty to her father ultimately makes her weak and powerless.

**4.Epistolary Novel**

An epistolary (pronounced eh-PI-stuh-lair-ee) novel is one where the story is told through written communication. Usually this means letters, but it can also include documents, diary entries, newspaper clippings, and any other form of written communication. "Epistolary" comes from the Latin word "epistola," meaning "letter." This form of narrative writing gained popularity in the 18th century, and it includes some famous novels such as Frankenstein, Dracula, and The Color Purple. The epistolary style is still used in literature, but oftentimes through text messages, email chains, blogs, notes, and social media posts rather than letters.

**The history of epistolary novels**

Since the letter predates the novel, it was common for writers to include letters as part of their narratives when novels first emerged in the 16th and 17th centuries in Europe. One of the first notable epistolary novels was called Love-Letters Between a Nobleman and His Sister, which was published anonymously beginning in 1684 and which has been attributed to Aphra Behn, a groundbreaking woman writer. This narrative explored historical events and themes of love, scandal, and politics through letters.

The word "epistolary" appeared in English around the 1740s to describe literary works composed of letters, which coincided with the surge in popularity of epistolary novels such as Samuel Richardson's Pamela, published in 1740. Often considered one of the most influential epistolary novels, Pamela explores themes of ethics and psychology through stream-of-consciousness-style writing in letters.

The epistolary form continued to thrive during the late 18th and early 19th centuries, with notable examples including Les Liaisons dangereuses (Dangerous Liaisons) by Pierre Choderlos de Laclos, published beginning in 1782, and Johann Wolfgang von Goethe's The Sorrows of Young Werther, published in 1774. In the 19th century, epistolary novels decreased in popularity, but out of this time period came the famous stories of Frankenstein, first published in 1818, and Dracula, in 1897.

Elements of epistolary writing are still widely used today. They incorporate documentation and intimate diary entries into storylines to give readers new perspectives on the characters and plot

**Why do authors write epistolary novels?**

There are a few reasons an author might use epistolary writing to tell their story:

1.Epistolary novels offer multiple first-person points of view.

2.Readers are given a deep sense of intimacy and authenticity through exposure to the characters' innermost thoughts.

3.Readers must be actively engaged in the story to understand how the characters' communications—and the supporting documents when those are presented—are building a plot.

4.Epistolary novels are great for exploring historical and cultural events in a narrative through firsthand accounts.

**Epistolary novel examples**

There are a few notable classics that are written as epistolary novels. Below are a few.

**Frankenstein, by Mary Shelley (1818)**

The story unfolds through letters exchanged, as well as the personal accounts of Dr. Frankenstein and the monster he creates.

**Dracula, by Bram Stoker (1897)**

Stoker's classic novel is presented in the form of letters, diary entries, and newspaper articles. The varied perspectives build suspense as characters chronicle their experiences with the iconic Count Dracula.

**84, Charing Cross Road, by Helene Hanff (1970)**

In this book, letters are exchanged between the author, Helene Hanff, a writer in New York, and the staff of a London bookshop. The letters cover a period of twenty years, creating an endearing story about a friendship that develops through a shared love for books.

**The Color Purple, by Alice Walker (1982)**

This Pulitzer Prize–winning novel unfolds through letters written by the main character to God and later her sister. The letters reveal the main character's struggles and personal evolution, exploring topics of race, gender, love, and resilience.

**The Perks of Being a Wallflower, by Stephen Chbosky (1999)**

This emotional, contemporary novel is told in a series of letters addressed to "Dear friend," an unnamed character to whom Charlie, the main character, confesses his most private insecurities.

Many popular contemporary novels use epistolary elements, such as The Handmaid's Tale, by Margaret Atwood, Daisy Jones & the Six, by Taylor Jenkins Reid, and The Silent Patient, by Alex Michaelides. While they are not written in the traditional epistolary fashion, they include personal accounts through documents or scripts that bring authentic and nuanced perspectives to them.

# *Short Story*

A short story is a brief work of fiction that typically focuses on a single event, character, or idea. It's a straightforward narrative that aims to arouse emotions, convey a message, or explore a theme within a limited space. Short stories usually have fewer characters and a simpler plot, but they can be just as impactful. They often contain elements like a clear setting, character development, a central conflict, and a resolution.

A short story is a work of prose fiction that can be read in one sitting—usually between 20 minutes to an hour. There is no maximum length, but the average short story is 1,000 to 7,500 words, with some outliers reaching 10,000 or 15,000 words. At around 10 to 25 pages, that makes short stories much shorter than novels, with only a few approaching novella length. A piece of fiction shorter than 1,000 words is considered a "short short story" or "flash fiction," and anything less than 300 words is rightfully called "microfiction."

**Characteristics of Short story :-**

- **Shortness**: Short stories are straightforward narratives with a limited word count, typically ranging from a few hundred to a few thousand words. They focus on a single incident, idea, or character.
- **Focused Plot:** Due to their shortness, short stories usually have a single plotline with a clear beginning, middle, and end. They often circle a central conflict or theme.
- **Character Development**: While shorter in length, short stories can still feature well-developed characters. Authors use straightforward descriptions and actions to reveal the characters' qualities and motivations.
- **Limited Setting:** Short stories often occur in a confined setting or a limited number of locations. This constraint helps maintain focus on the central theme or conflict.
- **Economical Use of Language**: Every word counts in a short story. Authors carefully choose words to convey meaning, emotion, and atmosphere efficiently.
- **Single Theme or Message**: Short stories manage to explore a single theme, idea, or message. Authors use the limited space to give depth through symbolism, imagery, or subtext.

**The key elements of a short story**

The **setting** of a short story is often simplified (one time and place), and one or two **main characters** may be introduced without full backstories. In this concise, concentrated format, every word and story detail has to work extra hard!

Short stories typically focus on a single **plot** instead of multiple subplots, as you might see in novels. Some stories follow a traditional narrative arc, with exposition (description) at the beginning, rising action, a climax (peak moment of conflict or action), and a resolution at the end. However, contemporary short fiction is more likely to begin in the middle of the action (*in medias res*), drawing readers right into a dramatic scene.

While short stories of the past often revolved around a **central theme** or moral lesson, today it is common to find stories with ambiguous endings. This type of unresolved story invites open-ended readings and suggests a more complex understanding of reality and human behavior.

The short story <u>genre</u> is well suited to experimentation in prose writing style and form, but most short story authors still work to create a distinct mood using classic <u>literary devices</u> (point of view, imagery, foreshadowing, metaphor, diction/word choice, tone, and sentence structure).

**The history of the short story**

Short-form storytelling can be traced back to ancient legends, mythology, folklore, and fables found in communities all over the world. Some of these stories existed in written form, but many were passed down through oral traditions. By the 14th century, the most well-known stories included One Thousand and One Nights (Middle Eastern folk tales by multiple authors, later known as Arabian Nights) and Canterbury Tales (by Geoffrey Chaucer).

It wasn't until the early 19th century that short story collections by individual authors appeared more regularly in print. First, it was the publication of the Brothers Grimm fairy tales, then Edgar Allen Poe's Gothic fiction, and eventually, stories by Anton Chekhov, who is often credited as a founder of the modern short story.

The popularity of short stories grew along with the surge of <u>print magazines</u> and journals. Newspaper and magazine editors began publishing stories as entertainment, creating a demand for short, plot-driven narratives with mass appeal. By the early 1900s, The Atlantic Monthly, The New Yorker, and Harper's Magazine were paying good money for short stories that showed more literary techniques. That golden era of publishing gave rise to the short story as we know it today.

**Different types of short stories**

Short stories come in all kinds of categories: action, adventure, biography, comedy, crime, detective, drama, dystopia, fable, fantasy, history, horror, mystery, philosophy, politics, romance, satire, science fiction, supernatural, thriller, tragedy, and Western. Here are some popular types of short stories, literary styles, and authors associated with them:

- **Fable**: A tale that provides a moral lesson, often using animals, mythical creatures, forces of nature, or inanimate objects to come to life (Brothers Grimm, Aesop)
- Flash fiction: A story between 5 to 2,000 words that lacks traditional plot structure or character development and is often characterized by a surprise or twist of fate (Lydia Davis)
- **Mini saga**: A type of micro-fiction using exactly 50 words (!) to tell a story
- Vignette: A descriptive scene or defining moment that does not contain a complete plot or narrative but reveals an important detail about a character or idea (Sandra Cisneros)
- **Modernism**: Experimenting with narrative form, style, and chronology (inner monologues, stream of consciousness) to capture the experience of an individual (James Joyce, Virginia Woolf)
- **Postmodernism**: Using fragmentation, paradox, or unreliable narrators to explore the relationship between the author, reader, and text (Donald Barthelme, Jorge Luis Borges)
- **Magical realism**: Combining realistic narrative or setting with elements of surrealism, dreams, or fantasy (Gabriel García Márquez)
- **Minimalism**: Writing characterized by brevity, straightforward language, and a lack of plot resolutions (Raymond Carver, Amy Hempel)

Famous short stories are "The Gift of the Magi" by O. Henry, "The Luncheon" by William Somerset Maugham, "Young Goodman Brown" by Nathaniel Hawthorne and "Araby" by James Joyce.

## *Essay*

The essay is a written piece that is designed to present an idea, propose an argument, express the emotion or initiate debate. It is a tool that is used to present writer's ideas in a non-fictional way. Multiple applications of this type of writing go way beyond, providing political manifestos and art criticism as well as personal observations and reflections of the author.An essay can be as short as 500 words, it can also be 5000 words or more. However, most essays fall somewhere around *1000 to 3000 words*; this word range provides the writer enough space to thoroughly develop an argument and work to convince the reader of the author's perspective regarding a particular issue. The topics of essays are boundless: they can range from the best form of government to the benefits of eating peppermint leaves daily. As a professional provider of custom writing, our service has helped thousands of customers to turn in essays in various forms and disciplines.

The type of essay will depend on what the writer wants to convey to his reader. There are broadly four types of essays.

**Narrative Essays:** This is when the writer is narrating an incident or story through the essay. So these are in the first person. The aim when writing narrative essays is to involve the reader in them as if they were right there when it was happening. So make them as vivid and real as possible. One way to make this possible is to follow the principle of 'show, don't tell'. So you must involve the reader in the story.

**Descriptive Essays:** Here the writer will describe a place, an object, an event or maybe even a memory. But it is not just plainly describing things. The writer must paint a picture through his words. One clever way to do that is to evoke the senses of the reader. Do not only rely on sight but also involve the other senses of smell, touch, sound etc. A descriptive essay when done well will make the reader feel the emotions the writer was feeling at the moment.

**Expository Essays:** In such an essay a writer presents a balanced study of a topic. To write such an essay, the writer must have real and extensive knowledge about the subject. There is no scope for the writer's feelings or emotions in an expository essay. It is completely based on facts, statistics, examples etc. There are sub-types here like contrast essays, cause and effect essays etc.

**Persuasive Essays:** Here the purpose of the essay is to get the reader to your side of the argument. A persuasive essay is not just a presentation of facts but an attempt to convince the reader of the writer's point of view. Both sides of the argument have to presented in these essays. But the ultimate aim is to persuade the readers that the writer's argument carries more weight.

## *Origins of the Essay*

Over the course of more than six centuries essays were used to question assumptions, argue trivial opinions and to initiatc global discussions. *Let's have a closer look into historical progress and various applications of this literary phenomenon to find out exactly what it is.*

Today's modern word *"essay"* can trace its roots back to the French *"essayer"* which translates closely to mean ***"to attempt"***. This is an apt name for this writing form because the essay's ultimate purpose is to attempt to convince the audience of something. An essay's topic can range broadly and include everything from the best of Shakespeare's plays to the joys of April.

The essay comes in many shapes and sizes; it can focus on a personal experience or a purely academic exploration of a topic. Essays are classified as a subjective writing form because while they include expository elements, they can rely on personal narratives to support the writer's viewpoint. The essay genre includes a diverse array of academic writings ranging from literary criticism to meditations on the natural world. Most typically, the essay exists as a shorter writing form; essays are rarely the length of a novel. However, several historic examples, such as John Locke's seminal work "An Essay Concerning Human Understanding" just shows that a well-organized essay can be as long as a novel.

## *The Essay in Literature*

The essay enjoys a long and renowned history in literature. They first began gaining in popularity in the early 16th century, and their popularity has continued today both with original writers and ghost writers. Many readers prefer this short form in which the writer seems to speak directly to the reader, presenting a particular claim and working to defend it through a variety of means. Not sure if you've ever read a great essay? You wouldn't believe how many pieces of literature are actually nothing less than essays, or evolved into more complex structures from the essay. Check out this list of literary favorites:

- **The Book of My Lives** by Aleksandar Hemon
- **Notes of a Native Son** by James Baldwin
- **Against Interpretation** by Susan Sontag

- **High-Tide in Tucson: Essays from Now and Never** by Barbara Kingsolver
- **Slouching Toward Bethlehem** by Joan Didion
- **Naked** by David Sedaris
- **Walden; or, Life in the Woods** by Henry David Thoreau

# Memoir

A memoir is a narrative, written from the perspective of the author, about an important part of their life. It's often conflated with autobiography, but there are a few important differences. An autobiography is also written from the author's perspective, but the narrative spans their entire life. Although it's subjective, it primarily focuses on facts – the who-what-when-where-why-how of their life's entire timeline. Booker T. Washington's Up from Slavery is an example of autobiography – the story begins with his childhood as a slave, proceeds through his emancipation and education, and ends in his present life as an entrepreneur.

To define memoir, we loosen the constraints of an autobiography. Memoir authors choose a pivotal moment in their lives and try to recreate the event through storytelling. The author's feelings and assumptions are central to the narrative. Memoirs still include all the facts of the event, but the author has more flexibility here because she is telling a story as she remembers it, not as others can prove or disprove it. (In fact, "memoir" comes from the French "mémoire" or "memory.") In Night, the Nobel Prize-winning title, Elie Wiesel tells his own story about one period of his life – how he survived his teenage years at Auschwitz and Buchenwald.

## *History of the Memoir*

In A.D. 397, St. Augustine of Hippo began writing The Confessions of Saint Augustine, telling the world of his sins: "It was foul, and I loved it. I loved my own undoing." Ever since, we've been hooked on the idea that we can get to know a stranger so intimately, even (and especially) a famous one. Although Confessions is technically an autobiography in structure, the intimacy of his narrative was a new phenomenon. From there, we can draw a straight line to all memoirs that followed.

Like a family tree, once a memoir type emerges, it gives rise to a number of sub-categories. In his book, Memoir: A History, Ben Yagoda gives a string of examples connecting Augustine's Confessions to the modern success of spiritual memoirs. Thus, Anne Lamott's Traveling Mercies: Some Thoughts on Faith and Elizabeth Gilbert's Eat Pray Love are a part of a long litcrary tradition. In turn, the success of books like Eat Pray Love fuels the demand for other "schtick lit" titles like The Happiness Project by Gretchen Rubin and Julie & Julia: My Year of Cooking Dangerously by Julie Powell. Also, let's note that Julie & Julia/i> follows the long tradition of "My year of..." memoirs, which includes beloved titles like Henry David Thoreau's Walden.

## *Types of Memoir*

There is no finite number of memoir sub-categories, just as there are no finite types of experiences we have as thinking, feeling human beings. So, what does memoir mean today? Most of them fall into several large types, but with a definite chance of overlap.

Transformation memoirs are written after an author has endured a great challenge. These stories almost always include a theme of redemption, whether it's achieved or missing. For example:

In **Finding Freedom**, Erin French first discovers her love for cooking as a young girl in her father's diner in Freedom, Maine. But in early adulthood, she struggles through prescription drug addiction, a daunting custody battle for her son, and multiple rock-bottoms, until she ultimately finds renewal through her community and love for food, opening the critically acclaimed restaurant The Lost Kitchen.

**Here We Are: American Dreams, American Nightmares** is Aarti Namdev Shahani's family immigrant story, of how an unknown dealing with a drug cartel led to her father being sent to Rikers Island, and a study in how difficult it is to make it in America.

**Educated** is Tara Westover's incredible account of how she overcame a childhood spent in survivalist camps in rural Idaho and worked her way into Harvard and Cambridge universities.

Confessional memoirs are unapologetically bold. The author shares painful or difficult secrets about themselves or their family and how it has affected them. For example:

Jean-Jacques Rousseau's **Confessions** shocked readers in that it was a secular coming-of-age story, and because it contained unexpected details of his life, like his sexual preferences.

**Running with Scissors** is Augusten Burroughs' childhood laid bare. His mother left him to be raised by her psychiatrist who lived in squalor, never sent him to school, and never protected him from the pedophile living in the back yard.

Professional or celebrity memoirs cover important moments in the author's rise to fame and success. Some examples include:

**I Am Malala** by Malala Yousafzai details her horrible attack by the Taliban, her recovery, and her decision to fight for girls' education worldwide.

**Just Kids** by Patti Smith is a beautiful recollection of her friendship with Robert Mapplethorpe in the years before they became famous.

Travel memoirs let us escape with the author and learn about a time and place through their experiences. For example:

Cheryl Strayed's **Wild** takes us on her emotional solo journey along the Pacific Crest Trail as she grieves the loss of her mother and her marriage.

**A Year in Provence** is Peter Mayle's heartwarming account of the year that he threw caution to the wind and moved his family into a crumbling, 200-year-old farmhouse in the French countryside.

# Biography

A biography is simply the story of a real person's life. It could be about a person who is still alive, someone who lived centuries ago, someone who is globally famous, an unsung hero forgotten by history, or even a unique group of people. The facts of their life, from birth to death (or the present day of the author), are included with life-changing moments often taking center stage. The author usually points to the subject's childhood, coming-of-age events, relationships, failures, and successes in order to create a well-rounded description of her subject.

Biographies require a great deal of research. Sources of information could be as direct as an interview with the subject providing their own interpretation of their life's events. When writing about people who are no longer with us, biographers look for primary sources left behind by the subject and, if possible, interviews with friends or family. Historical biographers may also include accounts from other experts who have studied their subject.

The biographer's ultimate goal is to recreate the world their subject lived in and describe how they functioned within it. Did they change their world? Did their world change them? Did they transcend the time in which they lived? Why or why not? And how? These universal life lessons are what make biographies such a meaningful read.

**Origins of the Biography**

Greco-Roman literature honored the gods as well as notable mortals. Whether winning or losing, their behaviors were to be copied or seen as cautionary tales. One of the earliest examples written exclusively about humans is Plutarch's _Parallel Lives_ (probably early 2nd century AD). It's a collection of biographies in which a pair of men, one Greek and one Roman, are compared and held up as either a good or bad example to follow.

In the Middle Ages, Einhard's _The Life of Charlemagne_ (around 817 AD) stands out as one of the most famous biographies of its day. Einhard clearly fawns over Charlemagne's accomplishments throughout, yet it doesn't diminish the value this biography has brought to centuries of historians since its writing.

Considered the earliest modern biography, _The Life of Samuel Johnson_ (1791) by James Boswell looks like the biographies we know today. Boswell conducted interviews, performed years of research, and created a compelling narrative of his subject.

The genre evolves as the 20th century arrives, and with it the first World War. The 1920s saw a boom in autobiographies in response. Robert Graves' _Good-Bye to All That_ (1929) is a coming-of age story set amid the absurdity of war and its aftermath. That same year, Mahatma Gandhi wrote _The Story of My Experiments with Truth_, recalling how the events of his life led him to develop his theories of nonviolent rebellion. In this time, celebrity tell-alls also emerged as a popular form of entertainment.

With the horrors of World War II and the explosion of the civil rights movement, American biographers of the late 20th century had much to archive. Instantly hailed as some of the best writing about the war, John Hersey's _Hiroshima_ (1946) tells the stories of six people who lived through those world-altering days. Alex Haley wrote the as-told-to _The Autobiography of Malcom X_ (1965). Yet with biographies, the more things change, the more they stay the same. One theme that persists is a biographer's desire to cast its subject in an updated light, as in _Eleanor and Hick: The Love Affair that Shaped a First Lady_ by Susan Quinn (2016).

**Types of Biographies**

**Contemporary Biography: Authorized or Unauthorized**

The typical modern biography tells the life of someone still alive, or who has recently passed. Sometimes these are authorized — written with permission or input from the subject or their family — like Dave Itzkoff's intimate look at the life and career of Robin Williams, _Robin_. Unauthorized biographies of living people run the risk of being controversial. Kitty Kelley's infamous _His Way: The Unauthorized Biography of Frank Sinatra_ so angered Sinatra, he tried to prevent its publication.

**Historical Biography**

The wild success of Lin-Manuel Miranda's _Hamilton_ is proof that our interest in historical biography is as strong as ever. Miranda was inspired to write the musical after reading Ron Chernow's _Alexander Hamilton_, an epic 800+ page biography intended to cement Hamilton's status as a great American. Paula Gunn Allen also sets the record straight on another misunderstood historical figure with _Pocahontas: Medicine Woman, Spy, Entrepreneur, Diplomat_, revealing details about her tribe, her family, and her relationship with John Smith that are usually missing from other accounts. Historical biographies also give the spotlight to people who died without ever getting the recognition they deserved, such as _The Immortal Life of Henrietta Lacks_.

**Biography of a Group**

When a group of people share unique characteristics, they can be the topic of a collective biography. The earliest example of this is Captain Charles Johnson's _A General History of the Pirates_ (1724), which catalogs the lives of notorious pirates and establishes the popular culture images we still associate with them. Smaller groups are also deserving of a biography, as seen in David Hajdu's _Positively 4th Street_, a mesmerizing behind-the-scenes look at the early years of Bob Dylan, Joan Baez, Mimi Baez Fariña, and Richard Fariña as they establish the folk scene in New York City. Likewise, British royal family fashion is a vehicle for telling the life stories of four iconic royals – Queen Elizabeth II, Diana, Kate, and Meghan – in _HRH: So Many Thoughts on Royal Style_ by style journalist Elizabeth Holmes.

**Autobiography**

This type of biography is written about one's self, spanning an entire life up to the point of its writing. One of the earliest autobiographies is

Saint Augustine's _The Confessions_ (400), in which his own experiences from childhood through his religious conversion are told in order to create a sweeping guide to life. Maya Angelou's _I Know Why the Caged Bird Sings_ is the first of six autobiographies that share all the pain of her childhood and the long road that led to her work in the civil rights movement, and a beloved, prize-winning writer.

**Memoir**

Memoirs are a type of autobiography, written about a specific but vital aspect of one's life. In _Toil & Trouble_, Augusten Burroughs explains how he has lived his life as a witch. Mikel Jollett's _Hollywood Park_ recounts his early years spent in a cult, his family's escape, and his rise to success with his band, The Airborne Toxic Event. Barack Obama's first presidential memoir, _A Promised Land_, charts his path into politics and takes a deep dive into his first four years in office.

**Fictional Biography**

Fictional biographies are no substitute for a painstakingly researched scholarly biography, but they're definitely meant to be more entertaining. _Z: A Novel of Zelda Fitzgerald_ by Therese Anne Fowler constructs Zelda and F. Scott's wild, Jazz-Age life, told from Zelda's point of view. _The Only Woman in the Room_by Marie Benedict brings readers into the secret life of Hollywood actress and wartime scientist, Hedy Lamarr. These imagined biographies, while often whimsical, still respect the form in that they depend heavily on facts when creating setting, plot, and characters.

## Autobiography vs. Biography vs. Memoir

## _Biography_

A biography, also called a bio, is a non-fiction piece of work giving an objective account of a person's life. The main difference between a biography vs. an autobiography is that the author of a biography is not the subject. A biography could be someone still living today, or it could be the subject of a person who lived years ago.

Biographies include details of key events that shaped the subject's life, and information about their birthplace, education, work, and relationships.

Biographers use a number of research sources, including interviews, letters, diaries, photographs, essays, reference books, and newspapers. While a biography is usually in the written form, it can be produced in other formats such as music composition or film.

If the target person of the biography is not alive, then the storytelling requires an immense amount of research. Interviews might be required to collect information from historical experts, people who knew the person (e.g., friends and family), or reading other older accounts from other people who wrote about the person in previous years. In biographies where the person is still alive, the writer can conduct several interviews with the target person to gain insight on their life.

The goal of a biography is to take the reader through the life story of the person, including their childhood into adolescence and teenage years, and then their early adult life into the rest of their years. The biography tells a story of how the person learned life's lessons and the ways the person navigated the world. It should give the reader a clear picture of the person's personality, traits, and their interaction in the world.

Biographies can also be focused on groups of people and not just one person. For example, a biography can be a historical account of a group of people from hundreds of years ago. This group could have the main person who was a part of the group, and the author writes about the group to tell a story of how they shaped the world.

Fictional biographies mix some true historical accounts with events to help improve the story. Think of fictional biographies as movies that display a warning that the story is made of real characters, but some events are fictional to add to the storyline and entertainment value. A lot of research still goes into a fictional biography, but the author has more room to create a storyline instead of sticking to factual events.

Examples of famous biographies include:

- His Excellency: George Washington by Joseph J. Ellis
- Einstein: The Life and Times by Ronald William Clark
- Princess Diana – A Biography of The Princess of Wales by Drew L. Crichton

# Autobiography

An autobiography is the story of a person's life written by that person. Because the author is also the main character of the story, autobiographies are written in the first person. Usually, an autobiography is written by the person who is the subject of the book, but sometimes the autobiography is written by another person. Because an autobiography is usually a life story for the author, the theme can be anything from religious to a personal account to pass on to children.

The purpose of an autobiography is to portray the life experiences and achievements of the author. Therefore, most autobiographies are typically written later in the subject's life. It's written from the point of view of the author, so it typically uses first person accounts to describe the story.

An autobiography often begins during early childhood and chronologically details key events throughout the author's life. Autobiographies usually include information about where a person was born and brought up, their education, career, life experiences, the challenges they faced, and their key achievements.

On rare occasions, an autobiography is created from a person's diary or memoirs. When diaries are used, the author must organize them to create a chronological and cohesive story. The story might have flashbacks or flashforwards to describe a specific event, but the main storyline should follow chronological order from the author's early life to their current events.

One of the main differences between an autobiography vs. a biography is that autobiographies tend to be more subjective. That's because they are written by the subject, and present the facts based on their own memories of a specific situation, which can be biased. The story covers the author's opinions on specific subjects and provides an account of their feelings as they navigate certain situations. These stories are also very personal because it's a personal account of the author's life rather than a biography where a third party writes about a specific person.

Examples of famous autobiographies include:

- The Story of My Life by Helen Keller
- The Diary of a Young Girl by Anne Frank
- Losing My Virginity by Richard Branson

## *Memoir*

Memoir comes from the French word mémoire, meaning memory or reminiscence. Similar to an autobiography, a memoir is the story of a person's life written by that person. These life stories are often from diary entries either from a first-person account or from a close family member or friend with access to personal diaries.

The difference between a memoir vs. an autobiography is that a memoir focuses on reflection and establishing an emotional connection, rather than simply presenting the facts about their life. The author uses their personal knowledge to tell an intimate and emotional story about the private or public happenings in their life. The author could be the person in the story, or it can be written by a close family member or friend who knew the subject person intimately. The topic is intentionally focused and does not include biographical or chronological aspects of the author's life unless they are meaningful and relevant to the story.

Memoirs come in several types, all of which are written as an emotional account of the target person. They usually tell a story of a person who went through great struggles or faced challenges in a unique way. They can also cover confessionals where the memoir tells the story of the author's account that contradicts another's account.

This genre of writing is often stories covering famous people's lives, such as celebrities. In many memoir projects, the celebrity or person of interest needs help with organization, writing the story, and fleshing out ideas from the person's diaries. It might take several interviews before the story can be fully outlined and written, so it's not uncommon for a memoir project to last several months.

Memoirs do not usually require as much research as biographies and autobiographies, because you have the personal accounts in diary entries and documents with the person's thoughts. It might require several interviews, however, before the diary entries can be organized to give an accurate account on the person's thoughts and emotions. The story does not necessarily need to be in chronological order compared to an autobiography, but it might be to tell a better story.

Examples of famous memoirs include:

- Angela's Ashes by Frank McCourt
- I Know Why the Caged Bird Sings by Maya Angelou

- Personal Memoirs of Ulysses S. Grant by Ulysses S. Grant

# Travelogue

Travel writing is a genre that is becoming increasingly popular. A travelogue is a truthful account of an individual's experiences traveling, usually told in the past tense and in the first person.

The word travelogue supposedly comes from a combination of the two words travel and monologue. In turn, the word monologue comes from the Greek words monos (alone) and logos (speech, word). A travelogue is then, in its most basic form, a spoken or written account of an individual's experiences traveling, which usually appears in the past tense, in the first person, and with some verisimilitude.Because a travelogue aims to be a true account of an individual's experiences traveling, descriptions of what the traveler sees, hears, tastes, smells, and feels in the external world while traveling are essential components. Of course, thoughts, feelings, and reflections are important parts of our experience of travel. So, descriptions of a traveler's inner world are not out-of-place in the travelogue.Likewise, notes and observations on history, society, and culture are also common features of travelogues, as we certainly learn about the world when we travel.

**What are the types of travelogue?**

A travelogue can exist in the form of a book, a blog, a diary or journal, an article or essay, a podcast, a lecture, a narrated slide show, or in virtually every written or spoken form of creation.

There are many examples of travelogues online in the form of "travel blogs."

However, not all travel blogs are travelogues in the pure sense of the term because some of their authors are less concerned with giving personal accounts of their own experiences traveling than capturing internet search traffic by providing tips, advice, or practical information about travel.

For example, they claim to present the "best things to do" in a particular destination instead of "what I did" there. Though, some travel blogs do publish hybrid travelogues that also provide tips and advice in order to market their travel services.

**Travelogue books**

Mark Twain's The Innocents Abroad is a good example of a travelogue in book form. While it was published as a book in the 19th century, it is perhaps best characterized as a travelogue by today's standards and not as a modern travel book. The frontispiece of the first edition in 1869 explains why:

**The Innocents Abroad Frontispiece**

In The Innocents Abroad, Twain gives us and "account of the steamship Quaker City's pleasure excursion to Europe and the Holy Land; with descriptions of countries, nations, incidents and adventures, as they appeared to the author." It is a descriptive account of his travels and thoughts, sometimes funny and often bigoted. He tells us what he saw and what he felt while also offering historical and cultural remarks on the places he visited.

While it is well-written, I'm not sure the book has a story, a plot, a narrative arc, or a storyline that holds everything together. These are features seldom found in travelogues, R. K. Wilson reminds us in his 1973 study The Literary Travelogue.A destination isn't a story. Neither is simply going from one place to another.Instead, The Innocents Abroad is an account of Twain's holiday, written as if were a letter to his mother half a world away. "Dear Mom," we imagine the book starting.

**Travelogues vs. travel books**

As we have seen in the example above, a travelogue can exist in the form of a book. But this does not mean that it is the same thing as a travel book as we understand it today. Indeed, terms like travelogue and travel book often get conflated. "Even [E.M.] Forster is uncertain what to call these things," Paul Fussell wrote in his book Abroad. "In 1941 he calls them travelogues, in 1949 travel books." Like Forster, Fussell conflates the terms.In the last 100 years or so, we have seen the travel book evolve from the travelogue and mature into a more rarefied thing with its own set of stylistic and formal expectations. Carl Thompson calls this the modern travel book, a concept he discusses in the early chapters of his academic study Travel Writing. While it can appear in book form and evoke a day-to-day account like a logbook, a ship's log, or a captain's log, a travelogue does not necessarily have the formal dimensions and stylistic conceits of the modern travel book.A travelogue does not necessarily have the formal dimensions and stylistic conceits of the modern travel book.This is not to say that travelogues are not insightful or uninteresting. Quite the opposite. They are incredibly revealing and can expose a tremendous amount of information about the world, the writer, and the reader.But the modern travel book is a different beast. Among other important distinctions, modern travel books and modern travelogues have stories, plots, and through-lines. A mission, quest, or journey isn't a story in and of itself.

Perhaps making a distinction between a travelogue and the modern travel book is an elitist or academic move. But perhaps it is no more pompous to say this than it is to say that a modern novel has a specific form and style different from its earlier iterations.

Is the travel book a "sub-species of memoir," as Fussell notes? Is travel writing even a genre? How do travelogues fit into the travel writing landscape?

Travel writing historians and scholars do not agree upon the definitions and boundaries of travel writing. The one thing they agree on is that there is no consensus on the definition. To that point, Thompson writes, "the boundaries of the travel writing genre are fuzzy, and there is little point in policing them too rigidly."

# Journal

Journal writing, also called journaling, in simple words is an informal way of writing or a method of penning down emotions, experiences, thoughts, events, etc. It can be a written or a typed medium of records where the person pens down the thoughts, observations, experiences, etc. This can be written on a daily or periodic basis, or when there is an urge to write. It can be a record of anything and everything. The journal entries are also a type of reflective writing. As journaling provides the freedom and liberty to examine various ideas and different forms of writing strategies, it can also be termed a type of exploratory writing as well.

**Purpose Of Journal Writing**

Journaling has many forms and serves varied purposes. Some of these can be creative, informative, or personal. Journaling helps in recording and maintaining thoughts, practicing the craft of writing, etc. Journaling is an informal writing process where the thoughts and experiences are penned down, which can be used either to identify, correct, and aim for either our mistakes and flaws or set future goals.

Keeping an everyday account of day-to-day routine through journaling betters us as a person as it helps us identify our previous mistakes or the wrong decisions taken and helps improve our writing skills as well.

**1.Improves Writing**

Practice makes a man perfect istrue. Hence, the more you practice writing, the better you get at writing. It helps improve the overall writing skills including better vocabulary and more knowledge of the relevant topics written. It encourages developing new techniques, styles, patterns, and content while increasing the range of the writer. It enhances creativity.

**2.Sharpens Mind**

When we pen down our experiences, we also tend to become more ardent observers. When we want to write about any particular topic, we pay more close attention to all the minute details of that topic. A regular habit of journaling knowingly or unknowingly ensures that we notice even the tiniest minuscule details of everyday life. This close observation of the world around us with great interest and inquisitiveness results in a heightening of senses.

**3.Passion/Love For Writing**

The most important reason for being a journal writer is the sheer love of journaling. It can provide a sense of pleasure, and comfort. It also may have a therapeutic effect on the journal writer when all the emotions and experiences are penned down. Reading our old journals helps revive our memories from the past.

**Main Types Of Journal**

Journaling, as we know, is an art of writing and recording our day-to-day events and thoughts, but apart from that, there are many other types of journals as well. Though, only a few are commonly used Let us get acquainted with the different types of journals.

**Blank Notebook Journal**
**The Dream Journal**
**Plant Journal**
**Gratitude Journal**
**Reading Journal**
**Food Journal**
**Artistic Journal**
**Travel Journal**

## *Benefits*

The practice of writing consistently has many benefits, especially with journal writing as it does not impose restrictions on the writing style or the pattern. It allows you to express yourself most informally and simply. We have made a list of some of the major benefits.

**Achieve Goals:** Goals are more easily achievable when you keep a track of the goals in your journal.

**Sclf-confidcncc:** Writing imparts self confidence.

**Improved skills of writing and communication:** Continuous and consistent writing improves writing skills as well as communication skills.

**Strengthen Memory:** When you are an avid reader and journal writer it strengthens your memory as you tend to read it over and over again as well as do lots of research being journaling.

**Tracking the Progress and Growth:** Maintaining a properly dated journal helps set goals as well as helps in tracking the growth and progress

Reduce Stress and Anxiety: Journaling is known to have a soothing and therapeutic effect on the writer.

# CHAPTER TWO

# Of Travel

## Of Travel

### *Francis Bacon*

TRAVEL, in the younger sort, is a part of education, in the elder, a part of experience. He that travelleth into a country, before he hath some entrance into the language, goeth to school, and not to travel. That young men travel under some tutor, or grave servant, I allow well; so that he be such a one that hath the language, and hath been in the country before; whereby he may be able to tell them what things are worthy to be seen, in the country where they go; what acquaintances they are to seek; what exercises, or discipline, the place yieldeth. For else, young men shall go hooded, and look abroad little. It is a strange thing, that in sea voyages, where there is nothing to be seen, but sky and sea, men should make diaries; but in land-travel, wherein so much is to be observed, for the most part they omit it; as if chance were fitter to be registered, than observation. Let diaries, therefore, be brought in use. The things to be seen and observed are: the courts of princes, especially when they give audience to ambassadors; the courts of justice, while they sit and hear causes; and so of consistories ecclesiastic; the churches and monasteries, with the monuments which are therein extant; the walls and fortifications of cities, and towns, and so the heavens and harbors; antiquities and ruins; libraries; colleges, disputations, and lectures, where any are; shipping and navies; houses and gardens of state and pleasure, near great cities; armories; arsenals; magazines; exchanges; burses; warehouses; exercises of horsemanship, fencing, training of soldiers, and the like; comedies, such whereunto the better sort of persons do resort; treasuries of jewels and robes; cabinets and rarities; and, to conclude, whatsoever is memorable, in the places where they go. After all which, the tutors, or servants, ought to make diligent inquiry. As for triumphs, masks, feasts, weddings, funerals, capital executions, and such shows, men need not to be put in mind of them; yet are they not to be neglected. If you will have a young man to put his travel into a little room, and in short time to gather much, this you must do. First, as was said, he must have some entrance into the language before he goeth. Then he must have such a servant, or tutor, as knoweth the country, as was likewise said. Let him carry with him also, some card or book, describing the country where he travelleth; which will be a good key to his inquiry. Let him keep also a diary. Let him not stay long, in one city or town; more or less as the place deserveth, but not long; nay, when he stayeth in one city or town, let him change his lodging from one end and part of the town, to another; which is a great adamant of acquaintance. Let him sequester himself, from the company of his countrymen, and diet in such places, where there is good company of the nation where he travelleth. Let him, upon his removes from one place to another, procure recommendation to some person of quality, residing in the place whither he removeth; that he may use his favor, in those things he desireth to see or know. Thus he may abridge his travel, with much profit. As for the acquaintance, which is to be sought in travel; that which is most of all profitable, is acquaintance with the secretaries and employed men of ambassadors: for so in travelling in one country, he shall suck the experience of many. Let him also see, and visit, eminent persons in all kinds, which are of great name abroad; that he may be able to tell, how the life agreeth with the fame. For quarrels, they are with care and discretion to be avoided. They are commonly for mistresses, healths, place, and words. And let a man beware, how he keepeth company with choleric and quarrelsome persons; for they will engage him into their own quarrels. When a traveller returneth home, let him not leave the countries, where he hath travelled, altogether behind him; but maintain a correspondence by letters, with those of his acquaintance, which are of most worth. And let his travel appear rather in his discourse, than his apparel or gesture; and in his discourse, let him be rather advised in his answers, than forward to tell stories; and let it appear that he doth not change his country manners, for those of foreign parts; but only prick in some flowers, of that he hath learned abroad, into the customs of his own country.

**Introduction to Bacon's Essays**

Francis Bacon (1561-1626), the English philosopher, was instrumental in the development of the Scientific Revolution in the late 18th century even though he had passed away centuries before. The "Scientific Revolution" was an important movement that emphasized Europe's shift toward modernized science in fields such as mathematics, physics, astronomy, biology, and chemistry (Grant). It was an extension of the Renaissance period, which then led to the Enlightenment which brought advances across all areas of human endeavor. Francis Bacon, in particular, is remembered today primarily for the "scientific method" as a way of establishing what is true from what is false perception (a method that still lies at the heart of modern science). Bacon's primary focus in his writings revolved around the practice of inductive reasoning, which he believed to be a complement to practical observation (Grant). Most people before this period followed the Aristotelian methodology for scientific arguments. This idea maintained that "if sufficiently clever men discussed a subject long enough, the truth would eventually be discovered" ("History – Francis Bacon."). However irrational this sounds, the Scientific Revolution helped replace this outdated system of thinking with Bacon's scientific method. Bacon argued that any proper argument required "evidence from the real world" ("History – Francis Bacon."). His revolutionary ideas about empirical information helped propel him toward political and societal importance and fame.

Bacon had a passion for metaphors, analogies, and vivid imagery. He was a rhetorical writer and his essays highlight his wisdom and incisive mind. His first book was released in 1597 followed by later editions with added essays that were released in 1612 and 1625. Each essay that Bacon wrote reveals his knowledge of Latin and draws on ancient Roman wisdom through axioms and proverbs. Additionally, Bacon uses wit as a way of getting his point across to his audience and this indeed causes the reader to reflect on his or her own beliefs and values. A key aspect of Bacon's literature is its "terseness and epigrammatic force" (De). By managing to pack all of his thoughts and ideas into quick, brief statements, Bacon deepens the reach and impact of his work. His writing deviated from the typical Ciceronian style of the time, which was characterized by "melodious language, clarity, and forcefulness of presentation" ("Ciceronian."). His statements are meaningful particularly because they are straight and to the point. The brevity of his ideas also facilitates the communication of his arguments, which is significant because, at the time, a solid, meaningful education was hard to come by. As such, Bacon's work helped spread the notions that would eventually bear fruit with the discoveries of the Scientific Revolution.

Francis Bacon's Essays cover a wide variety of topics and styles, ranging from individual to societal issues and from commonplace to existential. Another important aspect of the appeal of Bacon's essays are that they weigh the argument at hand with multiple points of view. Bacon's essays were received at the time with great praise, adoration, and reverence (Potter). He was noted for borrowing ideas from the works of historical writers such as Aristotle (Harmon), and, as such, he represents a continuation of this philosophical school of thought. Another important impact of the Scientific Revolution and Bacon's literature is that it allowed common people of the era to question old, traditional beliefs. They began to consider everything with reason, which led to a greater sense of self as well as moral and ethical standards. By having the opportunity to judge for themselves, the people were able to advance society a step closer to a form of democracy.

Francis Bacon Essays is a collection of eight of the famous philosopher's many essays. Each dissertation contains words of wisdom that have proven to be enlightening for many generations that followed. From "Truth" to "Of Superstition" and "Marriage and Single Life", Bacon covers a wide range of intriguing topics in order to challenge the human mind to think deeply; as he himself writes: "Read not to contradict and confute, nor to believe and take for granted, nor to find talk and discourse, but to weigh and consider" (Bacon). The philosopher not only provides a framework for the genre of the modern essay but also provides his readers a code to live by.

## Of Travel – Francis Bacon – Complete Explanation

**1.TRAVEL, in the younger sort, is a part of education, in the elder, a part of experience. He that travelleth into a country, before he hath some entrance into the language, goeth to school, and not to travel.**

**Explanation:-**When a young child travels around in alien places, he learns a lot from the sight and sound around him. In the process, his awareness grows and his learning process is accelerated. So, travel for a young child has good educational value. So, the countryside becomes a school for him, although in an informal way.

**2.That young men travel under some tutor, or grave servant, I allow well; so that he be such a one that hath the language, and hath been in**

the country before; whereby he may be able to tell them what things are worthy to be seen, in the country where they go; what acquaintances they are to seek; what exercises, or discipline, the place yieldeth.

Explanation:-A youngster travelling to an unknown place under the watchful eye of a knowledgeable chaperon is always desirable. By virtue of the knowledge and experience, the chaperon can guide the young traveler where to go, what to see, and the type of people to befriend. The able guide can also tell the youngster about the pastime, hobbies and crafts the places are famous for.

3.For else, young men shall go hooded, and look abroad little. It is a strange thing, that in sea voyages, where there is nothing to be seen, but sky and sea, men should make diaries; but in land-travel, wherein so much is to be observed, for the most part they omit it; as if chance were fitter to be registered, than observation.

Explanation:-Without the company of a guide, he will fail to observe the important and interesting things in the new places. While on a voyage in the sea, the sea farer gets to see nothing other than the vast expanse of blue water and the un-ending sky above. In such a case, the voyager should maintain a travel diary. When travelling over land, there is an overwhelming abundance of new sights and sounds and myriad things to observe. People generally fail to keep note of every detail of what they come across.

4.Let diaries, therefore, be brought in use. The things to be seen and observed are: the courts of princes, especially when they give audience to ambassadors; the courts of justice, while they sit and hear causes; and so of consistories ecclesiastic; the churches and monasteries, with the monuments which are therein extant; the walls and fortifications of cities, and towns, and so the heavens and harbors; antiquities and ruins; libraries; colleges, disputations, and lectures, where any are; shipping and navies; houses and gardens of state and pleasure, near great cities; armories; arsenals; magazines; exchanges; burses; warehouses; exercises of horsemanship, fencing, training of soldiers, and the like; comedies, such whereunto the better sort of persons do resort; treasuries of jewels and robes; cabinets and rarities; and, to conclude, whatsoever is memorable, in the places where they go.

Explanation:-So, maintain a diary is always a good idea. In the diary, one can record his observations about the following:

1. The royal courts of princes, kings and sovereigns. He can observe the opulence, splendor, courtiers, and the practices followed in the courts. The elaborate protocol followed while formally accepting the ambassadors from other countries is worth observing and noting.

2. The royal courts that hear pleas, and dispense justice also offer interesting sights. The practices followed in the Roman courts and those in the English clergy are also interesting.

3. The churches, monasteries, their architectural styles offer much visual delight. It is advisable to observe and record these in the diary.

4. The city walls, the fortresses and the watch towers that ring a city to ward off invaders are also very interesting to watch.

5. The beautiful towns and harbours also deserve to be seen with observant eyes.

6. The antiquities, the ruins standing as witness to past attacks of marauding invaders are worth seeing minutely.

7. Colleges, universities, centers of learning, town halls where debates are held, stadia etc. bear testimony to the intellectual vigour of any society. So, they should be visited too.

8. Shipping facilities and naval yards are the yardsticks of a nation's maritime prowess. So, they deserve to be keenly looked at.

9. Public office buildings are the citadels of power and authority. They are deliberately built majestically to tower over other private buildings nearby. They project the state's power. Similarly, parks and recreational open spaces speak about the taste and habits of the way people spend their leisure time. Their architecture reflect the aesthetic sense of the character of a race. So, these public places are to be visited and keenly observed.

10. Visit to the country's armoury and ammunition storage facilities is quite enlightening too.

11. Visits to warehouses, stock exchanges and wholesale markets are also of good educational value.

12. Seeing equestrian sports and horse rearing centers indicate the ability of the country to use horse for military and recreational purposes.

13. Visit to opera houses shows how cultured the upper sections of the society are.

14. Exhibition of fine jewelry, fine clothing, antiques etc. throws light on the wealth and taste of the people.

15. In this way, one needs to visit all places of interest to bring back a treasure trove of highly rewarding information and knowledge.

**5.As for triumphs, masks, feasts, weddings, funerals, capital executions, and such shows, men need not to be put in mind of them: yet are they not to be neglected.**

**Explanation:-**Social occasions like marriages, funerals, feasts, public executions, victory celebrations etc. are, no doubt, important, but they need not be documented or observed so keenly.

**6.If you will have a young man to put his travel into a little room, and in short time to gather much, this you must do: first, as was said, he must have some entrance into the language before he goeth; then he must have such a servant, or tutor, as knoweth the country, as was likewise said: let him carry with him also some card, or book, describing the country where he travelleth, which will be a good key to his inquiry; let him keep also a diary; let him not stay long in one city or town, more or less as the place deserveth, but not long: nay, when he stayeth in one city or town, let him change his lodging from one end and part of the town to another, which is a great adamant of acquaintance; let him sequester himself from the company of his countrymen, and diet in such places where there is good company of the nation where he travelleth: let him, upon his removes from one place to another, procure recommendation to some person of quality residing in the place whither he removeth; that he may use his favour in those things he desireth to see or know; thus he may abridge his travel with much profit.**

**Explanation:-**Bacon proceeds to give some 'do's and 'don'ts for a travel expedition to yield maximum value. These are as follows:

1. The youngster has to have some basic learning before he sets out on his journey.
2. He must have a dedicated and knowledgeable guide. This man must be well-conversant with the country he is visiting.
3. The guide should carry with him some books, catalogues or brochures about the places he has in his travel. These will prove to be handy in course of the travel.
4. The learner must have a diary where he can jot down whatever he sees as he moves from place to place.
5. He should not stay more than it is necessary to stay in one place.

6.  In case he stays in a city or a town for a longer duration, he must change his lodging, and move to another in the other end of the town to get the maximum exposure.

7.  While staying in a place, he must not choose to stay among people from his own place. Instead, he must choose to live among people of the host country, so that he gets to observe their habits.

8.  He must procure and carry with him letters of introduction from eminent people from his own locality to those in the places he is going to visit. This will ease travel, stay and availability of other conveniences.

**7.As for the acquaintance which is to be sought in travel, that which is most of all profitable, is acquaintance with the secretaries and employed men of ambassadors; for so in travelling in one country he shall suck the experience of many: let him also see and visit eminent persons in all kinds, which are of great name abroad, that he may be able to tell how the life agreeth with the fame; for quarrels, they are with care and discretion to be avoided: they are commonly for mistresses, healths, place, and words; and let a man beware how he keepeth company with choleric and quarrelsome persons; for they will engage him into their own quarrels.**

Explanation:-In the places where he goes, he must seek out people of eminence like ambassadors, senior bureaucrats, and other eminent people who can offer practical help in sight-seeing, gathering information, and in availing other comforts needed during travel in a new place. He should avoid getting into arguments, quarrels and fights with locals. He should avoid the company of mistresses and quarrelsome people, because these are the persons who drag him to unnecessary fights and unpleasant situations.

**8.When a traveller returneth home, let him not leave the countries where he hath travelled altogether behind him; but maintain a correspondence by letters with those of his acquaintance which are of most worth; and let his travel appear rather in his discourse than in his apparel or gesture; and in his discourse, let him be rather advised in his answers, than forward to tell stories: and let it appear that he doth not change his country manners for those of foreign parts; but only prick in some flowers of that he hath learned abroad into the customs of his own**

country.

**Explanation:**-On returning to his native home, he must not completely forget the people and places he has visited. He must maintain the link through correspondence with those eminent men who had extended courtesy and help to him during his sojourn. His heightened knowledge and awareness acquired during the journey are not to be shown off through elaborate attire or mannerisms of the foreign lands. This might invite ridicule and derision. On the contrary, his new wisdom must reflect in his talking and lectures to his fellowmen. He should be concise and factual in his accounts, and not weave stories. He must not give an impression that he has forsaken his country manners and dress to adopt those of the lands he has visited. He should selectively describe all the good things he has learnt abroad.

## Questions and Answers

**1.How is travel defined differently for the young and the old according to Bacon?**

Answer: For the young, travel is viewed as a part of education where they learn and explore new cultures. For the older generation, it represents a part of experience, accumulating wisdom and knowledge through their journeys.

**2.What are the essential preparations a young traveler should undertake before traveling?**

Answer: A young traveler should have some understanding of the local language, be accompanied by a knowledgeable tutor or servant familiar with the destination, carry a guidebook or map about the country, maintain a diary to record observations, and plan to stay varied in lodging and social circles.

**3. Why does Bacon emphasize the importance of keeping a diary while traveling?**

Answer: Bacon notes the irony that people keep diaries during sea voyages where few observations exist, yet neglect them in land travel where much can be observed. A diary helps in recording valuable experiences and insights that can be reflected upon later.

**4.What specific sites does Bacon recommend travelers to observe and why?**

Answer: Bacon urges travelers to observe various sites, including courts of princes, courts of justice, churches, fortifications, and cultural events, as these provide insights into the governance, culture, history, and social fabric of the country.

**5. How should a traveler approach making acquaintances in a foreign country?**

Answer: A traveler should seek to make connections with individuals who can offer insights and information, especially secretaries and ambassadors. Additionally, he should strive to connect with notable figures to gain a broader understanding of the country.

**6.What precautions does Bacon suggest concerning social interactions while traveling?**

Answer: Bacon advises avoiding quarrels and being cautious in choosing companions, suggesting that travelers should keep away from quarrelsome individuals to avoid being drawn into disputes.

**7.What should a traveler maintain after returning home from their travels?**

Answer: After returning, the traveler should keep in touch with acquaintances made abroad through letters and let their travel experiences enrich their conversation rather than exhibiting them through ostentatious apparel.

**8.How does Bacon suggest travelers integrate their foreign experiences into their home culture?**

Answer: He suggests that travelers should subtly incorporate what they learned abroad into their own culture, enriching their customs with new insights rather than wholly adopting foreign practices.

## *Of Travel –A critical Synopsis*

Francis Bacon is one of the most celebrated prose writers of the sixteenth century from where the modern age begins. This age is particularly noted for its religion, philosophy, science and travel. He represented the age in his works about its patriotism, high aims and lofty ideals. His earliest and chief interest in life was the reformation of scientific method of approach. He is considered 'the brightest, the wisest and the noblest of the humankind and he is known as the father of English Essay and Modern Prose.

Bacon's essays on verities of subjects apparently deal with the ethical qualities of men or with the matters pertaining to the governments of states. All his essays are full of practical wisdom of life. His style is aphoristic, formal, impersonal and informative. They are all full of quotable quotes.

In this essay, "Of Travel" Bacon expresses advantages and benefits of travels. He says that the travel is a part of education for the younger people and it is an experience to the elderly people. One must learn some knowledge of reading as well as writing of language before he/she undertakes a travel. Either some tutor or grave servant must accompany the young persons, while they undertake a travel. These people with their previous experience will help traveler to follow what exercises or discipline the country may demand while travelling in such a country.

He advised that the traveler must keep a diary with him and record his observations in it. It will be a strange thing in sea-voyages where there is nothing to be seen except the sky and the sea. However, in land-travel, there is so much to be observed and registered in his diary but most of it will be omitted. The enthusiastic traveler must observe and register in his dairy about the courts of princes especially when they give audience to ambassadors, the courts of justice, while they sit and hear the causes, the churches and monasteries, walls and fortifications of cities and towns, havens and harbours, antiquities and ruins, libraries, colleges, disputations, houses and gardens, great cities, warehouses armories, arsenals, magazines, exchanges, exercises of horsemanship, fencing, training of soldiers besides masks, feasts, weddings, funerals, capital executions and whatsoever is memorable in the places where they go.

He advised the travelers that they must carry a card or a book that can describe the country where he travels. He said that it is not advisable to stay one place for a long time in one city or a town and let him change his lodging from one part of the town to another and be isolate himself from the company of his fellow citizens. Let him see and visit the eminent persons who have great name and fame in those countries of abroad. Moreover, the travelers must be cautious of quarrels, quarrelsome people who will engage him into their quarrels and of contagious diseases like cholera and others. When a traveler returns home, he should not leave those countries behind but maintain correspondence with those of his acquaintances which of those most important. Finally, he advised that the traveler do not change his country manners for those of foreign parts but only prick some flowers of those that has learned abroad into the customs of his own country. Thus, Bacon reveled all the benefits of travel through his essay 'Of Travel'.

**Q. Write a short note on the Aphoristic Style of Francis Bacon**

Francis Bacon's fame as a writer depends most of all on the fact that he is the father of modern English prose. He evolved a prose style that proved for the first time that English could also be used to express the subtleties of thought, in clear and uninvolved sentences.

**Does Bacon have two styles?**

The critics have noticed that there is a marked difference between Bacon's earlier and later essays. Macaulay, by contrasting extracts from Of Studies (1597) and Of Adversity (1625) illustrates what he calls the two styles of Bacon.

Indeed it is true that there is a vast difference in the styles. But it is rather questionable whether this difference could be attributed to the fact that Bacon had gained a maturity of mind and intellect. This inference, as Hugh Walker shows, is not tenable. Bacon in fact wrote in more than one style; he suits his style to his subject. The style of Advancement of Learning shows an adornments as rich as that of Adversity. The stately movement of The Advancement of Learning has been achieved in 1605 itself. Does this mean that Bacon has achieved this maturity and development in mind and imagination in the space of eight years? This seems a rather unconvincing and unrealistic explanation for the change in his style.

The explanation lies in the fact that Bacon's very conception of the essay underwent a change. The first collection of essays is fully illustrative of Bacon's definition of the essay as 'dispersed meditations' set down rather significantly than curiously. The original idea was to make the essays into a sort of diary in which significant observations on various topics of practical importance, domestic, political, intellectual, moral, religious and social, were to be jotted down in a terse and pithy and concise language. These first essays were mere skeletons of thought, grouped around central themes with suitable titles. There was no attempt at polishing the style, or clothing the statements with literary beauty or imaginative grace. When, however, Bacon saw that his essays had gained an unexpected popularity, he thought it was worthwhile to spend some more time on them and make (item more polished and riches. Thus, the later essays acquired flesh and blood; the argument was amplified with the help of illustrations and analogies, the phrasing became more rounded and the style more supple and eloquent than before. The stylistic changes are prompted mainly by the desire to bring about greater clarity and richness. In the earlier essays, Bacon treated the subject in a very sketchy and incomplete manner. In the later essays, there is a warmth and colour and the introduction of connective clauses and conjunctions. In the earlier essays there is an extreme condensation that would not have been there if he had been treating the subject more fully.

Each sentence in these essays contains as some critics point out, matter for a paragraph. Having realized their popularity, Bacon felt it to be worthwhile taking the time to weave together the disjecta memba of his meditations". Though even in the later essays in the general conception of essays as an attempt is preserved, and the subject is still treated incompletely, the loose thoughts are no longer disconnected. His conception of the essay has developed.

**A Distinct Style**

Francis Bacon's writing has been admired for various reasons. Some admire his dazzling power of rhetoric, others, his grace, and yet others find him too stiff and rigid. But all admit that he is one of the greatest writers of English prose of his age. His essays have become a classic of the English language and they owe this position, not so much to their subject matter, as to their inimitable style and literary flavour. In Bacon we find a style which is distinct and at the same time characteristic of his age.

**Salient Features of his Style**

Bacon's style, while it includes a number of features common to the Elizabethans and the Jacobeans, has at the same time special characteristics of its own.

**1. Aphoristic Style**

The style of Bacon remains for the main part aphoristic, with the result that he is one of the most quotable of writers. There is a terseness of expression, and an epigrammatic brevity, in the essays of Bacon. His sentences are brief and rapid, but they are also forceful. "They come down like the strokes of a hammer', says Dean Church. This terseness is often achieved by leaving out superfluous epithets and conjunctions and connectives. It is seldom carried to the extent of causing obscurity, though one or two instances do exist where this extreme condensation has caused great difficulty in understanding the meaning. This is a remarkable power of compressing into a few words an idea which other writers may express in several sentences. The essays of Bacon in fact have to be read slowly because of the compact and condensed thought. There are a number of sentences which are read like proverbs Examples easily jump to one's mind:

1. A lie faces God and Shrinks from man. (Of Truth)

2. Suspicions among thoughts are like bats among birds. (Of Suspicion)

3. The ways to enrich are many, and most of them foul. (Of Riches)

4. A mixture of a lie doth ever add pleasure. (Of Truth)

5. It is a strange desire to seek power and lose liberty: or to seek power over others and lose power over a man's self. (Of Great Place)

6. The rising unto place is laborious, and by pains men come to greater pains. (Of Great Place)

There is not one essay which does not contain such capsules of common wisdom. The sentences are pregnant with meaning. They are often curt, telegraphic or stenographic in nature.

## 2. Antithetical Statements

The force of the aphoristic statements depend upon other stylistic devices which supplement them. Such devices are the 'balance' and antithesis' which mark the structure of most of his sentences. They range from simple two-pronged structure to the multi-pronged ones:

(a) Travel in the younger sort, is part of education; in the elder, a part of experience.

(b) For a lie faces God, and shrinks from man.

These are examples of two-pronged balance in the structure of sentences. In the essay, Of Studies, there is a consistent use of a three fold balance:

(a) Studies serve for delight, for ornament and for ability.

(b) Some books are to be tasted, others to be swallowed, and some few to be chewed and digested.

(c) Reading maketh a full man, conference a ready man; and writing an exact man.

(d) Read not to contradict, nor to believe, but to weigh and consider.

Other essays too exhibit this quality:

"Nuptial love maketh mankind; friendly love perfecteth it; but wanton love corrupteth and embaseth it." (Of Marriage and Single Life.)

Very often the two parts of a balanced sentence are made up of a statement and an explanatory analogy, so that the meaning remains 'suspended' till the end of the sentence:

"A simple life doth well with churchmen; for charity will hardly water the ground where it must first fill a pool."

Sometimes the explanation is a mere prolongation of sense completed in the first part:

"He that hath wife and child hath given hostages to fortune; for they are impediments to great enterprises either of virtue or mischief."

Bacon has the habit of weighing the pros and cons of every question that he deals with. When he makes a statement, he almost immediately counter-balances it. He scrupulously presents the advantages and the disadvantages of a particular issue; he gives both sides of the picture. Sometimes he draws definite conclusions after balancing the issues, but most of the time the reader is left to draw his own conclusion. In the essay Of Marriage and Single life, for instance, Bacon weighs the advantages of both the states in a cool and rational fashion. Thus, single men are good friends, good masters and good servants, but they are unreliable as good citizens, or when he says in his essay Of Parents and Children children sweetens labour, but they make misfortune more bitter, 'they increase the care of life, but they mitigate the remembrance of death.' In his essay, Of Simulation and Dissimulation, he clearly gives throe advantages and three disadvantages arising from dissembling. Such weighing and balancing makes his style antithetical. Each sententious statement is balanced by an opposite statement.

### 3. A Rhetorician

Bacon's style is definitely rhetorical. In this connection. Saintsbury has remarked that no one "knows better than..... (Bacon) how to have a single word to produce all its effects by using it in some slight *v uncommon sense, at setting the wits at work to discern and adjust this, or how to unfold all manner of applications and connotations, to open all inlets of side-view and perspective! That he dazzles, amuses half-delusively, suggests, stimulates, provokes, eddies, instructs, satisfies, is indeed perfectly true." His matter is not Always great, but almost always seems better than it is, but this vary fart is the greatest glory of his manner. He has great powers of attracting and persuading his readers even though he may not convince them.

"In prose rhetoric, in the use, that is to say, of language to dazzle and persuade, not to convince, he has few rivals and no superiors in English", says Saintsbury.

In this connection, one has to study another striking feature of Bacon's style.

### 4. His Imagery and Analogy

There is a constant use of imagery and figurative language in Bacon, especially in his later essays. The apt and extensive us of metaphors, images, similitudes and analogies is in keeping with the views of the rhetoricians of the ancient as well as the 'Renaissance. These devices were regarded by rhetoricians, and by Bacon, as functional or an integral part of the main object of the writer, namely to persuade, move and inform the reader.

Bacon draws his imagery from the familiar objects of nature, or from the facts of every day life. His similes are most of the time, apt, vivid and suggestive. Abstract truth is vivified by a concrete analogy of the unfamiliar thing with a familiar object, process or experience of common everyday life. And Bacon draws these analogies from a surprising range of sources. Classical mythology, the Bible, astronomy, philosophy, natural observation and domestic objects and functions, navigation, war, the sea or the garden, all these are pressed into service for communicating the meaning to the minds of the reader.

The analogies may take the form of similitudes simple and short, or complex and elaborate, or they may be short and suggestive as metaphors.

There are numerous examples to be found in the essays.

In his essay, Of Studies he says that distilled books are like common distilled water flashy things. In the essay, Of Marriage and Single Life, he says that some men value their freedom to such an extent that they "will go near to think their girdles and garters to be bonds and shackles." "Those that want friends to open themselves unto are cannibals of their own hearts", he says in his essay, Of friendship. In such examples comparison serves to intensify the aphoristic force of his wisdom.

Often he uses analogy to illustrate his ideas. Thus in the essay, Of Truth, Bacon communicates the idea of man's natural love of lie and proneness to mix falsehood with truth by taking the help of the analogy of dramatic performances which have a sense of beauty and reality only in the dim light of candles, bus lose all their fake brightness in the clear light of the day. He compares falsehood to an alloy in a coin of gold or silver. The alloy makes the metal work better, but it lowers the value of the metal.

An almost poetic figure of speech is found in the statement: "Certainly it is heaven upon earth to have a man's mind move in charity, rest in providence, and turn upon the poles of truth." Or when he adapts a passage from Lucretius:

"It is pleasure to stand upon the shore, and to see ships toss upon the sea; a pleasure to stand in the window of a castle, and to see the battles and adventures thereof below; but no pleasure is comparable to the standing upon the vantage ground of truth.....and to see .the errors, and wanderings and mists and tempests, in the vale below....."

In Of the True Greatness of Kingdom, there is an analogy drawn from the Bible which is rather elaborate:

"The blessing of Judah and Issachar will never meet: that the same people or nation should be both the lion's whelp and the ass between burthens: neither will it be, that a people overlaid with taxes should ever become valiant and martial."

He also aptly states the case against a clergyman marrying: "For charity will hardly water the ground where it must first fill a pool."

There are a number of similes and metaphors in the essay Of Friendship, such as:

"For a crowd in not company, and faces are but a gallery of pictures, and talk but a tinkling cymbal, where there is no love."

## 5. Allusions and Quotations

The essays bear witness to Bacon's learned mind in the extensive use of quotations and allusions drawn from various sources, classical fables, the Bible, History, the ancient Greek and Roman writers and the familiar collection of proverbs. But these allusions, like the images and metaphors are functional. In the essay Of Truth we have references to Pilate, Lucian, Lucretius and Montaigne, with quotations from two of them, hi the essay Of Great Place, there are allusions to Tacitus, Galba and Vespacian. Most of his allusions to Roman history are used to illustrate and support the argument in hand. The essay, Of Empire, abounds in this kind of allusions, hi the essay, Of friendship, a string of historical allusions are given in support of his argument.

Quotations likewise are used to illustrate and support Bacon's point of view or idea. At times, he even gives his own interpretation of quotations to make them fit the occasion. At times the quotations are rather inaccurate, made to be more serviceable to him than the exact words would have been. At times the quotations not only support the argument, but are themselves elucidated by the argument. In the essay Of friendship, for example, the argument is set in motion by a quotation by Aristotle. This is followed by Bacon's own comment upon it, which leads to a further elaboration of the meaning of solitude.

Bacon thus employs allusions and quotations in order to explain his point. They serve to make his style more scholarly and enrich it while lending weight to his ideas.

## 6. Flexibility

Though Bacon's style is heavy with learning, yet it is more flexible than any of his predecessors and contemporaries. The sentences are short and with this shortness came lucidity. The grammatical structure is sometimes loose, but the sense is rarely ambiguous. The new style of Bacon fitted itself as easily to buildings and gardens, or to suitors, as to truth and death. "It could be sunk to the familiarity of likening money to muck, not good unless it be spread, or rise to a comparison between movements of the human mind and the movements of the heavenly bodies." (Hugh Walker) Bacon shows a mastery of the principles of prose.

### 7. Wit

There is no humour in Bacon's essays, but there is ample of wit. He is a master of the skilful use of words. He could manipulate words cleverly to delight the reader:

"By pains men come to greater pains."

'Through indignities men rise to dignities."

### 8. Sources of Difficulty

Bacon on the whole is not difficult to understand, though his condensed style demands greater attention and more time on the reader's part. Yet at times this very condensation leads to a certain obscurity, though it is so in very few cases. There are a few Latinism in his essays which are difficult to follow. Dolours (pain), plausible (praiseworthy); foreseen (provided); creature (created tiling) are just a few examples of Latinisms. There are also a number of archaic words: 'leese' for 'lose'; 'fame' for 'rumour'; 'bravery' used in the sense of 'show' or 'ostentation'.

### Conclusion

The style of Bacon is not the personal, and chatty style of the subjective essayist like Montaigne or Lamb. It is dignified and aphoristic, full of learned quotations, and allusions, informed by striking though apt analogies. But what is most remarkable about this style is its terseness and brevity, the compact and condensed structure of sentences expressing the deepest thoughts in an economy of language. He was indeed a consummate artist who polished and chiselled his expressions and who could change his style to suit his subject. With him, English prose definitely took a long leap forward.

Reynolds, praising Bacon's style in the essays, "such expressions are the works of a great writer at his best, the highest efforts of an art that defies analysis, simple, unaffected, sublime,"

# CHAPTER THREE

# Mischiefs Of Party Spirit

### *Mischiefs Of Party Spirit*

Joseph Addison

My worthy friend Sir Roger, when we are talking of the malice of parties, very frequently tells us an accident that happened to him when he was a school-boy, which was at a time when the feuds ran high between the Round-heads and Cavaliers. This worthy knight being then but a stripling, had occasion to inquire which was the way to St. Anne's Lane, upon which the person whom he spoke to, instead of answering his question, called him a young popish cur, and asked him who had made Anne a saint! The boy being in some confusion, inquired of the next he met, which was the way to Anne's Lane; but was called a prick-eared cur for his pains; and instead of being shown the way, was told, that she had been a saint before he was born, and would be one after he was hanged. Upon this, says Sir Roger, I did not think fit to repeat the former question, but going into every lane of the neighbourhood, asked what they called the name of that lane. By which ingenious artifice he found out the place he inquired after, without giving any offence to any party. Sir Roger generally closes this narrative with reflections on the mischief that parties do in the country; how they spoil good neighbourhood, and make honest gentlemen hate one another; besides that they manifestly tend to the prejudice of the land-tax, and the destruction of the game.

There cannot a greater judgment befall a country than such a dreadful spirit of division as rends a government into two distinct people, and makes them greater strangers and more averse to one another, than if they were actually two different nations. The effects of such a division are pernicious to the last degree, not only with regard to those advantages which they give the common enemy, but to those private evils which they produce in the heart of almost every particular person. This influence is very fatal both to men's morals and their understandings; it sinks the virtue of a nation, and not only so, but destroys even common sense.

A furious party-spirit, when it rages in its full violence, exerts itself in civil war and bloodshed; and when it is under its greatest restraints, naturally breaks out in falsehood, detraction, calumny, and a partial administration of justice. In a word, it fills a nation with spleen and rancour, and extinguishes all the seeds of good-nature, compassion, and humanity.

Plutarch says very finely, that a man should not allow himself to hate even his enemies, because, says he, if you indulge this passion in some occasions, it will rise of itself in others; if you hate your enemies, you will contract such a venomous habit of mind, as by degrees will break out upon those who are your friends, or those who are indifferent to you. I might here observe how admirably this precept of morality (which derives the malignity of hatred from the passion itself, and not from its object) answers to that great rule which was dictated to the world about an hundred years before this philosopher wrote; but instead of that, I shall only take notice, with a real grief of heart, that the minds of many good men among us appear soured with party-principles, and alienated from one another in such a manner, as seems to me altogether inconsistent with the dictates either of reason or religion. Zeal for a public cause is apt to breed passions in the hearts of virtuous persons, to which the regard of their own private interest would never have betrayed them.

If this party-spirit has so ill an effect on our morals, it has likewise a very great one upon our judgments. We often hear a poor insipid paper or pamphlet cried up, and sometimes a noble piece depreciated, by those who are of a different principle from the author. One who is actuated by this spirit, is almost under an incapacity of discerning either real blemishes or beauties. A man of merit in a different principle, is like an object seen in two different mediums, that appears crooked or broken, however straight and entire it may be in itself. For this reason there is scarce a person of any figure in England, who does not go by two contrary characters, as opposite to one another as light and darkness. Knowledge and learning suffer in a particular manner from this strange prejudice, which at present prevails amongst all ranks and degrees in the British nation. As men formerly became eminent in learned societies by their parts and acquisitions, they now distinguish themselves by the warmth and violence with which they espouse their respective parties. Books are valued upon the like considerations: an abusive, scurrilous style passes for satire, and a dull scheme of party-notions is called fine writing.

There is one piece of sophistry practised by both sides, and that is the taking any scandalous story that has been I ever whispered or invented of a private man, for a known, undoubted truth, and raising suitable speculations upon it. Calumnies that have been never proved, or have been often refuted, are the ordinary postulatums of these infamous scribblers, upon which they proceed as upon first principles granted by all men, though in their hearts they know they are false, or at best very doubtful. When they have laid these foundations of scurrility, it is no wonder that their superstructure is every way answerable to them. If this shameless practice of the present age endures much longer, praise and reproach will cease to be motives of action in good men.

There are certain periods of time in all governments when this inhuman spirit prevails. Italy was long torn in pieces by the Guelfes and Gibelines, and France by those who were for and against the League: but it is very unhappy for a man to be born in such a stormy and tempestuous season. It is the restless ambition of artful men that thus breaks a people into factions, and draws several well-meaning persons to their interest by a specious concern for their country. How many honest minds are filled with uncharitable and barbarous notions, out of their zeal for the public good! What cruelties and outrages would they not commit against men of an adverse party, whom they would honour and esteem, if, instead of considering them as they are represented, they knew them as they are? Thus are persons of the greatest probity seduced into shameful errors and prejudices, and made bad men even by that noblest of principles, the love of their country. I cannot here forbear mentioning the famous Spanish proverb,

"If there were neither fools nor knaves in the world, all people would be of one mind."

For my own part I could heartily wish that all honest men would enter into an association, for the support of one another against the endeavours of those whom they ought to look upon as their common enemies, whatsoever side they may belong to. Were there such an honest body of neutral forces, we should never see the worst of men in great figures of life, because they are useful to a party; nor the best unregarded, because they are above practising those methods which would be grateful to their faction. We should then single every criminal out of the herd, and hunt him down, however formidable and overgrown be might appear: on the contrary, we should shelter distressed innocence, and defend virtue, however beset with contempt or ridicule, envy or defamation. In short, we should not any longer regard our fellow-subjects as Whigs and Tories, but should make the man of merit our friend, and the villain our enemy.

## An Introduction to Joseph Addison as an Essayist

Most of Joseph Addison's essays are the social documents of the eighteenth century English life of middle-class people. He wrote elaborately on religion, politics, death, woman and other contemporary issues. Myres, in this connection, says- "It is necessary to study the work of Joseph Addison in close relation to the time in which he lived, for he was a true child of his century....." Addison adopted the 'middle style'. It was associated with the graceful rhythm. Once Sr. Johnson praised the style of Addison- ;Give nights and days, sir, to the study of Addison if you mean to be a good writer, or , what is more worth, an honest man." Dr. Johnson again said- "His(Addison's)prose is the model of the middle style; on grave subjects not formal, on light occasions not grovelling; pure without scrupulosity, and extra without apparent elaboration; always equable, and always tempter, he performed; he is never feebler, and he did not wish to be energetic; he is never rapid, and he never stagnates. His sentences have nether not diligently rounded, are voluble and easy."

Addison used the language of the clubs and the coffee-houses. He too wished to refine the English language and to write with well-bred ease. But at the same time he saw a danger in common speech- "Since it often happens that the most obvious phrases, and those which are used in ordinary conversation, become too familiar to the ear , and contract a kind of meanness by passing through the mouths of the vulgar, a poet should take particular care to guard himself against idiomatic ways of speaking.........The great masters in composition know very well that many an elegant phrase becomes improper for a poet or an orator, when it has been debased by common use." (The Spectator, No.285.)

Mr. Addison wanted to avoid vulgarity. As a consequence, according to his sentiment, he created Sir Roger. He felt ease at the home of Sir Roger –"I am the more at ease in Sir Roger's family, because it consists of sober and staid persons: for as the knight is the best master in the world, he seldom changes his servants; and as he is beloved by all about him, his servants never care for leaving him; by this means his domestics are all in years, and grown old with their master." (SirRoger at home).

Mr. Addison was religious-minded. Naturally his essay was reflected with that ideology –"I am always very well pleased with a country. Sunday, and think, if keeping holy the seventh day were only a human institution, it would be the best method that could have been thought of for the polishing and civilizing of mankind." (Sir Roger at Church). In this essay he upholded the observance of Sunday on account of its social in influences rather than for its religious meaning-"Sunday clears away the rust of the whole week."

'The Drama-an allegory' is an excellent essay of Addison's style. Though this essay Addison tried to organize his humour-"Her name was Fancy. She led up every mortal to the appointed place, after having very officiously assisted him in making up his pack, and laying it upon his shoulders. My heart melted within me to see my fellow- creatures groaning under their respective burdens, and to consider that prodigious bulk of human calamities which lay before me."

Again in his Mischiefs of Party Spirit, he says Party spirit is harmful to man's morals and understanding. It may even lead to civil war and blood-shed –"A furious party –spirit, when it rages in its violence, exerts itself in civil war and blood-shed; and when it its under its greatest restraints, naturally breaks out in falsehood, detraction, calumny, and a partial administration of justice. In a world, it fills a nation with spleen, rancour, and exercise an exit of all the seeds of good-nature, compassion, and humanity".

Addison's style is marked for fantastic blending of humour and satire. There is no mannerism in his prose-style. He wrote without any effort. He also used irony and wit to mark his essay didactic. His essays were not 'art for the sake of art'. Critical investigation observes a mind approach of puritanical propaganda in his essays. Addison's aim and endeavour was "to enliven morality with wit, and to temper wit with morality."

Addison, regarded as one of the greatest prose stylists in English literary history, and the 'founder of modern English essay and modern English prose, was the pioneer of a style that was very simple, lucid, natural, moderate, free from extravagant expression, and called 'middle style'. It is a style of straightness, without any obscurities, ambiguities, complexities, or superfluities. "He perfected English prose as an instrument for the expression of social thought." Moreover, Addison, as an essayist, is often seen as a moralist, a preacher, a philosopher and critic, and also a humorist. In this writing we will discuss with reference from Addison's The Spectator essays.

Dr. Johnson for the first time mentioned Addison's style to be 'middle style'. He says well-

"His prose is the model of the middle style; familiar but not coarse, elegant but not ostentatious: on grave subjects not formal; on light occasions not groveling, but without scrupulosity, and exact without apparent elaborations; and always equable, and always easy, without glowing words or painted words or pointed sentences."

Actually, he is clear, fluent and understandable in what he wants to say.

Clearness and lucidity of expression is the most striking feature of Addison's style. There is no complexity or obscurity or difficulty in his expression. Even, a very long sentence can express clear ideas at the very first sight or reading. For example,

"sometimes he will be lengthening out a verse in the singing psalms, half a minute after the rest of the congregation have done with it; sometimes when he is pleased with the matter of his devotion, he pronounces amen three or more times to the same prayer, and sometimes stands up when everybody else is upon their knees, to count the congregation, or see if any of his tenants are missing." (Sir Roger at Church)

Here, more than one idea regarding Sir Roger's humorous activities is expressed with the help of many comas and semicolons. But each of the ideas is expressed clearly without any haziness.

However, Addison is also very expert, when situation demands, in using short sentences-

"As soon as the sermon is finished, no body presumes to stir till Sir Roger is gone out of the Church."

(Sir Roger at Church)

Again, Addison also writes many compact and succinct sentences having quotable quality like those of Bacon. For example –

"In this case, therefore, it is not religion that sours a man's temper, But it is his temper that sours his religion."

(Uncharitable Judgment)

Humour is one of the most notable qualities of Addison's style. Addison's humour is mainly ironical and satirical and sometimes funny. It is not harsh or bitter but gentle, genial and civilized with a view to correcting the society out of its follies and foibles. We can mention an example from the essay, "Sir

Roger at Church"-

"As Sir Roger is landlord to the whole congregation, he keeps them in very good order, and will suffer nobody to sleep in it besides himself; for it by chance he has been surprised into a short nap at sermon, upon recovering out of it he stands up and looks about him, and if he sees anybody else nodding, either wakes them himself, or sends his servants to them."

Here, the humorous irony towards Sir Roger's eccentricities is notable.

Addison's style is not highly figurative. Fanciful similes and metaphors are not found in his writings. Rather, when he thinks that his use of figurative language would be more useful and effective, only then he uses them. Such as:

"and his coachman has the looks of a privy –councillor"

(Sir Roger at Home)

Here, by 'the looks of a privy councilor', Addison wants to reveal the coachman's serious and wise looks with a touch of humour. Again –

"A sermon repeated after this manner, is like the composition of a poet in the mouth of a graceful actor."

(Sir Roger at Home)

Addison uses many allusions, anecdotes, references. Additionally, most of his essays are headed by quotations from classical or modern authors and these quotations are very apt to the subjects of the essays. For example, 'Sir Roger at Church' begins with the motto from Pythagoras –

"First, in obedience to thy country's rites,

Worship 'th' immortal God"

Apparently, it seems that Addison is not laborious in his expression and word selection as the reader is not to pay any labour to read and understand his writings. But, actually "Addison was extremely fastidious in his choice of words and laborious by polished and balanced hphrases." Here lies his difference from other prose writers. In fact, most of the prose of Milton, Bacon and Lamb demands simplified version and explanation. On the other hand, Addison himself is a simplified version.

Addison's style is near to the language of conversation, but not to the informal conversational style of Montaige. Sometimes, it seems that Addison is talking with the reader. Such as the speaker, the Spectator, that is, Addison is telling that –

"As I was walking with him [Sir Roger] last night, he asked me how I liked the good man [the Chaplain] whom I have just now mentioned, and without saying for an answer, told me, that he was afraid of being insulted with Latin and Greek at his own table." (Sir Roger at Home)

That is in the midst of the description of talking about the chaplain between the speaker and Sir Roger, the writer as well as speaker tells us whom he has just mentioned in previous paragraph.

In fine, we cannot but admit Addison's great service to English prose as well as English literature. He showed a perfect English prose style to a large extent, and freed it from extravagances and excesses of eighteenth century writers, and brought in it clearness, lucidity and exactness. Indeed, we can end the discussion with Dr. Johnson's tribute, regarded as classic, to it –

"Whoever wishes to attain an English style, familiar but not coarse, and elegant but not ostentations, must give his days and nights to the volumes of Addison."

## *Annotations*

**1.Guelfes and Gibelines:**-Or Guelphs and Ghibelines, names given to the papal and imperial factions who destroyed the peace of Italy from the twelfth to the end of the fifteenth century.

**2.the League:**-The Catholic league formed by Henry, Duke of Guise, in 1576, against the Huguenots or Protestants in France.

**3.prick-eared cur:**-But in Addison there is a special application to the Puritans, whose ears stood out prominently to view because they wore their hair short.

**4.good neighbourhood:**-Good feeling between neighbours.

**5.to the prejudice of the land-tax:**-To make the land-tax worse. It had been increased by the more accurate valuation of estates. Sir Roger attributes it to the malice of the Whigs towards the Tory land-owners.

**6.scheme of party-notions:**-Exposition of the principles held by a party.

## *MISCHIEF OF PARTY SPIRIT : SHORT QUESTIONS AND ANSWERS.*

**Q1: What is "party spirit" according to Addison?**

A: "Party spirit" is extreme attachment to a political group that divides people, causes hatred, and harms morals and judgment.

**Q2: Why does Addison tell the anecdote about Sir Roger?**

A: Sir Roger was insulted when asking for directions because people judged him by party labels, showing how party spirit causes misunderstanding and hatred.

**Q3: What division does Addison say is most harmful to a country?**

A: A country divided into opposing parties becomes like two separate nations, filled with hatred and social discord.

**Q4: How does party spirit affect morals and judgment?**

A: It destroys virtue, leads to hatred and falsehood, and makes people unable to judge others or works of merit fairly.

**Q5: What example from a philosopher does Addison mention?**

A: Addison cites Plutarch, who said a man should not hate even his enemies because hatred becomes a habit that harms even friends.

**Q6: What kind of writing is wrongly praised due to party spirit?**

A: Scurrilous or abusive writing is often praised as good simply because it supports a party's view.

**Q7: What solution does Addison offer against the mischief of party spirit?**

A: He suggests that all honest men should unite in an association to defend virtue and good sense, regardless of party loyalty.

**Q8: What can extreme party spirit lead to at its worst?**

A: At its worst, party spirit can lead to civil war and bloodshed.

**Q9: What does Addison say about the effect of party spirit on a nation's unity?**

A: Addison says party spirit divides a nation into two opposing peoples, making them strangers and enemies, which destroys unity, weakens the nation, and even gives advantages to common enemies.

**Q10: How does party spirit affect morals and understanding according to Addison?**

A: Party spirit harms people's morals and understanding, sinking the virtue of a nation, destroying common sense, and filling hearts with hatred, falsehood, and rancour if it becomes violent.

**Q11: What does Addison say about hatred through the reference to the philosopher Plutarch?**

A: Addison quotes Plutarch, who warns that hating even enemies breeds a poisonous habit of mind that eventually spreads to friends and indifferent people, thus worsening human relations.

**Q12: According to Addison, how does party spirit influence judgment?**

A: Party spirit distorts judgment; people fail to see truth or merit and judge others, books and writings based on party allegiance rather than real quality or worth.

**Q13: What does Addison consider a worse outcome when party spirit is restrained?**

A: Even if restrained, party spirit leads to falsehood, detraction, slander, partial justice, and deep bitterness, poisoning the nation's compassion and humanity.

**Q14: What is one example Addison uses to show party spirit's effect on personal interaction?**

A: Sir Roger's childhood experience shows party spirit leads people to insult him instead of helping, revealing how factional hostility destroys basic courtesy and neighborly relations.

**Q15: What is Addison's ultimate suggestion to combat the mischief of party spirit?**

A: He suggests that honest men, regardless of party, should unite to defend virtue and justice and prioritize character over factional allegiance.

## *Some Important long Questions and Answers*

## *1.What are the Mischief Of Party Spirit mentioned in the essay?*

The essay Mischief Of Party Spirit has been classed as one of the most fundamental texts on the subject of political rivalries based on the 18th century party politics. 18th century was marked for the immense expansion of party feuds between Whigs and Tories. Influence Party Spirit had an ill effect on the morals and judgements of the people knowledge and learning shuffled violently due to the pernicious effect of narrow party spirit. According to Joseph Addison when the effects of division rage in its full violence it exerts it self in civil war and bloodshed. Due to the enormous influence of party spirit there arises one kind of sophistry practised by all the parties.

That sophistry is nothing but taking any scandalous story that has been whispered or invented of a private man for a known, and doubted truth raising suitable speculations. Joseph Addison considered that there should never be a spirit of division among the country man due to the influence of pre judiciary party oriented politics. He thinks that in the country where previous a spirit of division then a person of merit of a different party principal always become the target of attacks from the opposition.

The biggest damage caused by party spirit arises when in a nation persons of the greatest merit are reduced into shameful errors and work inside a prejudice. Bad effects of party spirit influence meaning honest minds and because of this ill effect a good man of merit is filled with uncharitable and barbarous notions. Whenever in any Nation this kind of party politics takes place, then nothing but only damage and disaster is caused to the nation which hampers mens morality, social consciousness ethics and even private life also. These are the mischief caused by party spirit as discussed in the essay.

Joseph Addison as an essayist professed doctrine was to enhance the ethics and mores of his contemporary society. Social concern is considered as the central object of Mischief of the Party Spirit. He, says that such a impudent exercise of narrow partisanship will ultimately destroy virtue in once mind and heart. Addison's answer to this problem is that all honest men should unify into an association irrespective of political learning's and should stand against the common enemies of virtue, humanity and good sense. Addison's final concern toward the partisanship does not appear to be convincing. Though he unwillingly involved into a fallacious debate because he himself is advocating a clear breach of social thought on ethical grounds.

**2.Who was Plutarch? What is his relevance in the essay Mischief Of The Party Spirit?**

Plutarch was a celebrated Roman writer also a philosopher, who wrote lives of the ancient Grecians and Roman's.

Plutarch in the essay told one of the most remarkable true statements regarding political rivalries. According to Plutarch a man should never allow himself to hate even his enemies, because if the person indulge dispassion in any occasion, then that feeling of hatred will automatically rouse the sense of hatred among others.

The mention of Plutarch and his statement are extremely relevant in the essay. When Joseph Addison discusses some of the important negative aspect of political rivalries, then he mentions the name of Plutarch. Plutarch clearly reveals his opinion that one person should never encourage the feeling of jealousy and hatred in his mind, rather he warns us against such feelings because if anybody is found indulging in the feelings of hatred then it will automatically spread among the others. Plutarch statement is significant from the perspective of dealing positively with one's own political opponent. Thus the message which Plutarch has delivered here becomes extremely relevant in regard to the central concern of the essay that is the negative mischiefs caused by political parties.

**3.Who is Sir Roger in Mischief of the Party Spirit? Explain the anecdote in which Sir Roger was humiliated in his boyhood.**

Sir Roger de Coverley was an English squire at the Court of Queen Anne. He epitomizes the values of the old country gentry and is used as a figure of fun to ridicule Tory Politics and politicians of the time as old fashioned, out of touch and thus harmless in terms of politicaleffect and impact. When Addison and Sir Roger were talking about the malice of Parties, Sir Roger frequently tells Addison about an accident that happened to him when he was a child. He tells that in his Childhood days the feuds ran high between two parties namely, the Round-heads and the Cavaliers. For his purpose Sir Roger had to inquire "which was the way to St.Anne's Lane". When he asked this question to a person, instead of answering his question, the person called him "a young Popish cur" and asked him "who made Anne a Saint". At that very moment Sir Roger was totally confused. After sometimes Sir Roger asked another person "which is the way to Anne's Lane", then that person instead of showing him the way, told that she had been a Saint before he was born would be one after he was hanged and also called Sir Roger a "Prick-eard cur". After all these happened to Sir Roger he did not feel fit to repeat the former question, but going into every lane of the neighbourhood he asked what they called the name of that lane. Without giving any offence to any party, Sir Roger finally found out the place he inquired after. Sir Roger generally closes his narrative with reflection on the mischiefs that parties do in the country and how good neighbours were spoiled and how honest gentlemen are led to hate one another

**4. Who was Plutarch? What did he say in the essay Mischief of the Party Spirit?**

Ans- Plutarch was a Greek philosopher and biographer. In his essay Mischief of the Party Spirit Addison attacked the spirit of hatred which brings ruins to the peace and prosperity of a nation and individual. In this regard he cites the example of Plutarch, who said that a man should not hate even his enemies. According to Plutarch if a man hate his enemies than he will contract such a venomous habits of mind which by degrees will break out upon those who are his friends or those who are indifferent to him.

**5.Why sir Roger was confused in mischief of party spirit?**

Ans-Sir Roger de Coverley was an English squire at the Court of Queen Anne. He epitomizesthe values of the old country gentry and is used as a figure of fun to ridicule Tory Politics and politicians of the time as old fashioned, out of touch and thus harmless in terms of political effect and impact. When Addison and Sir Roger were talking about the malice of Parties, Sir Roger frequently tells Addison about an accident that happened to him when he was a child. He tells that in his Childhood days the feuds ran high between two parties namely, the Round-heads and the Cavaliers. For his purpose Sir Roger had to inquire "which was the way to St.Anne's Lane". When he asked this question to a person, instead of answering his question, the person called him "a young Popish cur" and asked him "who made Anne a Saint". At that very moment Sir Roger was totally confused. After sometimes Sir Roger asked another person "which is the way to Anne's Lane", then that person instead of showing him the way, told that she had been a Saint before he was born would be one after he was hanged and also called Sir Roger a "Prick-eard cur". After all these happened to Sir Roger he did not feel fit to repeat the former question, but going into every lane of the neighbourhood he asked what they called the name of that lane. Without giving any offence to any party, Sir Roger finally found out the place he inquired after. Sir Roger generally closes his narrative with reflection on the mischiefs that parties do in the country and how good neighbours were spoiled and

## 6.Prose style of Joseph Addison in Mischief Of Party Spirit

18th century in English literature is basically known as the age of prose and reason. And the age has produced some of the most intellectual authors like Joseph Addison, Steele. They are particularly marked for periodical writings. Addison's prose style in this regard may be mentioned, his prose style is neat and clean, with a high intellectual sense. Every sentence in the essay is arranged in a very simple manner which appear lucid, which all the readers can easily read and understand. In his prose style there is found the true maturity of an intellectual writer. Every words by Addison used in the essay have a weight of their own having a certain kind of depth, which definitely aroused our attention.

Then there is found another technique of Addison's prose style, which is found in his use of allusions. For instances in the essay Mischief Of Party

Spirit the allusion of the statement uttered by the great Roman Philosopher Plutarch is extremely significant, which contributes to the enrichment of his prose style. As a writer of periodicals Addison very well mentions the element of high intellectualism in his writing style. In his present essay Addison's prose style become highly appropriate to suits the subject matter of the essay.

Joseph Addison's final reverence to the partisanship does not appear to be conveyancing. He unwillingly falls into a fallacious argument because he himself is advocating a clear breach of Prose style though on moral grounds. There shall remain every possibility that in such cases of fission between virtuous and villainous, two parties will ultimately be formed which will once again stand the danger of endangering the party spirit.

**7.Influence of party spirit in the Mischief Of The Party Spirit.**

In the essay Mischief Of The Party Spirit, Joseph Addison has analysed all the negative sides of a furious party spirit. He thinks that, there cannot be a judgement of division among a country then a dreadful partition among the various political parties. That spirit of division divides government in to two distinct people and make them greater stronger and more averse to each other. The division is such that it makes a group of people as two separate Nations. The effect of such a division is extremely pernicious to the last degree, not only with the regard to those advantages which they give the common enemies, but those private evils which they produce in the heart of every common human being. This is how the influence of division is very fatal to both men's morals and their understandings, sinking the virtue of a nation destroying every common sense.

The party spirit does not only intertwine and raise men's morals, it paralyzed and dangers one's faculty of decision. One who is driven by this spirit becomes partial toward his reasoning, incapable of ascertaining real truth and appreciating real essence of beauty. As a consequence, a man of having ability and honour may appear to one as a dishonorable and vile person if he associate with different camp; a bad book may seems illuminating or an indecently offensive style of writing may be regarded as satire. Partisan lookout toward life by its prejudiced nature distorts knowledge and wisdom in man.

**8.Joseph Addison as a Social Critic with Special References to "Mischiefs of Party Spirit"**

**Joseph Addison: Illuminating Society's Frailties and the Evils of Party Spirit**

As an essayist Joseph Addison's professed doctrine was to improve the morals and mores of his contemporary society. Social criticism is by and large the core of his essay. In his Spectator essays, as also in some of his Tatler publications, Addison wrote to focus on the flames and depravities of his fellowmen and pointed out how these lacunae could be overcome. This is not to suggest that he had any professed political or ideological standpoint; nor was he motivated by any terrible reformistic zeal. He was a benign essayist at bottom and, accordingly satire or bitter criticism of human frailties was not his domain.

He, with a Chaucerian view, laughed good humorously at the foibles, specifically related to social manners and social health, with the purpose of killing as well as laughing with those faults of those persons he laughed at. In his essay entitled Mischiefs of Party Spirit, Addison focuses on the evils that are escalated in society through a zealous adherence to narrow and parochial party interest, as practiced by political personages. Joseph Addison's works often addressed various societal issues of his time, including the detrimental effects of party spirit. One of his most renowned essays, Mischiefs of Party Spirit, provides valuable insights into his perspectives on this subject.

**The Pitfalls of Party Spirit: Joseph Addison's Critique of Excessive Party Loyalty and its Detrimental Effects**

In Mischiefs of Party Spirit Addison criticizes the negative consequences of excessive party loyalty and the harmful influence it has on society. He highlights how party spirit can lead to the erosion of reason and rationality, replacing them with blind partisanship and animosity. Addison argues that when individuals become deeply entrenched in their political affiliations, they tend to abandon critical thinking and lose sight of the common good.

Addison emphasizes the dangers of party spirit in several ways. Firstly, he discusses how it fosters a divisive mindset that promotes the interests of one group over those of the entire nation. He warns that such narrow-mindedness can lead to the neglect of important issues and the adoption of policies that favor a particular party's agenda rather than the welfare of the people. He cautions, "There cannot a greater judgment befall a country than such a dreadful spirit of division as rends a government into two distinct people, and makes them greater strangers and more averse to one another, than if they were actually two different nations. "

**The Divisive Plight of Party Spirit: Joseph Addison's Critique of Intolerance and Betrayal in Politics**

Politics, Addison sees around him, is not guided by purely ideological motivations but by a violent intolerance of contrary opinion and a disrespect for anything and everything out of the straitened spheres of partisan political activity. Addison is of opinion that it is owing to the mischief's the parties do in the country that good neighborhood is spoiled and basically honest gentlemen are led to hate one another.

Moreover the major governmental policies which are supposed to work for the prosperity for the nation we also dictated by such narrow concerns of party interest, as a result of which the basic purpose of such politic are betrayed. For him, it is a great plight of a nation when a country, a government or the most major institutions are sharply divided into polar opposites as a result of the workings of this party spirit. It ultimately results in civil wars and bloodsheds: "A furious party-spirit, when it rages in its full violence, exerts itself in civil war and bloodshed; and when it is under its greatest restraints, naturally breaks out in falsehood, detraction, calumny, and a partial administration of justice. In a word, it fills a nation with spleen and rancour, and extinguishes all the seeds of good-nature, compassion, and humanity."

**Joseph Addison's Critique of Party Spirit: The Erosion of Civil Discourse and Impaired Judgments**

Addison criticizes the impact of party spirit on public discourse and reasoned debate. He laments that individuals driven by party loyalty often resort to personal attacks, character assassinations, and the distortion of facts to further their partisan goals. This, in turn, undermines the foundation of a healthy democratic society, where respectful dialogue and the exchange of ideas should prevail: "If this party-spirit has so ill an effect on our morals, it has likewise a very great one upon our judgments."

Addison argues that party spirit can impair individuals' ability to make objective judgments and form independent opinions. He believes that excessive allegiance to a political party can blind people to the merits of opposing viewpoints, hindering the pursuit of truth and progress. He advocates for the cultivation of a more inclusive and tolerant society, where individuals are encouraged to critically evaluate ideas and engage in constructive dialogue.

**Private Evils of Partisanship and its Moral Consequences**

Furthermore, Addison says that such a division by party politics, since it rends a country into two virtually makes a common enemy stronger, but he is not particularly interested in the international aspect of the mischief's of the party spirit, rather he is concerned with the 'private evil which the spirit private evil of partisanship breeds in the heart of every particular person. The influence of narrow partyism, for Addison, is ruinous "both to means morals and their understanding, it sinks the virtue of a nation".

It is a religious as well as a philosophical percept that once hate is given an entry into the human mind, it would naturally multiply itself, ultimately roving harbourer of hate its victim. The party spirit engenders the passion of hate in man. Addison is less concerned with the philosophical aspect of this insalubrious passion, he concentrates on the evils it thrust upon social life. He laments that the mind of many good men among us appear soured with party principals which defy both reason and religion.

**The Corrosive Influence of Party Spirit: Joseph Addison's Warning on Distorted Judgment and the Search for Unity**

The party spirit does not only confound and improve men's morals, it injures and dangers one's faculty of judgment. One who is guided by this spirit becomes one-eyed, incapable of discerning real truth and appreciating real beauty. As a result, a man of merit and honour may appear to one as a dishonorable and vile person if he belongs to different camp; a bad book may appear illuminating or an indecently opprobrious style of writing may be regarded as satire. Partisan attitude to life by its prejudiced nature distorts knowledge and learning in man.

Addison says that such a shameless practice will ultimately destroy virtue in good man it is the restless ambition of artful politician which thus splinters the integrity of nations and infects the innate virtue man. Addison's answer to this problem is that all honest men should unify into an association irrespective of political learning's and should stand against the common enemies of virtue, humanity and good sense:

*"Were there such an honest body of neutral forces, we should never see the worst of men in great figures of life, because they are useful to a party; nor the best unregarded, because they are above practising those methods which would be grateful to their faction. We should then single every criminal out of the herd, and hunt him down, however formidable and overgrown be might appear: on the contrary, we should shelter distressed innocence, and defend virtue, however beset with contempt or ridicule, envy or defamation. In short, we should not any longer regard our fellow-subjects as Whigs and Tories, but should make the man of merit our friend, and the villain our enemy."*

Addison's final solution to the partisanship does not appear to be convincing. He unwillingly falls into a fallacious argument because he himself is advocating a clear breach of social though on moral grounds. There shall remain every possibility that in such cases of cleavage between virtuous and villainous, two parties will ultimately be formed which will, once again, stand the danger of engendering the party spirit.

### Conclusion

Joseph Addison, through his essay "The Mischiefs of Party Spirit," presents a compelling critique of the detrimental effects of excessive party loyalty on society. His observations regarding the erosion of reason, the neglect of the common good, and the erosion of civil discourse continue to hold relevance even in contemporary times. Addison's work serves as a reminder of the importance of fostering a more rational and inclusive political culture, where the welfare of the nation takes precedence over partisan interests.

## 9. Joseph Addison's Enduring Social Critique in "Mischiefs ofParty Spirit

Influential eighteenth-century essayist Joseph Addison's "Mischiefs of PartySpirit," which appeared in Spectator No. 50 on April 27, 1711, offered a timeless societal critique. Addison's observations are still remarkably applicable in today's globe, where divisive political ideologies dominated society. Parties are like ignorant armies that clash by night, perpetuating mischiefs that tear the fabric of society. This narrow adherence to party interests, as scrutinized by Joseph Addison in 'Mischiefs of Party Spirit,'reveals a moral decadence that transcends ideologies,posing profound questions about the survival of democracy in a world plagued by divisive politics.To comprehend the significance of Addison's critique, it is imperative to delve into the nature of his writing and his role in the literary landscape.Addison, described as an essayist of a middle style, seamlessly combined Baconian objectivity with Lamb's subjectivity.His contribution tothe initiation of novel writing through spectator essays is monumental, setting the stage for a new era in literature.The crux of Addison's literary prowess lies in the charm and delightfulness of his essays, which extend beyond the realm of literature to influence life and manners.Addressing human vices, frailties, vanities, and affectations,Addison adopted a unique approach characterized by gentle humour rather than fierce attacks.This distinctive style is particularly evident in his celebrated essay, "Mischiefs of Party Spirit."In this notable essay, Addison directs his scrutiny towards the societal evils stemming from a narrow adherence to party interests, a theme strikingly relevant both in his era and persisting worldwide today.

His observations on the political world reveal a moral decadence that transcends ideological motivations, portraying a society intolerant of contrary opinions and disrespectful of diverse perspectives.Central to Addison's concerns is the divisive nature of party politics, which he perceives as fragmenting society into disconnected pieces.This Fragmentation,Addison argues, compromises the verybessence of democracy, raising questions about its survival in the face of escalating harm caused by parties.A poignant aspect of Addison's critique is his exploration of character assassination, drawing parallels between historical contexts and the contemporary misuse of social media platforms. He underscores the damaging effects of divisive politics on critical thinking and understanding,where misinformation and false narratives thrive.Historical examples further bolster Addison's argument, citing instances from European history, such as the Whigs and Tories, and the Guelfs and Guidelines. The persisting impact of party politics on modern international movements, exemplified by conflicts in Afghanistan, Iraq, Sudan, and Kashmir, underscores the enduring relevance of Addison's observations.In proposing solutions, Addison advocates for the formation of an association comprising honest individuals who can counteract the detrimental effects of party spirit. However, a critical analysis reveals a weakness in Addison's argument, as he seems to contradict his criticism of party culture by endorsing the formation of a neutral force.Despite this apparent inconsistency, Addison's overarching aim is clear—to criticize and improve rather than merely present a snapshot of contemporary society.His focus on countering the spirit of hatred that disrupts the peace and prosperity of a nation emphasizes the universal truth in his observations.To Addison, parties are not inherently detrimental; rather, it is the enslavement of party principles that poses a threat. In advocating for humanity as the prime factor in living, Addison encourages readers to rise above the divisive nature of party politics and embrace a broader, more inclusive perspective.To conclude, Joseph Addison's article "Mischiefs of Party Spirit" presents a thorough analysis of the social evils that are supported by specific political parties. The eternal significance of his insights emphasises the necessity ofa sophisticated comprehension of party politics and a dedication to the higher ideals of mankind. We might be inspired by Addison's appeal for harmony as contemporary readers and resist the polarising forces endangering society.

**IMPORTANT QUOTATIONS AND EXPLANATIONS**

**1. "There cannot a greater judgment befall a country than such a dreadful spirit of division as rends a government into two distinct people..."**

In this central quotation, Addison warns against the destructive force of rigid party spirit, which he sees as one of the worst calamities that can happen to a nation. A "spirit of division" refers to intense factionalism that splits society into opposing camps (historically between Whigs and Tories in Britain). According to Addison, when political rivalry becomes so fierce that people first identify as party members rather than as countrymen, social harmony collapses. The metaphor of "two distinct people" suggests that political factionalism creates quasi-separate nations under one government, each viewing the other with suspicion and hostility. Such division is "pernicious to the last degree" because it weakens not only national unity but also the ability of citizens to function together productively. They become strangers to each other and lose a shared sense of purpose. The phrase also implies that such internal division hands advantages to external enemies: a country divided against itself cannot defend its interests effectively. Importantly, Addison points out that the harm is both public and private: it affects national affairs as well as the hearts and minds of individuals, corroding morals and understanding. This quotation sets the tone for the rest of the essay, showing Addison's deep concern that partisan loyalty should never override loyalty to common humanity and reason.

**2. "A furious party-spirit, when it rages in its full violence, exerts itself in civil war and bloodshed..."**

Here Addison describes the worst consequences of unchecked party spirit. By calling it "furious," he emphasizes that extreme partisanship is not a rational political stance but an emotional frenzy that can escalate beyond debate into physical conflict. His reference to "civil war and bloodshed" evokes the English Civil War—a real historical example of what destructive factionalism can cause. Yet even when party spirit is constrained (i.e., not erupting into outright war), it still produces grave evils. These include falsehood, detraction, calumny, and a skewed justice system, where accusations and slander replace truth and fairness. In other words, even without violence, intense partisanship warps public discourse and undermines integrity. The list Addison gives—slander, malicious gossip, and partial justice—highlights how party loyalty corrupts society at every level. Instead of encouraging honest debate and examination of issues, people accept unverified and scandalous claims if they suit their political side. This enriches the negative social atmosphere with "spleen and rancour," filling hearts with bitterness rather than goodwill. The deeper message is that even when violent conflict is absent, a divided nation still suffers significant moral decay. Addison wants readers to see party spirit not as harmless competition but as a poisonous social force that must be resisted for the sake of justice, truth, and common humanity.

**3. "Plutarch says very finely, that a man should not allow himself to hate even his enemies..."**

This quotation reflects Addison's moral and philosophical stance on human emotions in politics. Citing Plutarch, the ancient philosopher, adds authority and depth to his argument. Plutarch's advice is simple yet powerful: hatred towards enemies should be avoided because hatred itself is a habit that can grow beyond its original object. According to this wisdom, once a person conditions themselves to hate, that emotion can spill over into relationships with those who were neutral or even friendly. Addison uses this idea to illustrate a key psychological effect of party spirit—it nurtures hatred beyond political disagreement. When individuals allow themselves to despise "the other side," they risk corrupting their own moral character and creating a chronic disposition of hostility. This insight goes beyond practical politics into ethics: political opposition should not degenerate into personal animosity. Addison implies that rational debate and mutual respect are essential for a healthy society. By including this quotation, he shows that party spirit is not just a political issue but a moral disease that affects the human heart and mind. This idea also ties back to his larger theme that partisan conflict destroys compassion, good-nature, and humanity. Instead of learning to coexist with differing views, people steeped in party spirit foster hatred that ultimately harms societal bonds and individual character.

**4. "How many honest minds are filled with uncharitable and barbarous notions... out of their zeal for the public good!"**

In this passage, Addison points out one of the ironies of party spirit: that even well-meaning people can be led astray by it. He recognizes that many individuals genuinely believe they are acting in the public interest — that their party's goals are noble and righteous.

However, loyalty to a party's cause often blinds them to reason and fairness. Their "zeal for the public good" — initially a virtue — becomes distorted. Instead of promoting real welfare, it fuels intolerance, prejudice, and hostility. People begin to judge others not by their character or actions, but by political labels and affiliations.

Addison's use of the words "uncharitable and barbarous notions" is significant. It highlights how party spirit doesn't just make people biased; it dehumanizes them. They are willing to hold harsh judgements, spread rumors, or engage in character assassination, all in the name of supporting their side.

This quotation serves as a warning: party spirit doesn't only empower the unscrupulous — it entices good people into harmful behaviour. Thus, he argues that principled independence and moral reasoning must be maintained even in political engagement. Otherwise, well-intended passion for public good becomes complicit in social division and moral decay.

**5. "Were there such an honest body of neutral forces..."**

Here Addison proposes his solution: he calls for an association of honest individuals who rise above party differences. Rather than judging people by faction, they would judge them by their character and actions.

In multiplying the metaphor of "neutral forces," Addison envisions a society where merit, virtue, and justice matter more than party loyalty. Such a group would prevent incompetent or unscrupulous individuals from gaining influence just because they serve a faction's interests. At the same time, it would recognize and support people of true worth, even if they refuse to follow party politics.

He envisions this body doing two things: (1) exposing and punishing real wrongdoing wherever it appears, and (2) protecting innocence and virtue even when it faces unjust criticism or ridicule. This represents a return to rational judgement, impartiality, and moral clarity — qualities that party spirit, in his view, obscures.

Ultimately, this quotation encapsulates Addison's optimistic belief that political life need not devolve into hatred and factionalism. If citizens are willing to think independently and ethically rather than succumb to partisan impulse, society can avoid the "mischiefs" he describes and build a healthier public life.

# CHAPTER FOUR

# TOASTED ENGLISH

**TOASTED ENGLISH**
**R.K.Narayan**

In the American restaurants they call for 'Toasted English', referring to English muffins which though being made in America, now retain 'English' as a sort of concession to their origin. The same may be said of their language too. Americans too, went through a phase of throwing out the British but retaining their language and letting it flourish on American soil; the resultant language is somewhat different from its British counterpart; it may be said to have gone through a process of toasting. One noticeable result of this toasting is that much of the formalism surrounding the use of English has been abandoned. In America, they have freed the language from the stifling tyranny of the Passive Voice. Where we should say ceremoniously 'Trespassing prohibited', their signboards, as I noticed in the parks of Berkeley merely say, 'Newly planted, don't walk'. Absolutely 'No Parking' leaves no room for speculation, and no motorist need spend too much time peering out and studying the notice. In a similar situation our authorities are likely to plant a twenty-line inscription on the landscape to say, 'Under Municipal Act so and so this area has been reserved, etc. etc., and any vehicle stationed thereon will be deemed to have contravened subsection so and so of the Motor Vehicles Act, etc. etc. I saw on many American office doors just 'Do not Enter'. The traffic signs at pedestrian crossings never mince words; they just say 'Go' or 'Wait' In a Hollywood studio I was rather startled to read, 'Mark Stevens—Keep out'. Mark Stevens is a busy television personality who does not like to be disturbed by visitors. Incidentally, it left me wondering why, if Mr Stevens does not like interruptions, he should announce his name at all on the door! But it is one of the minor mysteries that make travel through that country so engrossing. The 'toasting' of English has been achieved through other means also.

Americans have evolved certain basic key words which may be used anywhere, anyhow, words which have universal multipurpose use. I may make my point clear if I mention the example of the word 'Check' which may safely be labelled the 'American National Expression'. While British usage confines it to its bare dictionary definitions, the American uses it anywhere, this expression being so devised that one may blindly utter it and still find that it is appropriate for the occasion. I'll check means I 'll find out, investigate, examine, scrutinise, verify, or probe. 'You check' means your ticket, token or whatever you may have to produce. 'Check room' is where you leave your possessions for a while. 'Check girl' is one who takes care of your coat,umbrella,or anything else you may leave in custody. 'Check in' and Check out' (at first I heard it as 'Chuck out' and felt rather disturbed) refers to one's arrival in a hotel and departure therefrom. And there are scores of other incidental uses for the word. If you are ever hard-up for a noun or a verb you may safely utter the word 'check'and feel confident that it will fit in. 'Fabulous' is another word that is used in that country freely,without much premeditation. Of course everyone knows what fabulous means,but the American usage has enlarged its sense. I found a lady in Wisconsin declare 'Oh, those cats of mine are fabulous and meaning that they were eccentric. "Oh, so and so, he is fabulous!"may mean anything from a sincere compliment to an insinuation that so and so displays a mild form of charming lunacy. 'Ok' is another well-known example.It is the easiest sound that ever emanated from the human vocal cords.Everyone knows how comprehensive its sense can be. 'Okay' is a self-sufficient word which needs no suffix to indicate any special respect for the listener; it can stand by itself without a 'Sir' to conclude the sentence.In this respect it is like 'Yeah' which seals off a sentence without further ado. 'Yes sir', or 'Yes,darling', is conceivable but 'Yeah Sir', or 'Yeah darling', is unthinkable.'Yeah' is uttered in a short base-of-the-tongue grunt, which almost snaps off any further continuation of a sentence. 'Yes' involves time as the sibilant could not prolong. The refinements of usage in countries where English has a bazaar status are worth a study.On a London bus you will never hear the conductor cry, 'Ticket,ticket'. He approaches the passenger and says ' Thank you', and on receiving the fare says ' Thank you, sir'. I found out that one could calculate the number of passengers in a bus by having the total number of 'Thanks' heard.In any Western Country if a receptionist asks 'Can I help you?' it really means 'Have you any business here,if so, state it.'Or it may mean 'Evidently you have wandered off into a wrong place,go away.' A man who wants to pass you always says 'Excuse me', while he may with all justice burst out, 'What do you mean by standing there gaping at the world while you block everybody's passage? Stand aside, man!' When you send your card in, the busy-man's secretary appears and whispers in your ear, 'Would you like to wait?' Though the tone is one of consultation, you have really no choice in the matter. The thing to do is not to answer the question but say 'Thanks' and look for a comfortable seat in the waiting room, although you may feel like saying,'No, I wouldn't like to wait. I have other things to do.' The time has come for us to consider seriously the question of a Bharat brand of English. So far English has had a comparatively confined existence in our country, chiefly in the halls of learning, justice, or administration. Now the time is ripe for it to come to the dusty street, market place, and under the banyan tree. English must adopt the complexion of our life and assimilate its idiom. I am not suggesting here a mongrelization of the language. I am not recommending that we should go back to the days when we heard, particularly in the railway,"Wer U goin', man?" Bharat English will respect the rule of law and maintain the dignity of grammar, but still have a Swadeshi stamp about it unmistakably, like the Madras handloom check shirt or the Tirupathi doll.

- R.K. Narayan

**About the Lesson**

In Toasted English, R.K. Narayan shows the difference between American and British English. The essay is infused with humour. The author states that like Indians, Americans too, retained the English language and let it flourish even though they drove the British away. The Americans simplified the usage of English by eliminating the passive voice in the language. For instance in place of 'Trespassing Prohibited' the notice reads 'Newly planted, don't walk'. American English also includes words such as Ok, check and fabulous – words which can be used anywhere and in any context.

He further discusses the 'bazar status' of English in London. In day-to-day activities in London, English is used in a fine, polished way. The writer illustrates this by discussing certain expressions (as they are used in practical life) and what they connote. For instance "Can I help you?" actually implies "Have you any business here, if so, state it".

He concludes by proposing that Indians should follow a 'Bharat brand of English' in post independence India. The writer feels that like American English, Indain English should have its own flavour and style. There should be a "Swadeshi stamp"on it.

**GLOSSARY**

toasted English : toasted means to heat and turn brown bread. Here the expression toasted English means adding local flavour to English to suit local sensibilities.

**muffin** : a small, sweet, cup - shaped cake

**abandoned** : given up

**stifling** : suppressing and choking

**tyranny** : injustice and unfairness

**mince words** : to hold back words for the sake of politeness

**pedestrian** : person walking on a street

**inscription** : words carved or engraved on a rock

**trespassing** : going on to a privately owned land without permission

**speculation** : supposition, guessing

**Hollywood** : centre of the American film industry

**eccentric** : peculiar, not normal

**insinuating** : suggestive

**emanate** : to flow out from a source or proceed

**ado** : fuss

**sibilant** : characterized by hissing or a hushing sound like that of 's' or 'sh'

**mongrelisation** : mongrel means any cross between different things.

of the language : mongrelisation means to make mongrel in race, nature, or character. Here it means creation of a new language by mixing different languages.

## *Toasted English by R.K. Narayan*

**Summary**

In this essay "Toasted English" R.K. Narayan uses fantastic examples to demonstrate the differences between American and British English.

The author reminds us that, like Indians, Americans pushed the British out of their country but allowed the English to stay. By abandoning Passive Voice, the Americans simplified the use of English. On the notice-board, for example, instead of "Trespassing Prohibited" they put, "Newly planted, don't walk" R.K. Narayan refers to this process of altering the English language as "toasting" Americans have developed a set of basic core words that may be employed wherever, at any time—words with global multifunctional application. "O.K" "Yeah" and similar expressions are more regularly employed.

R.K. Narayan goes on to examine English's "the bazaar status" In London, English is utilised with finesse. On a London bus, the conductor will never say "Ticket, Ticket" but will just approach the passenger and say "Thank you" after receiving the fare and issuing the ticket.

Finally, he closes by adapting English to our needs, creating a "Bharat brand of English" He expressly states that he does not support "mongrelisation" or the hybridization of English. The author believes that Indian English should have its own distinct identity, a "Swadeshi Stamp" The author hopes that Indians build their own English that is more original and distinct than current English.

## *Short Questions and Answers*

**1. What does 'toasted English' refer to in American restaurants?**

Answer: 'Toasted English,' according to author R.K. Narayan, refers to English muffins that, despite being created in America, still bear the 'English' label as a nod to their heritage.

**2. What has happened as a result of the 'toasting' of English in America?**

Answer: The 'toasting' of English in America has resulted in the loss of formalism surrounding the use of the English language.

**3. How have the Americans simplified the language? Give examples.**

Answer: The Americans simplified the language by separating it from the suffocating tyranny of the Passive Voice. For example, in America, the phrase 'Trespassing Prohibited' on signboards has been replaced with 'Newly Planted', 'Do Not Walk', which is less straightforward than British English and provides no space for speculation. Additionally, many American office doors bear a notice that reads, 'Do Not Enter.' Simultaneously, the traffic signs at pedestrian crossings are unambiguous; they simply say 'Go' or 'Wait'.

**4. What does the author means by 'the American National Expression'? Why does it say so?**

Answer: The author expresses how Americans have evolved specific keywords that can be utilised anywhere in the world by using the phrase "the American National Expression."

He says this because expressions like 'check,' 'anywhere,' and 'anyhow' can be used carelessly and still be considered acceptable for the situation.

**5. The author approves and disapproves of American English in certain senses. Give examples to elaborate.**

Answer: The author agrees that Americans have built their own versions of English to fit their tastes and lifestyles, making it simpler, more conversational, and more informal. They liberated themselves from the suffocating tyranny of the Passive Voice in their use of the English language, making it simpler to express themselves. The author, on the other hand, disapproves since it does little to uphold the rule of law and the dignity of grammar. Giving out simplified instructions on the signboard where it is written 'Absolutely Little Parking' is an example of where the author approves of American English, as it provides no space for conjecture and one does not need to spend too much time peeking out and studying the signboard. Another point of contention for the author is the way American English disrespects the rule of law and the dignity of grammar when someone says something like, 'Were U going, man?'

**6. How according to the author, can the mongrelisation of English can be prevented?**

Answer: According to the author, the mongrelisation of English can be avoided by respecting the rule of law and preserving the dignity of grammar, which keeps the English language on track.

**7. How does the author visualize Bharat English?**

Answer: The author R.K. Narayan envisions Bharat English as upholding the rule of law and the dignity of grammar. He stated that the Bharat brand would have to come to the dusty street, the market place, and under the banyan tree with an unmistakable swadeshi stamp, much like the Madras handloom check shirt or the Tirupati doll.

**Some More Questions to Look at**

**1. What happened to English in America?**

It underwent a process of toasting. The American English retained the language but adapted it according to the American soil. They did away with much of the formalism.

**2 Give an example of the lack of use of the passive voice in American English.**

Example is where our boards would say 'Trespassing prohibited', their signboards (Americans) would say 'Newly Planted, Don't Walk' or 'Absolutely No Parking'.

**3. Why does a motorist need to spend a very short time reading a notice in America?**

A motorist needs to spend a very short time reading a notice because the message in the notice is very short, crisp and brief.

**4. Explain the line: but it is one of the minor mysteries that make travel through that country so engrossing.**

The author is intrigued by the nuances of the American English. He is surprised by the fact that a sign board reads 'Mark Stevens Keep Out'. If that person was so busy why did he put the sign board of his name at all.

**5. What is strange about Mark Steven's room?**

The strange part was that he did not want any interruptions, yet he announced his name on the sign board.

**6. How is the word 'fabulous' used in America? How is it used in England?**

According to the author the word 'fabulous' is used differently. And without any thought about its usage. He gives example of a woman from Wisconsin who used fabulous for her cats which was different from the regular usage of the word 'fabulous'. She meant they were eccentric. According to the American usage the word 'fabulous' could mean anything from a sincere compliment to an insinuation.

**7. What are the various meanings of the word 'check' in America?**

The various meaning of the word 'check' in America means: I'll check means I'll find out, investigate, examine, scrutinize, verify or probe; 'Your check' means your ticket, token ; 'Check room' is where you leave your possession; 'Check girl' is one who takes care of your coat, umbrella; 'Check in' and 'Check out' refer to one's arrival and departure in a hotel. Apart from this there are scores of other incidental uses for this word.

**8. What would the Bharat brand of English be like?**

The Bharat Brand of English would be to take English beyond the halls of learning, justice and administration. It would be to take it further to the dusty street, market-place and under the banyan tree.

**9. What shows you that America uses an informal version of English? Support your answer with details from the text.**

Signs like "Go" or "Wait" at pedestrian crossings, and the use of simple and direct language on notices, show that America uses a more informal and straightforward version of English.

**10. Comment on the title 'Toasted English'.**

He starts with how a simple English Muffin in America is called a 'toasted English'. The author takes it further from the restaurant towards the usage of English Language. How the language has been appropriated to flourish in the American soil. He gives ample examples to prove this point. Hence the title is justified.

**11. What does the writer's suggestions about developing a Bharat brand of English show you about his attitude towards languages?**

The writer seems open to the idea of languages evolving and adapting to the cultural context. The suggestion of a Bharat brand of English reflects an attitude of embracing linguistic diversity.

**12. Cite examples of humour in this essay.**

The humor comes from the author's observations about language use, like the "Mark Stevens—Keep Out" sign and the idea of calculating the number of passengers by the number of "Thanks" heard on a bus.

**13. Do you think we can learn something from the example of bus conductors from London?**

Yes, we can learn about politeness and indirect communication. Even though the bus conductors ask if you would like to wait, the expected response is not a direct answer but a simple "Thanks." It shows a cultural way of being thoughtful of others.

**Some long Questions and Answers**

**1. Humour is the quality of a literary or informative work that makes the character and/ or situations seem funny, amusing, or ridiculous.**
**Do you appreciate the humour in this piece? Support your answer with examples.**

Answer: Yes, I enjoy the essay's humour. The author expertly communicated his thoughts to the readers through an interesting narrative that would have otherwise been a completely different case. Several examples can be given to demonstrate the humour in the essay, such as Narayan referring to the American form of English as "toasted" English because, while the Americans preserved the English language after removing the British, they modified it and made it their own over time. His exaggeration that one can safely say "check" in every setting and believe that it will fit in is also an amusing way of ensuring the readers grasp the word's vast range of meanings in different contexts.

**OR**

This essay has an admirable sense of humour. The author uses humour deftly throughout the article to illustrate various scenarios. Numerous examples can be used to demonstrate the humour in this piece/essay. For example, the essay's portrayal of the English language's transformation into 'Toasted English' exemplifies the essay's comedy. Additionally, I find the author's exaggeration of the term 'check' as an American National Expression to be amusing. Additionally, the author's different examples of signboards are humorous, which is greatly appreciated.

**2. Do you agree with Narayan that we need a 'Bharat' brand of English? Why?**

Answer: Yes, I concur with the author, R K Narayan, that we require a 'Bharat' brand of English. Just as the Americans 'Toasted' English to create their own dialect, the time has come for us in India to seriously consider developing our own Bharat brand of English. Until now, English has been relegated to the halls of learning, administration, and courts of justice in India. Now is the time for it to make its way down the dusty street, to the market square, and beneath the banyan tree. English must adapt to the circumstances of our lives and make an attempt to assimilate its idiom. However, this does not imply a distortion of the grammar. Bharat English will adhere to the rule of law and the dignity of grammar while maintaining a Swadeshi flavour.

Yes, I believe we need a Bharat brand of English because English in India has had a relatively limited presence in the country—most notably in the halls of learning, justice, and administration. Now is the time for it to appear on the dusty street, in the market square, and beneath the banyan tree. English must take the hues of our lives and adapt its idiom. Bharat English would uphold the rule of law and the dignity of grammar while nevertheless bearing an unmistakable swadeshi mark.

**OR**

**3. Give examples of Indian words that have been incorporated into the English dictionary.**

Answer: Some of the English words that have been incorporated into the English dictionary are dhoti, hartal, guru, samosa, etc.

# CHAPTER FIVE

# Araby

## *Araby*

**James Joyce**

NORTH RICHMOND STREET being blind, was a quiet street except at the hour when the Christian Brothers' School set the boys free. An uninhabited house of two storeys stood at the blind end, detached from its neighbours in a square ground The other houses of the street, conscious of decent lives within them, gazed at one another with brown imperturbable faces.The former tenant of our house, a priest, had died in the back drawing-room. Air, musty from having been long enclosed, hung in all the rooms, and the waste room behind the kitchen was littered with old useless papers. Among these I found a few paper-covered books, the pages of which were curled and damp: *The Abbot,* by Walter Scott, *The Devout Communnicant* and *The Memoirs of Vidocq.* I liked the last best because its leaves were yellow. The wild garden behind the house contained a central apple-tree and a few straggling bushes under one of which I found the late tenant's rusty bicycle-pump. He had been a very charitable priest; in his will he had left all his money to institutions and the furniture of his house to his sister.When the short days of winter came dusk fell before we had well eaten our dinners. When we met in the street the houses had grown sombre. The space of sky above us was the colour of ever-changing violet and towards it the lamps of the street lifted their feeble lanterns. The cold air stung us and we played till our bodies glowed. Our shouts echoed in the silent street. The career of our play brought us through the dark muddy lanes behind the houses where we ran the gauntlet of the rough tribes from the cottages, to the back doors of the dark dripping gardens where odours arose from the ashpits, to the dark odorous stables where a coachman smoothed and combed the horse or shook music from the buckled harness. When we returned to the street light from the kitchen windows had filled the areas. If my uncle was seen turning the corner we hid in the shadow until we had seen him safely housed. Or if Mangan's sister came out on the doorstep to call her brother in to his tea we watched her from our shadow peer up and down the street. We waited to see whether she would remain or go in and, if she remained, we left our shadow and walked up to Mangan's steps resignedly. She was waiting for us, her figure defined by the light from the half-opened door. Her brother always teased her before he obeyed and I stood by the railings looking at her. Her dress swung as she moved her body and the soft rope of her hair tossed from side to side.Every morning I lay on the floor in the front parlour watching her door. The blind was pulled down to within an inch of the sash so that I could not be seen. When she came out on the doorstep my heart leaped. I ran to the hall, seized my books and followed her. I kept her brown figure always in my eye and, when we came near the point at which our ways diverged, I quickened my pace and passed her. This happened morning after morning. I had never spoken to her, except for a few casual words, and yet her name was like a summons to all my foolish blood.Her image accompanied me even in places the most hostile to romance. On Saturday evenings when my aunt went marketing I had to go to carry some of the parcels. We walked through the flaring streets, jostled by drunken men and bargaining women, amid the curses of labourers, the shrill litanies of shop-boys who stood on guard by the barrels of pigs' cheeks, the nasal chanting of street-singers, who sang a come-all-you about O'Donovan Rossa, or a ballad about the troubles in our native land. These noises converged in a single sensation of life for me: I imagined that I bore my chalice safely through a throng of foes. Her name sprang to my lips at moments in strange prayers and praises which I myself did not understand. My eyes were often full of tears (I could not tell why) and at times a flood from my heart seemed to pour itself out into my bosom. I thought little of the future. I did not know whether I would ever speak to her or not or, if I spoke to her, how I could tell her of my confused adoration. But my body was like a harp and her words and gestures were like fingers running upon the wires.One evening I went into the back drawing-room in which the priest had died. It was a dark rainy evening and there was no sound in the house. Through one of the broken panes I heard the rain impinge upon the earth, the fine incessant needles of water playing in the sodden beds. Some distant lamp or lighted window gleamed below me. I was thankful that I could see so little. All my senses seemed to desire to veil themselves and, feeling that I was about to slip from them, I pressed the palms of my hands together until they trembled, murmuring: "O love! O love!" many times.At last she spoke to me. When she addressed the first words to me I was so confused that I did not know what to answer. She asked me was I going to Araby. I forgot whether I answered yes or no. It would be a splendid bazaar, she said she would love to go."And why can't you?" I asked.While she spoke she turned a silver bracelet round and round her wrist. She could not go, she said, because there would be a retreat that week in her convent. Her brother and two other boys were fighting for their caps and I was alone at the railings. She held one of the spikes, bowing her head towards me. The light from the lamp opposite our door caught the white curve of her neck, lit up her hair that rested there and, falling, lit up the hand upon the railing. It fell over one side of her dress and caught the white border of a petticoat, just visible as she stood at ease."It's well for you," she said."If I go," I said, "I will bring you something."What innumerable follies laid waste my waking and sleeping thoughts after that evening! I wished to annihilate the tedious intervening days. I chafed against the work of school. At night in my bedroom and by day in the classroom her image came between me and the page I strove to read. The syllables of the word Araby were called to me through the silence in which my soul luxuriated and cast an Eastern enchantment over me. I asked for leave to go to the bazaar on Saturday night. My aunt was surprised and hoped it was not some Freemason affair. I answered few questions in class. I watched my master's face pass from amiability to sternness; he hoped I was not beginning to idle. I could not call my wandering thoughts together. I had hardly any patience with the serious work of life which, now that it stood between me and my desire, seemed to me child's play, ugly monotonous child's play.On Saturday morning I reminded my uncle that I wished to go to the bazaar in the evening. He was fussing at the hallstand, looking for the hat-brush, and answered me curtly:"Yes, boy, I know."As he was in the hall I could not go into the front parlour and lie at the window. I left the house in bad humour and walked slowly towards the school. The air was pitilessly raw and already my heart misgave me.When I came home to dinner my uncle had not yet been home. Still it was early. I sat staring at the clock for some time and. when its ticking began to irritate me, I left the room. I mounted the staircase and gained the upper part of the house. The high cold empty gloomy rooms liberated me and I went from room to room singing.

From the front window I saw my companions playing below in the street. Their cries reached me weakened and indistinct and, leaning my forehead against the cool glass, I looked over at the dark house where she lived. I may have stood there for an hour, seeing nothing but the brown-clad figure cast by my imagination, touched discreetly by the lamplight at the curved neck, at the hand upon the railings and at the border below the dress.When I came downstairs again I found Mrs. Mercer sitting at the fire. She was an old garrulous woman, a pawnbroker's widow, who collected used stamps for some pious purpose. I had to endure the gossip of the tea-table. The meal was prolonged beyond an hour and still my uncle did not come. Mrs. Mercer stood up to go: she was sorry she couldn't wait any longer, but it was after eight o'clock and she did not like to be out late as the night air was bad for her. When she had gone I began to walk up and down the room, clenching my fists. My aunt said:"I'm afraid you may put off your bazaar for this night of Our Lord."At nine o'clock I heard my uncle's latchkey in the halldoor. I heard him talking to himself and heard the hallstand rocking when it had received the weight of his overcoat. I could interpret these signs. When he was midway through his dinner I asked him to give me the money to go to the bazaar. He had forgotten."The people are in bed and after their first sleep now," he said.I did not smile. My aunt said to him energetically:"Can't you give him the money and let him go? You've kept him late enough as it is."My uncle said he was very sorry he had forgotten. He said he believed in the old saying: "All work and no play makes Jack a dull boy." He asked me where I was going and, when I had told him a second time he asked me did I know The Arab's Farewell to his Steed. When I left the kitchen he was about to recite the opening lines of the piece to my aunt.I held a florin tightly in my hand as I strode down Buckingham Street towards the station. The sight of the streets thronged with buyers and glaring with gas recalled to me the purpose of my journey. I took my seat in a third-class carriage of a deserted train. After an intolerable delay the train moved out of the station slowly. It crept onward among ruinous house and over the twinkling river. At Westland Row Station a crowd of people pressed to the carriage doors; but the porters moved them back, saying that it was a special train for the bazaar. I remained alone in the bare carriage. In a few minutes the train drew up beside an improvised wooden platform. I passed out on to the road and saw by the lighted dial of a clock that it was ten minutes to ten. In front of me was a large building which displayed the magical name.I could not find any sixpenny entrance and, fearing that the bazaar would be closed, I passed in quickly through a turnstile, handing a shilling to a weary-looking man. I found myself in a big hall girdled at half its height by a gallery. Nearly all the stalls were closed and the greater part of the hall was in darkness. I recognised a silence like that which pervades a church after a scrvicc. I walked into the centre of the bazaar timidly. A few people were gathered about the stalls which were still open. Before a curtain, over which the words Cafe Chantant were written in coloured lamps, two men were counting money on a salver. I listened to the fall of the coins.Remembering with difficulty why I had come I went over to one of the stalls and examined porcelain vases and flowered tea- sets. At the door of the stall a young lady was talking and laughing with two young gentlemen. I remarked their English accents and listened vaguely to their conversation."O, I never said such a thing!"

"O, but you did!"

"O, but I didn't!"

"Didn't she say that?"

"Yes. I heard her."

"0, there's a ... fib!"

Observing me the young lady came over and asked me did I wish to buy anything. The tone of her voice was not encouraging; she seemed to have spoken to me out of a sense of duty. I looked humbly at the great jars that stood like eastern guards at either side of the dark entrance to the stall and murmured:

"No, thank you."

The young lady changed the position of one of the vases and went back to the two young men. They began to talk of the same subject. Once or twice the young lady glanced at me over her shoulder.

I lingered before her stall, though I knew my stay was useless, to make my interest in her wares seem the more real. Then I turned away slowly and walked down the middle of the bazaar. I allowed the two pennies to fall against the sixpence in my pocket. I heard a voice call from one end of the gallery that the light was out. The upper part of the hall was now completely dark.

Gazing up into the darkness I saw myself as a creature driven and derided by vanity; and my eyes burned with anguish and anger.

**Footnotes**

1

Blindness supports one of the major themes in "Araby." In this first sentence, "blind" has two meanings. Literally, it refers to a cul-de-sac or dead-end street. However, figuratively, Joyce refers to the condition of the boy's, and other's, relation to reality, a kind of short-sighted naivety.

2

Many Christian Brothers' Schools were established throughout the world in the 19th century. The particular reference here is the O'Connell School, established in 1829 in North Richmond Street. It is the oldest of these schools in Dublin.

3

Joyce was a fierce critic of the Roman Catholic Church, and this specific word choice here provides a supportive example of this position: This little phrase suggests that religion has imprisoned the boys, and they are temporarily set free at the end of each day.

4

In establishing the setting in this first paragraph, Joyce presents the street as a representation of the Irish soul, uninhabited and detached. He personifies the houses here, making them more conscious and arguably more alive than the residents.

5

"Araby" is one of the stories in Dubliners, and Joyce uses the color brown frequently throughout these stories. The color here creates a discouraging and hopeless kind of mood for the story.

6

Joyce uses the house as a representation for all of Ireland. Since the previous tenant was a priest, who has since died, Joyce implies that the Church is also dead. Joyce hated Roman Catholicism, and the influences it had on him and others fuels one of his main themes in this short story as the young boy struggles to separate the secular from the sacred.

7

Joyce was raised as a Catholic in predominantly Catholic Ireland in the late 19th century. As he grew older, he rejected religion and criticized it in his work. There is much religious imagery in "Araby," acting as a sort of imposing and inescapable source of anxiety for the narrator.

8

Many of Joyce's adjectives in "Araby" create a drab and dull atmosphere. This technique is not subtle, and we can see here that choices like "musty," "waste," and "useless" all convey the lifelessness that surrounds the boy and pervades the neighborhood.

<u>9</u>

Sir Walter Scott's historical novel The Abbot, written in 1820, presents the life of Mary Queen of Scots in a religious and romantic way. The central character, Roland Graeme, is a young man who becomes involved in adventure and romance, much like the narrator of "Araby," who goes on his own quest. Joyce's inclusion of this text represents the complexity and confusion of romantic, religious, and materialist love that the boy faces in "Araby."

<u>10</u>

The Devout Communicant could refer to one of three texts with the same name. However, the more likely text is the popular Catholic work written by Pacificus Baker, a Franciscan Friar, published in 1761 and noted for its pious language that perhaps influences how the boy talks about Mangan's sister. The important take-away from this book's inclusion in this list of three is that it influences boy's language and perspective on life.

<u>11</u>

Francois-Jules Vidocq published The Memoirs of Vidocq in 1829. This popular 19$^{th}$-century novel was about a Parisian Police Commissioner and thief who was able to conceal his own crimes. The book's inclusion here presents and supports the theme of deception in the story. The presence of these three novels further strengthen the deception, because readers can understand their purpose but the boy himself remains ignorant of their meaning and influence.

<u>12</u>

Joyce gives readers a first look at the boy's romantic and naive view of life in this line. Readers can understand the the allegorical and symbolic meanings of the texts, and this line quickly reveals the identity of the narrator: He is a young boy who lacks an understanding of such figurative language and doesn't use it self-consciously.

<u>13</u>

Joyce's inclusion of an apple tree is a reference to the Garden of Eden from the Bible. Since the story of the apple involves Adam and Eve falling from grace by eating forbidden fruit and having their "eyes opened," the inclusion of this allusion helps provide context and foreshadow the events later in "Araby." In particular, pay attention to how many times Joyce uses the word "fall," especially around the end of the story.

<u>14</u>

The rusty bicycle-pump has been hailed as one of the treasures in Joyce's work. The rust on the pump represents the passing of time: the comparison of the priest's garden to Eden as After the Fall reinforces Joyce's position that the time of the Church has passed. He also foreshadows the boy's confusion of religion and sex by positioning the phallic, rusty bicycle pump within the garden.

<u>15</u>

The frequent hypocrisy of religion is a familiar theme in Joyce's work. This description hides a disconcerting question that Joyce uses to point out the hypocrisy of religion: if the priest was so charitable, how could he have had so much money at the time of his death? While the narrator doesn't understand such hypocrisy, readers know that "all" suggests a lot of money, particularly when referring to donations to institutions, and that leaving one's possessions to family, such as the sister here, is not true charity.

<u>16</u>

In this third paragraph, Joyce shows us the dreariness of Dublin by using increasingly darker and dreadful adjectives to describe the setting: "sombre houses," "feeble lanterns," "silent street," "dark muddy lanes," "dark dripping gardens," etc.

<u>17</u>

The boys' bodies glowing is an important image to contrast the dreary adjectives and descriptions Joyce puts into this paragraph. Toward the end of this passage, readers will notice that Joyce repeats the word "shadow" three times. This repetition, coupled with the other adjectives here, portray the people of Dublin as ghosts. However, since the boys "played till [their] bodies glowed," readers know that they are still alive; their youth and souls haven't yet been claimed by the dreariness of Dublin.

<u>18</u>

The repetition of the letter "d" in these words is an example of alliteration. This literary device has many uses, and the sound here helps add to the cadence of the passage and anchor the dark descriptions in the readers' minds.

<u>19</u>

In this passage, Joyce uses olfactory cues to create a run-down, working-class image of the city. Memory is closely linked to smell and certain scents can conjure strong emotions, as shown in this passage. Smell became a more prominent mode of representing sensory perception among modernists in the early 20th century.

20

By "the areas," Joyce means the places in front of many Dublin houses below the level of the sidewalk. Such spaces are also prevalent in the older brownstone buildings in New York City.

21

One reason for the choice of the name "Mangan" could be the Irish Romantic poet James Clarence Mangan, whose poetry Joyce admired. This reference would gesture to the history and tradition of female muses as divine inspiration for poets in medieval and Renaissance romantic poetry. This would be fitting, as romantic tropes and images appear throughout "Araby."

22

The inclusion of "railings" here is important because Joyce could count on his readers making the connection with the altar rails in Catholic churches. These rails separate the congregation from the altar and serve as locations for the faithful to kneel, pray, and take communion. By standing by these rails to watch Mangan's sister, the boy conflates her with the Virgin Mary as an object of religious veneration. However, he doesn't understand or recognize—perhaps due to repressive, religious influences—his sexual attraction to her. This confusion persists and is elaborated on in more detail.

23

The choice of "Mangan" for the girl's last name also serves another interesting purpose. In Gaelic, the family name "Mangan" refers to someone with an abundant amount of hair on their head. English readers may see a connection between the original Gaelic "mong," which means "hair," and the word "mane."

24

The color brown returns to describe the figure of Mangan's sister. This association informs us that she's older than the boys, and consequently the drab lifelessness of Dublin has already started to affect her.

25

A "litany" is a resonant or repetitive chant. Joyce uses this word to invoke its religious connotations, as a "litany" is also a specific type of prayer in a church service. By doing so, he connects religion with consumerism and materialist culture. This word choice parallels the narrator's own inability to separate religion from secular activities and desires.

26

A "come-all-you" was a type of street song that dealt with current events and popular heroes. These songs were also sung in pubs and other popular gathering places.

<u>27</u>

Jeremiah O'Donovan Rossa (1831–1915) founded the Irish Republican Brotherhood (IRB), which served as the main proponent of republicanism during the campaign for Ireland's independence. Rossa earned the nickname "Dynamite Rossa" for organizing one of the first Irish bombings of an English city.

<u>28</u>

Joyce combines the story's themes of romantic, religious, and materialist love in this paragraph through a routine shopping trip with the boy's aunt. Notice how the boy imagines this mundane task to be more like a sacred adventure, much like a knight on a medieval quest for the Holy Grail (the "chalice" he mentions).

<u>29</u>

The narrator's feelings of love for Mangan's sister interrupt his daily activities, many of which include religious rituals. Joyce suggests that religion tries to suppress and ultimately confuses the boy's romantic and sexual feelings. As seen with the earlier comparison of Mangan's sister to the Virgin Mary, the boy's struggle to separate his secular emotions from his religious upbringing continues as a pervasive theme in "Araby."

— <u>30</u>

Note the religious terms the boy uses when thinking about Mangan's sister: "litanies," "chalice," "adoration," etc. While the narrator professes to not understand certain things, readers have a deeper understanding of the significance of these religious undertones and the situation in which the boy finds himself: he is struggling with his conceptions of romantic and religious love.

<u>31</u>

Joyce's choice of words in this sentence masterfully conveys the boy's confusion about love and sexuality. The language the boy uses here is overly sentimental and even a little ridiculous, and he even ruins the mood of the simile by incorrectly calling the harp strings "wires."

<u>32</u>

The shift from the previous scene to this one occurs without a transitional paragraph; in fact, Joyce doesn't try to portray the story of "Araby" within a continuous time frame; we don't know how much time occurs throughout this entire narrative. This is characteristic of modernist writers, who prefer to focus on intense, emotional moments rather than the 19th-century, Victorian style of providing specific details about weather, clothing, food, views, houses, etc. However, the lack of time-focused transitions can sometimes make reading a modernist work more difficult than other kinds of literature with clearly detailed timelines.

33

Notice how the boy personifies his senses by saying that they are the ones who have the desire instead of him. This strategy gives readers the impression that the boy is trying to separate his mind from his body in order to understand his confusion.

34

Joyce uses the veil to encapsulate the blinding and stifling nature of religion. The metaphorical veil represents the narrator's lack of clarity surrounding his feelings for Mangan's sister due to his religious upbringing that has taught him to suppress those kinds of emotions.

35

Alone in the house (a classic masturbatory situation), the boy nearly engages in sexual activity. Instead, he presses his hands together and murmurs like he's in church. The culmination of his activity shows how the boy's religious upbringing has so suppressed his sexual feelings, with the religious completely obscuring the sexual in his mind and body.

36

This paragraph exemplifies an important modernist technique: Joyce shows the boys confusion after she speaks to him by making the prose itself abrupt and fragmented (stunned). This style is again a reaction against many of the 19th-century Victorian traditions that simply described all that the characters were feeling.

37

The Araby bazaar was a highly anticipated, annual event in Dublin in the 19th century that introduced foreign concepts such as music, literature, styles, and goods. Joyce's bazaar, Araby, was called "A Grand Oriental Fete: Araby in Dublin" and was held in May, 1894, to benefit a local hospital.

38

Notice how the narrator can only describe Mangan's sister as a bunch of disembodied parts and accessories (hands, hair, clothes, and jewelry). As "Araby" is told from the narrator's limited point of view, these descriptions speak to his distorted and superficial conception of her as an object of affection, rather than as a fully fleshed-out person.

<u>39</u>

Joyce builds on the theme of religion in the story here by showing how the girl's religious retreat takes precedence over her desire to enjoy the bazaar. The twirling of her silver bracelets also hints at a kind of nervous, and possibly sexual, energy that her religious obligations have also suppressed.

<u>40</u>

In Roman Catholicism and other religious or spiritual organizations, a "retreat" refers to location of privacy for a period of seclusion that allows the participants time to pray, meditate, receive advice, and discover ways to improve their moral lives.

— Wesley, Owl Eyes Editor

<u>41</u>

The details in this section are reminiscent of the biblical scene during the crucifixion of Jesus Christ, where the Roman soldiers are throwing dice over the possession of Christ's clothes. This image of the crucifixion is further supported by the spike (such as those in Christ's hands and feet) that Mangan's sister is holding and the earlier comparison of her to the Virgin Mary.

<u>42</u>

The strong presence of religion in this paragraph is continued as Joyce describes the light from the lamp shining on her hair, which gives readers an image of a halo and a light streaming from heaven.

<u>43</u>

This sentence melds the boy's confused feelings of religion and sexuality, and builds on two earlier established elements of the story: the Catholic altar rails and the Garden of Eden comparison. Here, the placement of "railing" between "falling" and "fall" strongly suggest and foreshadow the boy's coming fall from innocence.

<u>44</u>

A "petticoat" is a light, loose undergarment typically worn by women underneath a skirt or dress. The inclusion of this detail at the end of a paragraph full of religious imagery parallels the girl's twisting of the silver bracelet in the first line, effectively mixing the religious and sexual imagery that will continue to define Mangan's sister for the rest of the story.

<u>45</u>

Since the girl has just explained why she cannot go, this expression appears to carry overtones of envy and potentially bitterness. However, the boy appears to not notice this because of how deluded he is in his own fantasy.

46

As mentioned earlier with the romantic notions of the bazaar, this statement represents the foundation of story's climax. The boy makes a vow to the girl, which strongly suggests the quest of a knight.

47

The theme of consumerism and materialism occurs again in this line. The narrator's promise to Mangan's sister suggests that he believes expressions of love can be contained in objects and traded like commodities.

48

The word choice here emphasizes the boy's romantic fascination with Araby (and the enchanting idea of the Middle East). His romantic quest has consumed his reality and hindered his ability to operate on a day-to-day basis. However, there is also a hint of a new understanding on the boy's part; he appears critical of his own past, as demonstrated by his recognition of his "innumerable follies."

49

"Araby" is not only the name of the bazaar (a market in Middle Eastern countries). The boy romanticizes Araby as a symbol of the mystical allure of the Middle East. We've seen how his romantic and religious love have manifested thus far in how he imagines himself as a knight on a holy quest, and this continues when he offers to attend the bazaar in order to purchase a gift for Mangan's sister.

50

The Freemasons are an international order that was established on the principles of mutual help and friendship. The aunt's surprise and apprehension is based on Freemasonry's position as primarily a Protestant organization. Since Ireland is predominantly Roman Catholic, such organizations would be feared and mistrusted at this time and place.

51

The color brown appears for the third time in the story when the boy imagines seeing Mangan's sister. Notice how his image of her is an echo of the earlier scenes, in which she is depicted religiously (the lamplight at the curved neck) and sexually (the border below the dress).

<u>52</u>

The name "Mercer" is derived from the Old French word "mercier" or "merchier," which means a merchant. Joyce chose this name to continue the theme of mercantile love. Notice how Mrs. Mercer is also the widow of a pawnbroker, and she also collects used stamps to sell for money to donate to the church. Again, the material is mixing with the religious similar to how it was in the paragraph about the boy's shopping trip with his aunt.

<u>53</u>

Instead of saying that the uncle is drunk, Joyce lets the reader figure this out along with the boy. This technique also serves another purpose: it shows how the boy has started to correctly interpret signs, demonstrating some growth on his part. This development foreshadows his final interpretation of his trip to Araby.

<u>54</u>

Many of Joyce's readers would understand his inclusion of Caroline Norton's poem and its relationship to "Araby." In the poem the Arab boy sells his beloved horse for money. However, in the end he regrets this decision and returns the gold to get his horse back. Such a reference hits on the boy's confusion between materialist and romantic love in "Araby."

<u>55</u>

Florins are a form of currency that originated in the city of Florence during the Renaissance. The coins had a likeness of St. John the Baptist on one side and one of the Virgin Mary on the other. This little fact not only subtly supports the confusion between the material and the romantic in the story, but florins from the late 19th century also depicted the British Queen Victoria on one side with a phrase on the other: "by the grace of God, defender of the faith." Since Ireland was still under British rule, this subtly reminds readers of colonialism, because the young Irish-Catholic boy has to carry around a coin that represents the authority of the Queen and the British (and Protestant) Church of England.

<u>56</u>

This train station in south Dublin is now known as the Dublin Pearse railway station. Notice how in this paragraph Joyce uses certain words to indicate the boy's making a special journey: "twinkling," "special," and "magical." This convey a sense of magic about the boy's quest and builds up our expectations as he arrives at the bazaar.

<u>57</u>

There are a few words in this paragraph that provide clues, but Joyce still uses a rather specific simile to ensure that readers make the connection between the Araby bazaar and a church. However, the quiet and the dark makes the scene more closely resemble a church after its service has finished.

<u>58</u>

Throughout Europe, such cafés typically had singers, dancers, and other entertainers perform for patrons. The food and entertainment were not of very high quality, so the presence of this café at Araby suggests that the bazaar not the grand wonder that the boy has made it out to be.

<u>59</u>

Since Joyce has made the comparison between Araby and a church explicit, then this line provides a very stark image of how money and religion are mixed in this place: The two men counting money inside a church likely alludes to the story of Jesus Christ in Matthew 21:12-13 in which he throws the money changers out of the temple, and a "salver" refers to the plate on which a wine cup sits for communion in church.

<u>60</u>

The word "fall" makes another appearance in this passage, again supporting the notion that like Adam and Eve in the Garden of Eden, the boy is about to experience his own "fall" from innocence.

<u>61</u>

This short scene represents the turning point of the story as the boy's situation worsens. Joyce's inclusion of English accents indicates that this Irish boy is in unfriendly territory because the British are running the bazaar. The short conversation they have is so ordinary as to be vulgar, and the boy begins to realize that his quest was not the sacred journey he thought it was.

<u>62</u>

Joyce termed this type of final scene as an epiphany in that it provides a moment of sudden revelation or insight even in an apparently ordinary situation or conversation. Joyce's epiphany shows how the boy acquires an intuitive grasp of reality: he is defeated; he failed his quest to buy a gift, but most of all, his self-deception and ego defeated him by making him believe that his quest was sacred. This epiphany represents the boy's fall from innocence and his change into an adolescent dealing with the harsh realities of life.

— Wesley, Owl Eyes Editor

<u>63</u>

The boy began with a florin, valued at two shillings or 24 pence. After his roundtrip train ticket and the unnecessary spending of a shilling at the entrance, he has two pennies and a sixpence, in total valued at eight pence. This small sum proves ironic in that he is left with not enough to purchase a gift, even if one were available.

<u>64</u>

Disillusioned by what he sees at the bazaar, the boy finally sees himself as readers have seen him for much of the story. He realizes his own vanity and foolishness, his unprofitable use of time, the futility of life in Dublin, that Mangan's sister likely has no interest in him, and that there is no magical "Araby" in Ireland.

**James Joyce (1882-1941):- A short Introduction**

James Joyce is generally regarded as this century's greatest prose stylist in English. The basis of this judgment is the extraordinary achievement of but three novels, A Portrait of the Artist as a Young Man (1916), Ulysses (1922), and Finnegans Wake (1939), and one book of short stories, Dubliners (1914). Had Joyce written nothing other than these four books, his position in English literature would be altered little if any at all. However, Joyce also wrote an interconnected series of elegant love poems loosely modeled after the style of Ben Jonson entitled Chamber Music (1907); another slim volume of poetry, Pomes Penyeach (1927); and a play of great challenge and complexity, Exiles.

**Dubliners:-A short analysis**

Like many important artistic works of the early twentieth century (the paintings of Joyce's contemporary Wassily Kandinsky, for instance, or Louis Armstrong's music), Dubliners appears deceptively simple and direct at first, especially compared with James Joyce's later works of fiction: A Portrait of the Artist As a Young Man, Ulysses, and Finnegans Wake. It is certainly his most accessible book — relatively easy to comprehend and follow, whereas the others mentioned tend to challenge even the most sophisticated reader.

It was in Dubliners that Joyce developed his storytelling muscles, honing the nuts-and-bolts craftsmanship that would make the high modern art of A Portrait of the Artist As a Young Man, Ulysses, and Finnegans Wake viable. In Dubliners, he does not yet employ the techniques of mimetic narrative (characteristic of A Portrait) or stream-of-consciousness (Ulysses), but he paves the way here for those technical breakthroughs. Dubliners is somewhat comparable to Picasso's so-called Rose and Blue periods, in which the painter perfected his skills at realistic portrayal with paint before pioneering cubism and other abstract styles. Joyce even introduces characters (Lenehan from "Two Gallants" and Bob Doran from "The Boarding House," for instance) who reappear in his later books.

Mainly, Joyce worked and played in Dubliners at plotting and characterization, description and dialogue, and (especially) point of view (the technical term for who is telling a story, to whom, and with what limitations). What is amazing is that such a relatively immature work succeeds almost without exception. And just as Picasso's realist works have not only lasted but are actually preferred by many museum goers to his more difficult-to-appreciate later paintings, Dubliners is the favorite James Joyce book of many readers.

The setting of Dubliners is, logically enough, in and around the city of Dublin, Ireland. Though the capital city of Ireland, the Dublin in which Joyce grew up was a provincial place — far less cosmopolitan than a number of other Western European cities of similar size (Venice, for instance). Unlike France, Spain, and Italy, Ireland had never been a center of continental culture; unlike England and the Netherlands, it had never been a trade hub. Nor, in contrast to then recently united Germany, was Ireland yet industrialized. (In fact, the country would remain almost exclusively rural for decades to come.) It was a kind of third-world nation, really, before the term existed. Though Dublin was a genuinely urban locale, with electric lights and streetcars, competing daily newspapers and even a museum, the city remained fairly unsophisticated at the time when Joyce wrote about it.

To some degree, this was a function of Ireland's geographical remoteness from the rest of the continent in the days before radio and air travel (much less television and the Internet). It is an island off an island (Britain) off the coast of Europe, and therefore somewhat inaccessible. James Joyce himself, however, blamed two other factors for the backwardness of his home city: the Roman Catholic Church and the neighboring country of England.

According to legend, St. Patrick had brought Christianity to Ireland in the Middle Ages; ever since, most Irish have observed a rigorous and rather literal brand of the religion, one that is perhaps more superstitious than the Christianity practiced by French Catholics, for instance. In story after story in Dubliners as well as in the novels he wrote later in his career, Joyce holds the Roman Catholic Church accountable for the failure of the Irish to advance in step with the rest of Europe. He was particularly bitter about the way in which the Church often recruited intellectuals like himself to serve in the priesthood — rather than encouraging them to use their minds in the service of progress, as doctors, scientists, or engineers.

Joyce also blamed England for what he saw as Ireland's backwardness. On July 1, 1690, at the Battle of the Boyne, the Protestant forces of King William III of England had defeated the Roman Catholic Jacobites of James II, causing the downfall of Catholic Ireland. Until 1922, when British Parliament granted independence to the country (while retaining control of what is to this day the province of Northern Ireland, the inhabitants of which tend to be Protestant rather than Catholic), Joyce's homeland would remain, in effect, a colony of England. Joyce and many other Irish saw this era of over 200 years as one of outright occupation by an overtly hostile enemy.

The period during which Dubliners is set follows the brutal so-called Potato Famine of the late 1840s — for which many Irish held the British responsible — after which a movement for Irish independence (led by the nationalist Charles Stewart Parnell) occurred. This movement, however, failed ignominiously when Parnell was betrayed by his own countrymen, and in the Dublin of Joyce's novels, the defeat still stings. (For evidence of this, see "Ivy Day in the Committee Room.") The Irish Revival, a movement begun in the 1880s to foster understanding and respect for Celtic and Gaelic language and culture, is referred to in Dubliners as well (in "A Mother" and "The Dead"). From the very first story onward, the book is rife with examples, obvious and less so, of the treachery of England and the English, at least in the opinion of Joyce and his characters.

The stories of Dubliners are united by the city itself — Dublin is rendered in Joyce's book with a concreteness and specificity that was unprecedented at the time of its writing. The other aspect that unites these disparate works of narrative prose is shared themes. Though the protagonist of "Araby" and that of "Clay" could hardly be more different with respect to age and temperament (the same goes for the main characters of "Eveline" and "The Dead"), all these stories are united by the ideas that the tales dramatize: paralysis, corruption, and death. In story after Dubliners story, characters fail to move forward, tending rather to forge outward and then retreat, or else circle endlessly. They are stuck in place. Examples of corruption — that is, contamination, deterioration, perversity, and depravity — occur throughout. Finally, Dubliners begins with a death and ends with a death (in a story titled, logically enough, "The Dead"), with numerous deaths either dramatized or referred to in between.

All of this knits the book's many and varied stories together in a web of place, time, and meaning. Each successive story gains in momentum and weight by virtue of following those that came before. (For instance, Gabriel Conroy from "The Dead" is more completely understood if thought of as the grown-up protagonist of "Araby.") And after reading the book, it will be hard to think of one Dubliners tale without remembering others.

## *Araby by James Joyce Analysis*

### Introduction

Araby is one of the short stories taken from James Joyce's collection of sketches and short stories entitled Dubliners. It is one which has received universal praise both for its exposition of matter and for the manner of its presentation. It is one in which the evocation of a mood is more important than the presentation of a neat, round narrative. Its theme is concerned with dream and disillusionment.

### Autobiographical Elements

The Story bears some autobiographical elements. It reflects the own childhood of Joyce. It refers to North Richmond Street to which Joyce and his family moved. Again the Joyce lived in a house corresponding exactly to the one described in the story. We further learn that the Christian Brother's School of the story is the one which Joyce attended during this early years. It also describes the plays in which he took part as a boy.

### Topical Allusions

The contemporary scene of Dublin has been finely caught in 'Araby. It is marked by a realism for which we cannot but have a high praise, In it Joyce refers to 'flaring streets' from which we learn that the streets had gas-lit lamps instead of electric lights. Streets around the market were often crowded, and shoppers were pushed every now and then by drunken men and bargaining women. They were also full with diverse kinds of noises. One could hear, for example, the curses of labourers, the shrill cries of shop-boys for the sale of pigs' cheeks kept in barrels over which they kept guard to prevent their stealing, and the nasal singing of patriotic songs and ballads about the troubles of Ireland under the British rule. The ballad come-all-you through which the nationalist leader O'Donovan Rossa gave a stirring call to the Irish is another topical matter. Another contemporary event was Araby itself, the Grand Oriental Fete which was held in Dublin from May 14 to

May 19, 1894.

**Sordidness of Dublin**

The sordidness of Dublin has been brought to a focus here. It was Joyce's explicit purpose that his countrymen should at least have one good look at themselves in his nicely-polished looking-glass in the form of this short story. And the picture that was reflected is far from flattering. Possibly the author presented the seamy sides of life so that the Irish could rectify and improve. There is first the reference to the blind street, the narrow passage in a slum open only at one side. We next hear of dark muddy lanes behind the houses where people of despicable character ('the rough tribes) lived in dilapidated cottages. Finally, the author mentions of the dark dripping gardens where ashpits gave out a foul smell and of stinky stables where a conchman smoothed and combed the horse or shook music from the buckled harness. All these help to produce the picture of a poor, foul-smelling, and shabby-looking place which the capital of Ireland was turned into at the time when 'Araby' was written.

**The Human Figures**

The human figures also produce another picture of Dublin. The author has described how in rows of brown houses lived decent people not capable of being excited. The story presents a fine picture of middle class people who remain contended with themselves and do not usually get involved in any neighbourly matters. The boys here are like those to be found everywhere. Play is to them what lifeblood is to a living being, Home life seems to have no attraction. Old men like the boy's uncle return late at night and often in a tipsy state. Women go on talking endlessly on small matters over evening meals. Women like Mrs Mercer want to be engaged in pious activities but not at their own cost. Outside they haggle over prices. Elderly men like the boy's uncle are miserly in nature. They try to dissuade young boys from one recreation that attracts them intensely. Thwarted in their aim, they pretend to be keen in boys' enjoyment and quote stale proverbs in support of their view. Religion is a strong force in Ireland and the story bears enough proof of that. The boy attended the Christian Brothers' School run by the Roman Catholics. The girl could not go to Araby because of a retreat to be observed at that time in her convent school. The former tenant of the house in which the boy lived was a priest who had left all his money to religious institutions. The keeping of girls indoors after school hours indicates the conservative nature of the people. Thus, the author succeeds in presenting the contemporary picture of Dublin having mostly middle-class conservative, religious-minded, economically weak, and unenterprising people who singularly lacked dynamism in their lives.

### The Boy's Love for the Girl

In 'Araby' Joyce draws an interesting sketch of the boy's love for the girl. It is entirely platonic, noble and pure in nature. The boy did not know whether he would ever speak to her. What worried him was the thought whether he would be able to convey her adoration in his state of emotional confusion. His body was like a harp and her words and gestures were like fingers running upon the wires. The girl was an object of endless fascination for him. Overtly or covertly he used to look at her. At evening when she stood on the doorstep to call her brother in to tea, he went along with him and stood near their railings looking at her. At the time of going to school he followed her, keeping her brown figure always in front of him. Every morning he lay on the floor in the front parlour and sought to look at her through a slit in the window. One rainy evening when he was alone in an empty and dark room the thought of her suddenly flashed in his mind, and it became unbearable for him to contain the uncontrollable emotions. So he held the palms of his hands tightly together and began to repeat in a low voice: "O my love! O my beloved" sometimes her name sprang to his lips in strange prayers and praises but its cause he did not understand. Sometimes his eyes were full of tears and he could not tell why. Occasionally a flood of emotions from his heart seemed to pour itself out into his bosom. The girl occupied his mind most of the times. Her image accompanied him even in places most hostile to romance. Love to him was like a chalice which he bore safely through a throng of foes. This finely stresses the holy nature of the boy's love for the girl.

### Depiction of the Girl

In the story both the boy and his beloved remain unnamed. The latter is simply known as Mangan's sister (obviously Mangan is the name of one of the friends of the boy). In the story the author has not directly stated that she was a beautiful girl; but he has left enough hints that point to her beauty. We are told of her brown figure : this does not mean that her skin was brown; it simply means she frequently wore a brown dress on her body. The boy loved to look at her while he stood by the railings. Her dress swung as she moved her body, and the soft rope of her hair tossed from side to side. She became a lovely figure at evening when the light fell on one side of her body. The light caught the white curve of her neck, lit up her hair that rested there, and shone on her hand that lay on the railing. The light fell over one side of her dress and caught the white border of her petticoat, just visible when she stood bowing her head towards the boy. Besides her figure, her name was like a summons to all his foolish blood.

**Dream and Disenchantment**

Araby is concerned with dream and disenchantment. The boy's love for the girl initiated the dream. It flowered when one day she spoke to him and asked whether he would go to Araby. She encouraged him to go there adding that there would be a splendid bazaar there. Visibly moved, he replied that if he went there, he would certainly bring something for her. The dream began to spread a sweet fragrance from that evening when she first spoke to him. His waking and sleeping hours were spent in innumerable follies. He wished to annihilate the tedious days that must yet pass before he could go to the bazaar. He neglected his studies. His master began to suspect him to be idling. Her image stood before him and his page when he attempted to study. He had hardly any patience with the serious work of life which seemed to him ugly monotonous child's play. The only thing that mattered was Araby and a gift for his beloved. Here the dream reached its fullest development. Afterwards starts the gradual fading of the dream. On the appointed day his uncle reached home too late. He was also unwilling to let him go. With his aunt's assistance he at last got the permission but reached there when it was ten minutes to ten. Most of the stalls were closed and a major part of the hall was in darkness. All he could hear was the sound of the counting of cash and of a young lady's small talk with a pair of young gentlemen. After the examination of porcelain vases and flowered tea-sets when two great jars drew his attention as fit gifts for this beloved, suddenly the young lady asked if he wished to buy anything. Her tone was most discouraging. The boy checked his money and found it too small for the jars. He replied in the negative. He let fall his pences that vocalized his incapacity. Meanwhile the lights in the upper gallery were turned off. His dream of bringing a gift for his beloved came to an end. He was filled with disenchantment and despair.

**Symbolic Significance**

The boy's going to Araby has a symbolic significance. On one level it is his quest for beauty in the drab surroundings of his country. On another level it is man's universal search for the ideal amidst choking realities. This symbolic meaning is suggested by the reference to the 'chalice' which reminds us of the Grail Legend. In the end the boy's quest for beauty is foiled by the rude blast of his unhelpful surroundings and own dependence. This is like man's search for the ideal universally frustrated by the harsh touch of reality.

**Theme**

The theme of 'Araby' is escape the boy's attempts at escape from the sordid and grim realities of life with the help of love which was like a chalice to him- a chalice that he strove to bear safely through a throng of foes – a group of unromantic men and women who drank and cursed, bargained and cried to the top of their voice for sale, sang or chattered aimlessly for hours' over the evening meal. Dream and disenchantment the contrast between dream and reality- might also be regarded as one of the themes of this story. An additional theme of the story is the 'paralysed uneventfulness to which the modern city reduces the lives of its citizens.'

**Evocation of a Mood**

In 'Araby' the author has put more emphasis on the evocation of a mood rather than on the smooth narration of a story. Indeed the plot of the story is very simple-a boy's desire of bringing a gift for his beloved from a bazaar and its frustration. But the story finely realises a poetic mood through which he passes. It is seen in the description of the winter evening sky with its colour of ever changing violet, the boy's looking at the swing of his beloved's dress, the tossing of her hair from side to side, and the white curve of her neck, his imagining that he was bearing his chalice safely through a throng of foes, that his body was like a harp on which played her words and gestures and that she was uttering the syllables of Araby to him through the silence of the night, the dark rainy evening with no sound in the house, the fall of raindrops on the sodden flower beds, the uncontrollable emotions making him tighten his palms and cry softly 'o love ! O love!' and the perceiving in the bazaar a silence that prevails in the church after a service. It is to be noted that the mood serves various functions: it sheds light on the nature of the principal character, it helps the story to move on; and but for it the disenchantment and despair that take place in the end would not have been so telling

**Araby Epiphany**

The author has characterized all the stories and sketches of Dubliners as 'epiphanies'. In that sense Araby which is included in Dubliners is also an epiphany. By this religious term Joyce made most clear what he was after. By an epiphany he meant, as he himself stated in his Stephen Hero, 'a sudden spiritual manifestation, whether in the vulgarity of speech or of gesture or in a memorable phase of the mind itself.' He believed that it was for the man of letters to record these epiphanies with extreme care, seeing that they themselves are the most delicate and evanescent of moments'. It was in this epiphany that the author found "the supreme quality of beauty."

In 'Araby' Joyce mentioned such a moment of epiphany. It was when the boy in his nurture of love amidst drab surroundings and harsh sounds imagined himself bearing the chalice safely through a throng of foes.

**Araby as A vivid waiting**

It is well-known that when Joyce's Dubliners were being rejected by publishers for his outspokenness, Ezra Pound the American poet and critic came to his stout support and praised his book in high terms. Regarding Araby he remarked : 'It is much better than a "story"; it is a vivid waiting'. By this remark Pound wanted to emphasize that 'Araby' is not like an average story in which all the problems are happily solved before it inevitably reaches its expected conclusion. For example, many issues in 'Araby' remains unresolved : We do not know what finally happens to the uncle or the aunt or Mrs Mercer, nor do we know what happens to the boy's love for the girl. But the story's superiority lies in enkindling a clear sense of waiting in us. We wait to see what happens to the boy's love for the girl even after the bursting of his dream. We further wait to see whether Dublin whose grim realities and stereotyped figures that are responsible for the frustration of the boy's dream can overcome these and help once again in the matter of the blooming of his love.

**Self-awareness of the Boy**

The most important aspect of 'Araby' is the sudden self-awareness of the boy. Before his arrival at 'Araby' he was leading as it were a curtained life. Nothing mattered to him except love and romance. Though there remained the odours of ashpits and stables, the rough treatment at the hands of cottagers who lived in dark muddy lanes, the harsh and unpleasant noises near markets, Mrs Mercer's long and tiring talk over the evening meal, and the uncle's non-cooperative attitude, the boy did not take them seriously as he imagined himself bearing his chalice safely through a throng of foes. But his sensitive and romantic nature received a severe jolt when the young lady rudely asked him if he wanted to buy anything thereby reminding him of his cash position-a poor position that did not permit him to buy the jars even after his selection of them as fit objects of gift for his beloved. As the light went out, he realized for the first time that it was his vanity-his high notion about himself that he would be able to buy a fine gift for his beloved–that brought him to the bazaar. This vanity proving empty was also responsible for his humiliation. He suffered from anguish–the cause of his great mental pain being his inability to buy the thing he promised to his beloved. His eyes also burned in anger at himself at his dependence on others, at his powerlessness in giving a present to one whom he loved best.

### Joyce's Manner of Story-Telling

In Araby Joyce used a method of narration different from others. While most stories have sensational events that make up the main point of their interest and entertainment, 'Araby' is mostly free from such events. Its author applied the open structure in the presentation of the narrative. According to it, the story moves along with the flow or experience of the main character of the piece-the boy's looking at the girl, his following her at school time, her name sending a summons to his foolish blood, her talk to him regarding Araby, his promise to bring something for her, his final going to the bazaar and shocking disillusionment. When required the author could make close observation of a particular situation the sordidness of Dublin, for example. Harry Levin who has studied his manner of narration remarks: As the part, significantly chosen, reveals the whole, a word or detail may be enough to exhibit a character or convey a situation. For example, the word 'chalice' conveys that the boy's love is noble, pure and platonic; without this our knowledge about him would be incomplete. Again the word 'humbly-his looking humbly at the great jars suggests a situation in which the boy felt humiliated (obviously for his incapacity to buy a gift for his beloved). An analysis of his sentences will also convince us that Joyce is a master artist in his use of words with which he evoked such moods as he liked.

## *Joyce's "Araby" Short Questions- Answers*

**1. Where was North Richmond Street? When was it quite disturbed?**

Answer: North Richmond Street was located in Dublin, Ireland. It was quite disturbed during the winter season.

**2.What is the meaning of Araby?**

Answer: The meaning of Araby refers to an idealized and exotic place, often associated with romance and adventure. In the context of James Joyce's story, it represents the boy's infatuation and desire for something beyond his mundane surroundings.

**3.North Richmond Street being blind, where and when did the boys in Araby play?**

Answer: The boys in "Araby" played in the street, which was adjacent to North Richmond Street. They played in the evenings when the street was empty.

**4.When and why did Mangans' sister call her brother? Did her brother obey her at once?**

Answer: Mangans' sister called her brother in the evening to ask him to go to the bazaar called Araby. Her brother initially refused, but eventually agreed to go after some persuasion.

**5. "This happened morning after morning "- What happened morning after morning?**

Answer: The phrase "this happened morning after morning" refers to the boy's infatuation with and observation of his neighbor, Mangans' sister. He would watch her from his window as she passed by on her way to school.

**6.Who was the former tenant of the house in which the boy-narrator of "Araby" lived?**

Answer: The former tenant of the house in which the boy-narrator of "Araby" lived was a priest who had passed away. The boy mentions finding religious books and a bicycle pump belonging to the priest.

**7."Her image accompanied me even in places most hostile to romance" - Mention the places most hostile to romance.**

Answer: The places most hostile to romance mentioned in the story are the market where the boy's uncle does business, the drapery shop where his aunt shops, and the street where he sees men loading barrels onto carts.

**8.The nasal chanting of street-stagers who sang a 'come all you' about O'Donovan Rossa. What is 'come all you'? Who is O'Donovan Rossa?**

Answer: "Come all you" is a phrase that introduces or invites people to listen to a story or song. O'Donovan Rossa was an Irish Fenian leader and a prominent figure in the Irish nationalist movement.

**9.Whose body is referred to here? Whose words and gestures were like fingers running upon the wires? Stripped of the metaphor, what does the sentence mean?**

Answer: The body referred to here is the boy's body. The words and gestures that were like fingers running upon the wires belonged to Mangans' sister. Stripped of the metaphor, the sentence means that the boy's body was tense and responsive to every word and gesture of Mangans' sister.

**10."At last, she spoke to me "- Who spoke to whom? What did she speak?**

Answer: Mangans' sister spoke to the boy. She initiated a brief conversation with him, inquiring if he was going to the bazaar and expressing her inability to attend due to staying at a retreat.

**11." I bore my chalice safely through a throng of foes "- says the boy in James Joyce's "Araby." What is meant by chalice?**

Answer: In this context, the word "chalice" is used metaphorically to represent the boy's hopes and aspirations, his idealized view of the bazaar and the possibility of obtaining a gift for Mangans' sister.

**12.What is meant by Freemason affair? What is meant by 'it'?**

Answer: In the context of the story, a "Freemason affair" refers to a secretive organization or event associated with Freemasonry, a fraternal society. The narrator's aunt expresses surprise and hopes that the event the boy is attending (the bazaar) is not related to Freemasonry. The "it" refers to the event or affair that the boy is participating in.

**13.: Who is the speaker? Why did the master's face pass from amiability to sternness?**

Answer: The speaker is the boy-narrator of the story. The master's face passed from amiability to sternness because the speaker arrived late for school, which displeased the master.

**14.: When did the boy in 'Araby' intend to go to the bazaar?**

Answer: The boy in 'Araby' intended to go to the bazaar on Saturday evening.

**15."When I came downstairs again, I found Mrs. Mercer knitting at the fire. "-Who was Mrs. Mercer? When did she leave for her home? How did she appear to the speaker?**

Answer: Mrs. Mercer was a neighbor of the boy's aunt. She left for her home after dinner. To the speaker, she appeared to be a friendly and ordinary neighbor engaged in knitting.

**16. "My uncle said he was sorry he had forgotten. "What had he forgotten?**

Answer: The uncle had forgotten to give the boy the money he had promised for the bazaar.

**17.How much did the boy in 'Araby' take with him to the bazaar? What was finally left with him?**

Answer: The boy in 'Araby' took one pound with him to the bazaar. In the end, he only had two shillings left with him.

**18.When did the boy reach the bazaar?**

Answer: The boy reached the bazaar quite late, around 9 o'clock in the evening.

**19. "He asked me, "Did I know 'the Araby's Farewell to his steed'?" Who asked whom? What is 'the Araby's Farewell to his steed'?**

Answer: The boy's friend asked him if he knew 'the Araby's Farewell to his steed.' The 'Araby's Farewell to his steed' is a poem or song that was likely part of the cultural or literary references surrounding the bazaar.

**20.What was the state of the bazaar when the 'boy hero' in Joyce's Araby reached there?**

Answer: When the 'boy hero' reached the bazaar, it was in a state of almost complete darkness. Many of the stalls were already closed, and there were few people remaining. The atmosphere was disappointing and anticlimactic for the boy.

## *Some more Araby Questions and Answers*

**1. What description has Joyce left about North Richmond Street?**

Ans. North Richmond Street, situated in Dublin, was one whose one end only remained opened, the other being blocked by houses. It was a quiet street except at the hour when the school-boys came to play on it. It had brown, calm houses on its either side that looked on at one another.

**2.What was the name of the school in which the boy hero was educated?**

Ans. The name of the school in which the boy hero was educated was Christian Brothers' School, one that was run by the Catholics.

**3.Who was the former tenant of the house in which the boy lived? What do you know of him?**

Ans. The former tenant of the house in which the boy lived was a priest who was no more.

His reading of The Abbot and The Memoirs of Vidocq indicates that he was fond of historical romances and stories of adventure which hardly agreed with his religious duties. In his will he left all his money to institutions and the furniture of his house to his sister. This shows that he was more interested in his name after his death than in really helping his own relations.

**4.What did the boys do during the short days of winter?**

Ans. During the short days of winter dusk fell even before the boys had finished their tiffins. There was, however, light in the sky which made the street lamps shine feebly. Despite the cold air the boys played till their bodies glowed. The silent street was resounded with their shouts. The course of their play brought them through dark muddy lanes behind the house, where the cottagers treated roughly with them, to the back doors of the dark wet gardens where ashpits spread out a foul smell, and to the dark stinky stables where a coachman smoothed and combed the horse or shook music from the attached harness. When they returned to the street, it was already filled with light that came out of the kitchen windows.

**5. Who was Mangan? Why did his sister come out in the evening? What did the boy do at that time?**

Ans. Mangan was one of the playmates of the boy.

In the evening Mangan's sister used to come out on the door-step of their house to call her brother in to his tea.

The boy went along with Mangan upto their house. He waited near the railing for the return of his friend. Meanwhile he looked at her. The movement of her dress and the tossing of her hair from side to side caught his attention and filled him with delight.

**6. How did the author trace out the arousal of love in the boy's heart?**

Ans. The author showed uncommon skill in tracing out love in the boy's heart. First, the boy went along with Mangan upto their house and stood by the railings looking at his sister. The swing of her dress and the tossing of the soft rope of her hair' from side to side filled him with much delight. Secondly, he tried to look at her from a distance. Every morning he lay on the floor of the front parlour watching at her through the narrow opening of the window keeping himself completely hidden. When she came out on the door-step his heart leapt up in joy. On way to school he followed her keeping her brown figure always before his eyes. When the point where their ways parted came he quickened his pace and passed her by. Thirdly, he felt his heart to be full of uncontrollable feelings one rainy evening and pronounced her name repeatedly as if out of intense joy. Finally, when she spoke to him and urged him to visit <u>Araby</u>, he felt the syllables of <u>Araby</u>

pouring honey on his mouth and sensed that his bringing a gift for her would be the fulfilment of his quest for the ideal, of his search for the unfading beauty. He carried his love like a chalice in his heart from which we may conclude that the boy's love was of the purest kind.

**7.'Yet her name was like a summons to all my foolish blood.' Who is the speaker? What does this extract suggest?**

Ans. The speaker here is the boy hero of James Joyce's short story 'Araby'.

The extract suggests the depth of the boy's love for his beloved, Mangan's sister. Even though they had seen each other many a time no word had passed between them. The boy did not know whether he would ever speak to her. Nor was he certain about her feelings towards him. What he was fully confident was that his own heart was full to the brim with love for her. Such being the case whenever he heard her name uttered immediately he felt a tremendous sensation in his blood. He did not know why this occurred nor was he able to resist it. Hence he described his blood as the foolish one. Again, just as a receiver of summons from the court cannot but appear before the magistrate, he, too, could not but respond whenever her name was uttered.

**8.How has Joyce described the market scene of Dublin on Saturday nights?**

Ans. In his short story 'Araby' James Joyce has described a contemporary market scene of Dublin in a fine and faithful manner. On Saturday nights the streets were covered with harsh glaring light. When one walked through a street near a market there was every possibility of one being pushed by drunken men or bargaining women. One could also hear, the Curses of labourers, the shrill cries of shopboys eager to sell pigs' cheeks kept in barrels and the nasal singing of a patriotic song come-all you about O'Donovan Rossa or of a ballad depicting the hardship of Ireland under the British rule.

**9.'Her image accompanied me even in places the most hostile to romance'.-Who is the speaker ? Whose image is referred to here ? Which places were most hostile to romance ?**

Ans. The boy hero is the speaker of the above extract. The image referred to above is that of the sister of Mangan, one of the friends of the boy. The image is the impression that she let on his heart.

The boy has mentioned certain places which were helpful neither for the blooming nor for the development of love which was like a romance to him. Among such places mention may be made of the flaring streets near the market where one was likely to be jostled (=pushed) by drunken men and bargaining women, amid the curses of labourers, the shrill cries of shop-boys sitting by the barrels of pigs cheeks, and nasal singing of street-singers who sang patriotic songs about O'Donovan Rossa or ballads about the woes of Ireland under the British rule. These places were so dull, disturbing or noisy ones that far from developing romance they were sure to destroy it by all means.

**10.Who is O'Donovan Rossa? In which song is he referred to? What does the song signify?**

Ans. O'Donovan Rossa is the popular name of the nineteenth century Irish nationalist leader Jeremiah Donovan.

O'Donovan Rossa is referred to a street-ballad come-all-you, so called because these were its opening words.

The song is a stirring call by the nationalist leader O'Donovan Rossa to all the people of Ireland to be united in their struggle for freedom against the British rule.

**11.'These noises converged in a single sensation of life for me- Who is the speaker? What were the noises referred to above? How did they converge in a single sensation of life? What does the single sensation of life meant?**

Ans. The speaker of the above extract is the boy, the central character of James Joyce's famous short story 'Araby'.

The noises referred to were those heard on Saturday nights near a market place in contemporary Dublin. They were the harsh and unpleasant sounds made by drunken men and bargaining women. In addition there were the curses of labourers, the shrill cries of shop-boys guarding over barrels of pigs cheeks, and the nasalized voice of street-singers singing either a patriotic song about ODonovan Rossa, a nationalist leader, or a ballad depicting the woes of Ireland under the British rule.

These dull and prosaic noises came from all sides. They were different in nature and the sources of their origin were also different. Yet they were united for a single purpose. Here their meeting together for a single interest has been described as a kind of convergence.

The single sensation of life means that despite their different nature and different sources of origin the noises produced but a single strong feeling in the boy's mind. It was that they were all enemies and that they were united for the single purpose of destroying his tenderly love for the girl.

**12.'I imagined that I bore my chalice safely through a throng of foes.'- Who is the speaker? What does the word 'chalice' allude to and which does it imply? What does the extract suggest?**

Ans. The boy hero in James Joyce's short story 'Araby' is the speaker of the above extract.

The word 'chalice' which means a wine-cup is associated with the legend of the Holy Grail. Chalice is the wine-cup which was used by Jesus for his Last drink. After his crucifixion Josek, of Arimathea contained some drops of Jesus's blood into the cup which was later brought to England. Because no guardian was worthy of it, it disappeared. Though many were in quest of it, only a few noble and pure knights like Galahad and Perceval were able to see the cup, the symbol of supreme bliss. The word 'chalice' here implies the holy and untainted love of the boy for the girl

The above extract suggests the utmost care that the boy took in respect of his love. Though love sprouted in his heart it was the most delicate and tender object that he could conceive of. At the same time it was as precious and as pure as chalice which the enemies could stain or destroy the moment they would come to know of its existence. To the boy the overall drab and commercial atmosphere of Dublin together with its Jostling drunken and bargaining scenes near the market and a host of dull and prosaic cries and noises was most hostile to the development and survival of his delicate love. It was like a host of enemies determined to destroy the chalice he was carrying. Hence he had to guard his love most carefully from the polluting touches of such inimical atmosphere and noises.

**13. When did the girl's name spring to the boy's lip ? What other emotional experience did he undergo ?**

Ans. Occasionally the girl's name sprang to the boy's lip at the time of his strange prayers to and praises of God. Because of his immature age and lack of experience he did not understand why such a thing occurred. Actually of course he was deifying his beloved quite unconsciously.

Among other emotional experience which the boy had one was that his eyes were often full of tears and the other was that at times a flood (of emotion) from his heart seemed to pour itself out into his bosom. In these cases, too, he did not understand why they occurred.

**14. I thought little of the future. Who is the speaker ? What kinds of future activity could be contemplate ? Why did he think little of the future?**

Ans. The speaker is the boy hero of James Joyce's short story 'Araby'.

The kinds of future activity that the boy could contemplate are the possibility, or otherwise of his speaking to his beloved at any time and the feasibility or otherwise of conveying his adoration to her in his state of confusion.

The boy did not trouble himself by thinking about the future because he was contented with his present state of looking at his beloved from a distance or having a pleasant sensation in his blood occasioned by any reference to her name.

**15.'But my body was like a harp.' – Who is the speaker ? What is a harp ? Why did the speaker compare his body to a harp?**

Ans. The boy hero of James Joyce's short story 'Araby' is the speaker.

A harp is a self-standing musical instrument with vertical strings played with the fingers.

A musician plays with his fingers on the strings of a harp to music. In the same way the girl's sweet words and her gestures (like the swing of her body or the tossing of her hair from side to side) were like fingers that ran on his sensitive body and produced in it a series of pleasant sensations.

**16.What experience did the boy have one dark rainy evening in the empty back drawing-room ?**

Ans. One evening the boy went into the empty back drawing-room when the house was without any sound. It was a dark rainy evening when he heard the rain striking the earth and saw numerous fine needles of water playing in the sodden (-soaked) flower-beds. In the dark he could see little but it helped in bringing about his concentration. Suddenly it seemed to him that all his senses (i.e. sight, hearing, smell, taste, and touch) were eager to veil themselves and that he was about to slip from them. There also arose in his heart such uncontrollable feelings of love that he strove to balance himself by pressing the palms of his hand together until they trembled. At the same time he went on, as if hysterically, murmuring many times the words: 'O my beloved ! O my sweetheart !

**17."At last she spoke to me.'-Who is the speaker? Who is "she'? What did she speak? What was the speaker's reply?**

Ans. The speaker is the boy hero of James Joyce's short story 'Araby'. She is the sister of the boy's friend Mangan with whom he fell in love.She asked the boy whether he was going to Araby. She said that it would be a splendid bazaar. She added that she could not go as there would be a retreat that week in her convent school. Her final recommendation was that it would be well for him.

The boy replied that if he went there, he would bring some gift for her.

**18.'She could not go, she said.'–Who is "she'? To whom did she say the above words ? How did she appear to the addressee? Where couldn't she**

**go and why?**

Ans. She is Mangan's sister with whom the boy hero of Araby' fell in love.

She said the above words to her young lover, the boy hero of 'Araby'.

To her young lover she appeared to be extremely beautiful. While she spoke the words she turned a silver bracelet round and round her wrist.

She held one of the spikes of the railings bowing her had to her lover who was standing below. The light that came from outside fell on the white curve of her neck, lit up her hair that rested there, and caused her hand that lay upon the railings to look bright. It also fell over one side of her dress and made just visible, as she stood at ease, the white border of a petticoat she was wearing below her dress.

She could not go to Araby, the Grand Oriental Fete, that was being held that time in Dublin.

She could not go there on account of a retreat to be held that week in her convent school. The retreat is a Roman Catholic religious observance which is marked by withdrawal from all worldly festivities. It was for this that she could not go to Araby.

**19.What is a retreat ? What effect did it have upon Mangan's sister ?**

Ans. A retreat is a religious occasion observed by the Roman Catholics. It is generally held for a week or for the last three days before Easter. It is marked by holy thinking, abstention from alcoholic drinks and sexual enjoyments and withdrawal from merriment and wordly festivities.

Since the retreat was being observed that week and since she read in a Roman Catholic institution. Mangan's sister could not go to Araby, a bazaar providing amusement and rejoicing.

**20."What innumerable follies laid waste my waking and sleeping thoughts after that evening! Who is the speaker ? What was the evening referred to above ? Mention some of the follies as committed by the speaker.**

Ans. The speaker is the boy hero of the story "Araby'.

The evening as referred to above was the one in which Mangan's sister, his beloved, spoke to the boy for the first time. She asked him whether he would go to Araby where a splendid bazaar would be held. She regretted she could not go there on account of a retreat which would be observed that week in her convent school. She remarked that it would be well for him to go Araby.

Since the evening the girl spoke to him first the boy suffered from a restlessness both in his waking and sleeping hours. At the same time he committed innumerable follies. He wished, for example, the day for his going to 'Araby' to come at once and wanted the tedious intervening days to be destroyed completely. He felt vexed at his school work. Her image flashed upon his mind at night in his bedroom and by day in his class-room. The syllables of the word 'Araby' seemed to call him through the silence of the night (a fancy in which his soul loved to luxuriate) and cast an eastern enchantment over him. He answered few questions in class for which his master became angry with him. He was unable to bring back his wandering thoughts at one place. He had no patience with any serious work of life (e.g. study, church-going, carrying parcels etc.) which seemed to him ugly monotonous child's play. These follies laid waste a lot of his waking and sleeping hours.

**21.Who was Mrs. Mercer? What was her hobby? Why couldn't she wait longer?**

Ans. Mrs Mercer was obviously a friend or neighbour of the boy's aunt. A pawnbroker's widow, she was an old and garrulous (=talkative) woman.

Mrs. Mercer's hobby was to collect used stamps and to use them for some pious purpose.

Mrs. Mercer could not wait longer than eight o'clock as the night air was bad for her health.

**22.'I'm afraid you may put off your bazaar for this night of Our Lord.'- Who is the speaker and to whom were the words used? What is the meaning of the word "bazaar"? Why should it be put off? What is the meaning of the expression 'this night of Our Lord'?**

Ans. The speaker is the boy's aunt. She used these words to her nephew.

The word 'bazaar' menas a place where goods are sold for the purposes of charity and where some arrangement is made for providing amusement to the public.

The anut was afraid her nephew might have to postpone his going to Araby on account of the excessive delay in his uncle's returning home.

This night of Our Lord' means this night as counted from the birthday of Jesus Christ. The night was most probably the Easter Eve (which in India is known as Easter Saturday).

**23.'I could interpret these signs.'-Who is the speaker? What were the signs? What could the speaker interpret from these signs?**

Ans. The speaker is the boy hero of James Joyce's short story 'Araby'.

When his uncle returned home at night he made certain signs. First, he turned the latchkey in the hall door. Secondly, he talked to himself. Finally, he threw his heavy overcoat on the hall-stand that made it rocking

From these signs the boy interpreted unerringly that his uncle had returned home in a tipsy or drunken state.

**24. What is come-all-you? What is the Freemason affair? What is The Arab's Farewell to his Steed?**

Ans. Come-all-you is the name of a street-ballad in which these words are used as its opening words. Through this patriotic song O'Donovan Rossa, a nineteenth-century Irish nationalist gave a stirring call to his countrymen to join Ireland's struggle for freedom against the British rule.

The Freemason affair is one of the Freemasons, an old-established secret society having lodges (i.e. branches) all the world over. The Freemasons are known for their anti-Catholic attitude. As the boy avoided crowded places his wish to visit Araby led the aunt to suspect that her nephew had probably joined the secret society of the Freemasons, a staunch Protestant organization reputed for its anti-Catholic stand.

The Arabs Farewell to his Steed is the name of a sentimental poem written by the nineteenth-century minor poetess, Caroline Norton, who was also the granddaughter of the famous dramatist, R.B. Sheridan. In the present short story the boy's uncle mentioned this poem when the former's wish to go to Araby made him discover some similarity between Arabia and Arab in the poem he knew. Excepting this similarity in names there is no likeness between the bazaar and the poem. Obviously the uncle attempted to recite the poem to show his learned nature, and thereby the author subtly draws our attention to the dull nature of the boy's uncle.

**25. Describe the boy's journey to Araby.**

Ans. When the boy came out to go to Araby he had to cross streets crowded with buyers and glaring with gaslight. Then he reached a station and took his seat in a third-class carriage of a deserted train. After an intolerable delay the train started passing ruinous houses and a twinkling river. At Westland Row Station a crowd wanted to get into the carriages but the porters moved them back saying that it was a special train. The boy remained alone in the carriage. At last when the train stopped beside a temporarily constructed wooden platform, he got down at 2-50 p.m. and reached his destination

**26. 'In front of me was a large building which displayed the magical name.'- Who is the speaker? What was the large building meant for?**

**What is the magical name and why is it magical?**

Ans. The speaker is the boy hero of James Joyce's short story "Araby'. The large building was meant for the accommodation of the bazaar.

The magical name displayed on the building is 'Araby'. The name is magical because it was the boy's beloved who first uttered its syllables. In addition the name had an eastern enchantment cast over it.

**27.What is a Cafe' Chantant? What is Araby?**

Ans. It was ten minutes to ten when the boy reached Araby. Already most of the stalls were closed and a large part of the building in which the bazaar was being held was in darkness. The spectators and buyers had mostly left the place. Only a few sellers stood round the stalls that were still open. The boy perceived in the place a deep silence which prevails in the church when the service is done.

Cafe' Chantant (literally 'singing cafe') is a kind of coffee house or restaurant where light refreshments were provided to customers for whom there was also arrangement for music and entertainments. Through such restaurants have fallen into disuse at present they were quite popular in the first decade (ten years) of the twentieth century. The boy of the present story saw the words Cafe' Chantant written in coloured lamps over the curtain of an open stall.

Araby is the name given to a 'Grand Oriental Fete' held in Dublin from 14th May to 19th May, 1894. The boy went there to take part in its bazaar, a special event at which goods were sold for the benefit of charities and sideshows were provided for amusement

**28.'The tone of her voice was not encouraging.'-Who is the speaker? Whose voice is referred to here? Why was the tone of the voice not encouraging ?**

Ans. The speaker of the above extract is the boy hero of James Joyce's short story 'Araby'.

The voice referred to above is that of a young lady serving as a sales woman in one of the open stalls.

The tone of the young lady's voice was not encouraging because as an experienced sales girl she found in the boy something which convinced her that he would not be able to buy anything from her stall. So when she asked him if he wished to buy anything she asked merely out of a sense of duty, not out of a feeling that he would buy anything. Such being the case, the tone of her voice did not appear encouraging to him.

**29.'I looked humbly at the great jars. Who is the speaker ? Where did he find the jars? How did he describe the jars ? Why did he look humbly at them?**

Ans. The speaker is the boy hero of James Joyce's short story 'Araby

The boy found the jars in one of the open stalls of Araby where a young lady was keeping guard over them.

The boy was extremely delighted to see the jars. He called them great because they moved him with surprise. The bazaar had an oriental name and the jars were in keeping with that tradition. It seemed to him that they were like a pair of eastern guards placed at either side of the dark entrance to the stall. The expression 'eastern guards' conveys an erotic and enchanting air and suggests about their large size, handsome appearance and colourful form. The boy thought the jars to be a magnificent gift that be presented to his beloved

The boy looked humbly at the fine jars because he realized that however lovely or interesting they might appear to him he could not afford to buy them with the meager money his uncle had given him.

**30.'I lingered before her stall, though I knew my stay was useless.'- Who is the speaker? Why did he linger before her stall? Why was his stay felt to be useless?**

Ans. The speaker is the boy hero of James Joyce's short story 'Araby'.

To the young lady's question whether he wished to buy any wares – things) from her stall the boy had already replied in the negative. After that it was useless to wait any longer in her stall. But the tone of her voice was discouraging. From it he guessed that the young lady had possibly taken her to be one unable to buy anything. He, however, did not like her to have such an unfavourable impression about him. Hence he lingered before her stall to make his interest in her wares seem the more real. Therefore, the motive behind his lingering was to efface the wrong idea she had about him.

He felt his stay to be useless as he knew that he had no sufficient money with him with which he could buy anything from her stall.

**31. I allowed the two pennies to fall against the six pence in my pocket. Who is the speaker? Why did he allow the two pennies to fall? Does the fall signify anything?**

Ans. The speaker is the young lover in James Joyce's short story Araby.

The boy got a florin (=two shillings) from his uncle at the time of his going to Araby. Out of it he spent one shilling for admission into the bazaar and four pennies for his railway journey. He was left with eight pennies of which six lay in his pocket and two in his hand. When he realized that this small amount was not at all sufficient to buy anything from the stall he could not but allow the two pennies to fall against the six pence in his pocket.

The fall signifies the drooping of his spirit, the failure of his head to keep itself high, the defeat of dream and idealism before the rude touches of reality and commercialism, and the frustration of the quest for beauty in a depressing atmosphere of dullness and dryness.

**32. "Gazing up into the darkness I was myself as a creature driven and derided by vanity; and my eyes burned with anguish and anger."- Who is the speaker? What assessment did he make about himself? Why did his eyes burn with anguish and anger?**

Ans. The speaker is the young lover in James Joyce's short story "Araby

The extract helps us to recognize the boy's assessment about himself. It was at his beloved's request that he decided to visit Araby. She lured him by saying that there would be a splendid bazaar there. The syllables of the word Araby cast an eastern enchantment over him. They began to call him through the silence of the night. It became difficult for him to pass time without feeling restless. He thought his arrival at Araby would be the end of his quest for the ideal, his quest for beauty. In keeping with his romantic nature he further said that he would bring a gift for his beloved. By so doing, he felt, his carrying of the pure and priceless chalice through a throng of foes would be over and it would finally reach its cherished goal. But all this high talk about himself and his mission came to nothingness when he reached Araby and found it to be almost deserted and plunged in darkness with a few sellers counting cash. Thus his romantic vision about Araby was broken to pieces. He realized that it was his vanity that brought him there. As regards giving a gift to his beloved (and he found a pair of great jars quite suitable for this purpose) he realized that the paltry sum he had with him was not sufficient to buy anything, not to speak of the jars that caught his fancy. Thus his vanity of letting her have a look at the chalice by way of offering her a gift was likewise blasted, and he found himself standing there as an object of general shame and ridicule.

The boy's eyes burned with anguish (extreme pain) when he noticed that his dream and quest for the ideal as well as for beauty had been spoilt and utterly lost, and they blazed with anger at his own helpless and dependent state.

**Araby James Joyce Characters**
**The Boy or The Young Lover**

Like his female counterpart the boy in Joyce's Araby remains unnamed. Being the principal character of the story he has every right to be called its hero. Very likely he had lost both his parents at an early age and was now living in the house of his uncle and aunt.

The boy was very much sensitive and imaginative by nature. For this he had often to face unpleasant situations. His play took him to places he did not like at all. In the dark muddy lanes he was roughly treated by cottagers. He passed by dark dripping gardens whose odorous ashpits offended his delicate taste. Sometimes stables too gave out a foul smell making it hard for him to stay there. On Saturday evenings he had to accompany his aunt for the sake of carrying some of her parcels. This made him come near crowded places where he had to face a number of unpleasant experiences like getting pushed by drunken men and bargaining women and hearing curses coming from labourers, shrill cries from shop boys and nasal chanting from street-singers. All these appeared to him like a throng of foes and he imagined that he bore his chalice–his pure love for the girl safely through them. This shows that he loved to raise himself to the position of a dauntless knight.

Though he could give vent to his anger before his aunt by clenching his fists, he was somewhat afraid of his uncle. So he hid himself in the shadow as soon as he saw his uncle turning the corner and did not come out of it until he saw him safely housed. From certain signs he could easily understand when his uncle returned home in a tipsy state. Understanding little of his difficulty his aunt frequently detained him in the tea-table when she was engaged in long boring gossip with Mrs Mercer.

The boy loved the girl intensely. His hungry heart loved to look at her. The swing of her dress, the movement of her body, the tossing of her slender hair, the white curve of her neck, and the sight of the border of her petticoat either roused his curiosity or gave him joy. He devised clever tricks for the sake of seeing her. Every morning he lay on the floor in the front parlour watching her door through a small opening in the window. When he came out his heart leaped up in joy. He ran to the hall, seized his books and followed her. He kept her brown figure always in front of him and when they came near the point at which their ways diverged, he quickened his pace and passed her.

Besides seeing her, he adopted other means to keep her always in the focus of his attention. Her name was like a summons to all his foolish blood. Her name sprang to his lips in strange prayers and praises he could • not tell why. He felt that his body was like a harp and her words and gestures were like fingers playing upon the wires. He was so full with emotions for her that his eyes were often full of tears and at times a flood from his heart seemed to pour itself out into his bosom. One rainy evening when there was no sound in the house he felt the pressure of emotions so much on him that it seemed he was about to slip from his senses, and pressing his palms tightly together he murmured repeatedly : O love! O love! He also dreamed of her. One evening we went upstairs, stood there for an hour, and leaning his forehead against the cool glass he saw nothing but the brown-dad figure of the girl cast by his imagination. From the time when she spoke to him and urged him to go to the bazaar his soul luxuriated in the thought that she was calling the syllables at the word Araby to him through the silence of the night.

Despite the meanness and sordidness of his surroundings the boy was able to help himself about from them. With the help of imagination he thought himself as one capable of fulfilling his desires. With high expectation went to Araby dreaming that he would be able to bring a nice object for his beloved. The closed stalls, the darkness of the hall, the sound of the counting at cash, and the small talk among the young sellers chilled his spirit to some extent But the discouraging tone with which the young lady asked if he wished to buy anything gave a severe jolt and placed him face to face with reality. He felt his money to be too small for the Na jars he selected for her and returned home there without any gif for her. He realized that it was his vanity that brought him to the bazaar and turned him into a laughing stock. His powerlessness and dependence on his uncle made him suffer from deep anguish and burned his eyes in anger at himself.

The boy is vitally important for the story for its theme dream and disillusionment would have found no figure for its representation except him.

**Mangan's Sister or the Girl**

The girl or Mangan's sister is an important character of Araby. Her name has not been disclosed by the author. She is simply known as Mangan's sister because she happened to be the sister of Mangan, a friend of the boy. In the story she occupies such an important position than it will be no exaggeration if we take her to be the heroine of the narrative.

The houses of the boy and the girl were situated on either side of a narrow street. When the boys played on the street till evening, Mangan's sister came out on the doorstep to call her brother in to his tea. It was a kind of pleasure to them to see from their shadow whether she would remain on the door-step peering up and down the street or go back. If she remained they came out of their shadow and walked up to her steps. The boy particularly stood by the railings looking at her. He got much joy when her dress swung as she moved her body, and when the soft rope of her hair tossed from side to side.

The girl did not know that the boy watched her every morning through a chink of the window keeping himself unobserved. Nor did she know that she was followed by him when she went to school. What is clear is that she did not have any antipathy or dislike for the boy.

When the necessity of conversation arose it was she who took the lead. She did not feel confused as the boy did. On the other hand, she was free and frank in her speech. It was she who informed him that there would be a splendid bazaar in Araby. When she explained why she could not go there, we understand that she was a student in a convent that had asked her to observe the retreat and that like every good girl she must observe this Roman Catholic practice. It was for her encouragement that the boy decided to go to Araby and bring a gift for her from there.

The girl knew how to draw the attention of the boy. While she spoke she turned a silver bracelet round and round her wrist. Again, she stood in such a manner that the light that fell on her from one side revealed the beauty of the white curve of her neck, of her hair and of her hand that lay on the railing. As she bowed her head towards him the white border of her petticoat which she wore below her skirt became just visible to the great joy and curiosity of the boy.

There is no doubt that Magnan's sister was an object of infinite attraction to the boy. The main function served by her is the gradual arousal and full flowering of the feeling of love in the boy's heart. Had she not encouraged him, the boy would not have gone to the bazaar where he meet with disenchantment and self-awareness which is the main objective of the author. We, thus, conclude that the girl had a vital role to play in Joyce's short story 'Araby'.

**The Priest**

The unnamed priest, obviously a Roman Catholic, is one of the characters of James Joyce's short story Araby. He was the former tenant of the house in which the boy hero later came to live along with his uncle and aunt. That he was not methodical and tidy is clear from his keeping the extra room behind the kitchen littered with old useless papers, from letting his garden have a wild look, and from throwing his bicycle-pump into some irregularly spreading bushes.

The priest was perhaps not as much religious-minded as could be expected from such a person. His reading attests to this. Excepting The Devout Communicant, a manual which every priest must keep, he read only light entertaining books. One of his favourite books was The Abbot by Sir Walter Scott, a book depicting the life of a disappointed lover who finally became a monk. Another was The Memoirs of Vidocq, a book delaing with the adventures of one who played in the roles of a soldier, thief, and detective.

'He was', the author ironically comments, 'a very charitable priest'. In his will, he bestowed all his money to religious institutions leaving only his used furniture to his sister. Thereby he forgot the proverb that charity begins at home. Thus we notice some discrepancy between his professional duties and his day-to-day deeds.

We must observe that the priest is not vitally important in the plot development of the story. This character has been introduced for the sake of padding. However, the priest has some role to play in the raising of the overall sordidness of Dublin which was one of the objectives of Joyce.

**The Uncle**

Though the boy's uncle does not occupy much space of 'Araby' he is undoubtedly an interesting character. He exhibits all the characteristics of a flat character and provides enough amusement to readers by his attempts to keep up a genteel exterior which his weak economic position constantly conspires to crack

Had he been a loving and kind-hearted character the boys would not have wanted to avoid him. As soon as they saw him turning the corner, at once they hid under the shadow until they saw him safely housed. An old man, he used to fuss at the hallstand looking for the hat-brush or any other thing at the time of going out. After spending long hours outside when he came back he used to talk to himself and threw his heavy overcoat on the hallstand making it to rock. The boy could interpret these signs as his returning home in a tipsy state.

When the boy reminded him that he wished to go to the bazaar he replied glibly that he knew it. However, he was most unwilling to let his nephew have some amusement, at his cost outside home. That is why he intentionally came home quite late at night on the appointed day. He tried to dissuade the boy from going to the bazaar by telling first that the people were already in bed, and then adding that they were after their first sleep then. He also intentionally forgot the boy's purpose. Miser by nature, he was not at all willing to part with money. When his wife intervened on behalf of the boy, he escaped from the unpleasant situation by giving him two shillings with which he could buy little. From a discourager he quickly changed himself to an encourager by foolishly quoting the old proverb : All work and no play makes Jack a chill boy. He even tried to assume the stance of an intellectual before his wife by reciting a few lines from a minor poem The Arab's Farewell to his Steed. The uncle, thus, presents himself as a self-centered, pleasure-loving, closefisted man before us.

The uncle is an example of Joyce's capacity of drawing the sketch of an impressive figure with as few words as possible. He has an important role in the short story for by giving only a florin to the boy he was entirely responsible for the breaking of his dream-the dream of giving a nice present to his beloved. This rude shock also serves to make the boy realize his foolish vanity and his object dependence which filled him with anguish and anger. By creating characters like the uncle Joyce was also able to hold his highly-polished looking-glass in the form of a story before the contemporary people of Dublin, so that they might have look at their meanness and rectify.

**The Aunt**

The aunt is a sketchy character, she has not been as developed as her husband. She is an old loving lady, much sympathetic to her young nephew. On Saturday evenings she took him to the market to let him carry her parcels although she knew that such crowded places were not at all liked by him. Therefore she felt surprised when he proposed to go to the bazaar on Saturday night. A pious Roman Catholic by nature, she suspected her nephew's involvement in some affair of the Freemasons members of a secret Protestant organization reputed for their anti-Catholicism. There is enough hints that like an average Irish woman she liked to haggle over prices while out on shopping. When her husband did not turn up and the boy began to walk up and down clenching his fists, she tried to soften him by stating that perhaps he would have to postpone his visit to Araby till another day. Her kindness to her nephew is clear when she energetically argued with her husband and succeeded in making him give the money to the boy to let him go to the bazaar that very night. However, like other Irish women of her age and status, she was fond of a long gossip over the evening tea.

Whatever may her shortcomings be, we must admit that she is a more likable person than her own husband. She serves one important purpose in the story. Without her intervention the boy could have received permission and money to go to Araby and to meet his eventual disillusionment there.

## Mrs Mercer

Mrs Mercer is a minor character of Araby'. She was an old, garrulous woman and a companion of the boy's aunt. A pawnbroker's widow, her hobby was to collect used stamps from neighbours so that they could be used for some pious purpose. This she did not so much for neighbourly charity as for her own benefit that would result when her individual contribution for it would be much less than what it would have been in the absence of such a collection. Like the boy's aunt she was also too much fond of a long evening gossip caring little how such tedious talk would tell upon young ones who happened to be present at the tea-table. She made no attempt to rise before eight o'clock when she remembered of the cold night air that would be bad for her health. Whether or not she suffered from rheumatism, it is clear that she took much care about her health, having no desire to pass away all on a sudden.

She contributes nothing to the advancement of the plot. The author introduces her possibly to show how dull and insufferable middle-class Irish homes could be in the evening when they are peopled with such women as Mrs Mercer and her likes.

**Long Questions and Answers**

### 1.Significance of the Title Araby by James Joyce

The title of James Joyce's short story ' Araby' is highly symbolic. It is the name given to a 'Grand Oriental Fete' (i.e. festival; rejoicing) held in Dublin from May 14 to May 19, 1894. It was practically a bazaar which means 'a special event at which goods are sold for the benefit of charities, and sideshows are provided for amusement.'

In the story it was Mangan's sister, beloved of the boy hero, who, to his great surprise, one day asked him whether he would go to Araby. She said that there would be a splendid bazaar there. She added that she would have loved to go there had there been no retreat (=withdrawal from external merry-making) that time in her convent school. Then with a tone of encouragement she entreated him to go there. With deep emotion he replied that he would certainly bring something for her if he went there.

Her image lay impressed in his mind. He remembered how she was turning a silver bracelet round and round her wrist while she spoke to him. He could also bring to mind how the light opposite their door caught the white curve of her neck, lit up her hair that lay on her neck, and shone brightly the hand that rested on the railing. He could also distinctly remember how the light fell over one side of her dress making the white border of a petticoat (short, light, and sleeveless garment worn below the skirt) just visible as she bowed herself towards him holding the railings. Naturally a request coming from such a sweet and beloved girl was for him something which could not but be complied with.

Since the evening she had made the proposal he was engaged in innumerable follies that laid waste both his waking and sleeping thoughts. He wished to annihilate the tedious days that were vet to pass. He was vexed with the work of school. Her image flashed on the pages as he attempted to read. His master suspected he was idling and became angry. It became difficult for him to bring together his wandering thoughts. He had hardly any patience with the serious work of life which eventually became ugly monotonous child's play. Nothing but the bazaar could hold his attention. He began to imagine that the girl was uttering to him the syllables of the word Araby through the silence of the night. It was a fancy in which his soul luxuriated.

The word Araby cast an Eastern enchantment over him. Imaginative by nature, the boy thought his going to Araby would be a kind of fulfilment. His sensitive nature made him feel his journey there was nothing but the end of his quest for beauty, his quest for the ideal. His buying a gift from there and giving it to her might be felt by him as a pure and chivalrous knight's restoration of the chalice (=the wine-cup that Jesus used during the last supper) to its proper place after carrying it carefully and secretly through a throng of wicked and malicious foes.

' Araby' is, however, associated not only with enchantment and romance, dream and desire, it is also linked up with sorrow and frustration, anger and anguish. From the time when he sought permission to go to Araby till his reaching there the boy had to go through s series of dejection and difficulties. Despite his prior intimation the uncle reached home too late at night forgetting all about the boy's purpose. He also tried to dissuade him from going there telling that the people were already in bed. Had not the aunt intervened, he would have got no permission to go to the bazaar. His miserly uncle gave him only a florin with which he could buy little.

At last when he reached there a few minutes before ten, he found most of the stalls were already closed and a major part of the hall was in darkness.

The only sound that he heard was that of the counting of cash or a young lady's senseless talk with two gentlemen about some insignificant matter. Before he could examine the porcelain vases and flowered tea-sets, she asked in a discouraging tone if he really intended to buy anything. He looked humbly at two great jars that caught his fancy-humbly because he found he had no cash with which he could buy them as proper gifts to his beloved. He also felt humbled and insulted, fearing that the practiced eye of the young lady had found him out as one unable to buy anything. This and his failure to bring a gift for his beloved filled him with tremendous anguish and anger. His dream was not fulfilled, and his eyes were filled with samarting tears.

The title of the story has, thus, become significant because of its association with dream and dischantment, with yearning and frustration.

**2.Araby as a Story of Adolescent Psychology**

The protagonist in Joyce's short story Araby is a boy. The author speaks in the first person through the boy, who is as such his own self. Joyce actually interprets here his own boyhood experience and his adolescent psychology during his stay in the city of Dublin with his uncle and aunt.

Of course, Araby is no conventional story of the external action and sensations. It is, in fact, all about a young boy's fascination for a young girl, not much known to him, and his lingering longing for Araby. The story also highlights utter frustration and disillusionment of the boy hero after visiting Araby, considered so much as a place of ideal beauty and charm. The central character here is not merely an individual but rather the symbol of the frustrated human search for the ideal of beauty and romance. The character of the boy is to be studied from the deep psychological insight of adolescent period.

The symbolic aspect of the story serves to present the boy from a psychological angle. What is more conspicuous in the boy's nature is his romantic sensibility. He is no normal figure of the world. He is possessed of too much vigour of the romantic sensibility that is found active all through. The romantic sensibility draws the boy somewhat inexplicably to Mangan's sister. His romantic mind is fascinated by her. He is eager to have a little sight of or contact with her. Of course, he has the least communication with her, and there is no scope for the development of any relationship between them. But the boy is haunted with her dream and her image seems to accompany him even in a most noisy commercial environment of Dublin.

The boy's romantic sensibility seems to develop a kind of passion of love in him. Of course, he is too young to understand what love is or to know the significance of sex. Yet, somehow or other, he is drawn to her absolutely and this is nothing but love, though different from the conventional view of love. The boy's own words to himself reveal the inexplicable sense of love that possesses his mind. He murmurs within himself 'O love!, O love!' many times.

Another strongly noted feature in the boy's psychology is his strong imaginative power. Of course, this follows naturally from his romantic temper. He is fascinated by the vision of Araby. His romantic imagination is allured by the call of Araby which he looks upon as an ideal centre of pomp and splendour. He has no actual knowledge of Araby, noted for oriental magnificence. But in his mind's eye, he has an enchanting vision of Araby that spells him.

"The syllables of the word Araby were called to me through the silence in which my soul luxuriated and cast an Eastern enchantment over me."

Of course, the boy does not know what is this love. His mind hungers for the realization of love, heard by him on other occasions. This is here, through his boy, Joyce strikes adolescent psychology

The adolescent stage is just between boyhood and youth–the stage that begins to realize the impulse of love without knowing what this actually is. The boy's adolescent mind was drawn to the girl rather irresistibly and he was in a state of helpless bewilderment. He seemed to look before and after and pined for what was not. This is perfectly indicative of the restlessness of an adolescent mind. The boy was eager to see her, to talk with her, to have a contact with her. He looked at her secretly, watched her lingeringly and longed intensely for getting intimate with her. That was all the thoughtless, restless mood of adolescence. Joyce catches that mood with a rare psychological insight.

When the boy chanced to speak with her at last, there was an exchange of a few words between them. He fumbled in his reply to her. She asked him whether he would be going to Araby and advised him to go there. That would be 'a splendid bazaar', but she could not go because of a retreat in her convent. The boy was under a spell. He was lost in the vision of her, forgot his surroundings and could only promise to bring something for her. It was his adolescent mind, terribly stirred by the meeting, that seemed to bewitch and haunt him and dumb all his powers of reasoning and judging.

Again, an adolescent boy or girl is readily impulsive and easily impressionable. His or her mental balance is scarcely firm, and may be stirred by every gush of passion. This is clearly evident in Joyce's self-portrayal in the boy of the story Araby. The boy there, sensitive in nature, grew impertinent and restive in the matter of his proposed visit to Araby. He failed to concentrate his mind or attend seriously to anything. His own words bear out that restlessness of an adolescent mind-

"I had hardly any patience with the serious work of life which, now that it stood between me and my desire, seemed to me child's play, ugly monotonous child's play".

The adolescent stage constitutes an important phase in the transition of the human nature from boyhood to manhood. As the boy grows into a young man, his mind is subjected to various impressions that confront him here and there. He is naturally drawn to diverse factors of life and longs for things that touch him and impress his heart. All this is found patent in Joyce's boy, attaining adolescence. He has particularly a new feeling–the feeling of love, though as already stated, the full implication of love was not at all clear to him. Mangan's sister attracted the boy and his mind was absorbed in his thought of her, as indicated in his own words:

"I did not know whether I would ever speak to her or not or, if I spoke to her, how I could tell her of my confused adoration. But my body was like a harp and her words and gestures were like fingers running upon the wires."

A state of confusion and restlessness occupied much of his adolescent mind.

The second factor is his fascinating attachment to Araby where he was advised to go by Mangan's sister. The intervening period between his resolve to go there arid his actual visit was all restless to him. His adolescent mind could not bear the delay involved and grew violently impatient and restless as evident in his admission below:

"The syllables of the word Araby were called to me through the silence in which my soul luxuriated and cast an Eastern enchantment over me."

Joyce's success in capturing and representing adolescent psychology in his self-portrayal in the boy of his short story Araby is truly clear and commendable.

**3. Assess James Joyce's Araby as a Short Story or Araby as a Modern Short Story**

A short story, as defined by Edgar Allan Poe, one of the finest storywriters, is a brief prose-narrative. He even claims that this requires from half an hour to one or two hours for its perusal. Hudson calls that prose narrative a short story which can be read at a single sitting.

Brevity is, thus, the essential element in a short story. But mere brevity is not the whole of a good short story which has other features, as a narrative of some incidents or events. As a work of art, it depends specifically on the impression produced. The brevity of the short story is achieved in an artistic way through the singleness of the situation and the singleness of the impression. There is the artistic concentration which adds to the impressiveness of the story.

Again, the short story, because of its limited length, cannot entertain a good many characters. The paucity of characters is a part of its brevity. Of course, the characters are well developed and remain quite alive even within a limited range. They are not all sketchy and some of them may be lively and engaging enough.

The brevity of the short story is also artistically achieved through the structural design in which there is a smooth progress from the exposition through the development to the climax. The singleness of the story and the situation is nowhere missed. The impression, as emphasized, too, remains single all through.

Lastly, the short story follows an utmost economy in its words and expressions, so necessary to achieve brevity. Whether in dialogue or in narration, stringent economy is observed in a good short story. Of course, its literary quality should, in no case, be sacrificed at the altar of brevity.

James Joyce's Araby is a specimen of the modern short story. It covers some six pages, and is truly brief in length. In respect of brevity, Araby, just like Katherine Mansfield's The Fly, is a true specimen of the short story.

Of course, Joyce's Araby, an autobiographical story deals with a matter of profound psychological interest of a young boy's fascination for what he considered to be his ideal life. Naturally, this is no conventional tale. The story has no regular exposition or development from the point of view of the plot. It is all about the psychology of a boy who was drawn inexplicably to a girl, the sister of his friend, and was haunted with the dream of Arabys, an oriental fete held in Dublin. The climax of the story comes with the author's utter frustration, after his visit to Araby, where he went with much expectation and returned, dejected and disillusioned.

The plot of the Araby story is, thus, intricate enough, based on the state of a boy's mind, but the unity of impression is well retained through the singleness of the situation. The author's attachment to Mangan's sister and his longing for Araby are harmonized into one impression through the boy and his eager and romantic visualization. Though there is no conventional structure, the singleness of the effect is achieved through the boy's psychology.

The course of the plot, in fact, has a smooth development, although the story element, as stated, is not conventional here. The author's longing lingering look at Mangan's sister, her talk with him, his proposal to go to Araby and his actual experience there form the subtle chain of development of the story which has a psychological interest rather than incidental. The modernity of this story is affirmed here.

In the second place, Araby is a typical short story in which the number of characters is but a few. The main two figures in the story are the boy and Mangan's sister. But even the latter is kept more as an impression than as an active real being. Of course, the author's uncle, aunt, friends, neighbours and the sales hands of Araby are mentioned, but they are no characters, in the strict sense of the term. For its extremely few characters, Araby testifies to the condition of a good short story.

Lastly, the precision found in this story is to be mentioned and admired. Joyce is not found to play with words, but has employed the concise and right expressions all through. His artistry is here unique, for the story remains a happy reading, despite the intricacy of its psychological probe into a young mind. Joyce's masterly craft, as a story-teller, retains all through the interest of the story. Indeed, Araby is a good short story–a good modern short story with its modern technique of storytelling through the psychological introspection

Araby as a Realistic Short Story with Symbolic overtones

In Araby, there are, two types of elements – realistic and symbolic, and because of their happy co-existence the story has received universal praise. The author has shown his skill in the depiction of the reality while dealing with the boy's home life. We also find a beautifully accurate realism in the details of Dublin's life that the story contains.

Another way through which Joyce has shown his skill in realism is the depiction of uncle's characterization. The boy's experience in Araby has also been described with an eye to realism. Though he saw outside the magical name, inside he found altogether different events waiting for him. While dealing with the boy's dream – his earnest desires – the author's language becomes poetic and turns to have symbolic overtones.

The denouncement is found in the boy's return from the bazaar empty handed and his self discovery that he was no better than "a creature driven and derided by vanity." The conflict of the story arises out of a clash between dreams and reality.

**4.Symbols in Araby**

In its simplest sense a symbol is something that stands for something else (and its meaning is more or less fixed by tradition). Symbolism is the use of objects or actions through which authors suggest ideas or emotions. In Shakespeare's Macbeth we find the use of symbolism in Lady Macbeth's washing of hands which signifies her desire to cleanse herself of guilt.

Symbolic Literature is one which is characterized by the dominance of symbols. There may be the achievement of a single symbolic meaning in the totality of a work or plurality of symbolic meanings in it. Melville's Moby Dick or Coleridge's The Rime of the Ancient Mariner are examples of symbolic literature

In literature, symbolism is the use of objects or actions to suggest emotion or ideas. This has been finely elaborated by Murrary. 'Symbolism,' he says, may be described as the art of expressing emotions not by describing them directly nor by defining them through overt comparisons with concrete images, but by suggesting what the ideas and emotions are by recreating them in the mind of the reader through the use of unexplained symbols. These symbols help to convey a mood to the subconscious mind rather than an appeal to the rational faculties.

Sometimes an entire work may be taken as a symbol. Thus, the mariner's voyage in Coleridge's The Rime of the Ancient Mariner may symbolize the universal journey into the depths of despair and return to a state of spiritual and psychological stability. It may be pointed out that some plays of Shakespeare are structurally symbolic. J. A. Cuddon notes : 'In Macbeth there is a recurrence of the blood image symbolizing guilt and violence. In Hamlet weeds and disease symbolize corruption and decay. In King Lear clothes symbolize appearances and authority and the storm is symbolic of cosmic and domestic chaos to which "un-accommodated man' is exposed'.

In 'Araby' we get in touch with certain objects which may be loosely regarded as symbols loosely because their literal interpretation can explain them quite satisfactorily. In this sense the blind allay is symbol. It signifies the narrowness of the lives and attitudes of the people who dwelt in it. There is, again, a cluster of images that point to the sordidness of the place- rough tribes, odours, ashpits, and stables. The same cluster we notice in the market-place. Jostling and bargaining, cursing, crying in shrill voice, and chanting in nasal tone, and barrels full of pigs' cheeks all show the shabby and distasteful nature of the people as well as the place. Summons to blood and body as harp stress the imaginative nature of the boy, the delight obtainable from love.

Light and darkness are referred to in the story for a number of times. While light reveals charms and focuses on weak spots, darkness points to poverty, emptiness, and defects. The boy's clenching of fists and mounting the staircase suggest his protest an attempt to gain liberation respectively. Long and idle gossip at the tea-table and fear of the night air indicate the lethargy and care for health found among middle-class people. The fall of the coins has two meanings : to the seller it suggests gain and to the boy frustration. The overall picture which these objects and actions suggest is one of poverty, sordidness, and despair.

The present short story contains only three literary symbols chalice, Araby, and journey to Araby and back. The word 'chalice' is associated with the Grail Legend. It is the wine-cup or platter that Jesus Christ used at the Last Supper. Joseph of Arimathea took it to the Crucifixion and caught some of Christ's blood in it. During years of imprisonment Joseph kept it and it mysteriously supplied him with food. Then he took it to Britain. Because no guardian was worthy of it, it disappeared. This tale was linked to Arthurian romance, and the quest of the lost Grail was a dominating inspiration to the Knights of the Round Table. Those knights who took part in the quest were Perceval, Gawain, Lancelot, and Galahad. At first an instrument of healing and regeneration, the Grail later became a symbol of plenty and grace. According to tradition one who could see it clearly reaches a state of perfect bliss which affirms union with God. In the German version of Wolfram Von Eschenbach the Grail become a symbol of man's search for an ideal and true religion. According to the legend only two knights (because of their distinguished purity) succeeded in seeing the Grail (which first appeared, accompanied by lighting, before the four knights mentioned above) —Galahad (who died in ecstasy after seeing it in a remote castle) and perceval (who became a monk and died two months later).

In Joyce's Araby there is a reference to the boy's imagining that he bore his chalice safely through a throng of foes. As the knights in quest of the chalice encountered a number of dangers and difficulties coming from those who sought to stop their journey, the boy similarly thought the distasteful surroundings and unpleasant noises as inimical to his cultivation of love which was to him the source of supreme bliss and the provider of inexplicable joy. The word 'chalice' also suggests that his idea of love is something extremely noble and holy, and, that being a bearer of it he has been distinguished for his bravery and purity of character.

The next literary symbol is Araby which to a Western mind is associated with Arabia, the famous country of the East, and with the Arabian Nights wherein are narrated the tales of Aladin and of the magic carpet. To a young boy accustomed to play in a narrow and suffocating street and to live in an empty and lonely house with a pair of elderly people, the word 'Araby' could quite reasonably arise in his mind the picture of the gorgeous East with its fabulous wealth, its dazzling brilliance, its magic and romance, its domed palaces and black-haired damsels. It gained added importance for the boy when the girl herself said that there would be a splendid bazaar there and when she pressed him to go there recommending it profusely. After this 'Araby' became a sort of a wonderland to him, a place that could give him the joy he sought, a bazaar that could fulfill his dream. As a result of it we find him restless to go there even though he hated crowds. He wished to annihilate the intervening days. He had no patience with school work and all the serious work of life seemed to him but child's play. Araby absorbed his entire attention. His soul loved to luxuriate on the fancy that she was calling the syllables of the word Araby to him through the silence of the night. Indeed it cast an Eastern enchantment over him. So the image Araby stands for beauty and romance, charm and joy of an extraordinary kind.

The final literary symbol is the boy's journey to Araby and back (Incidentally it is linked with other journey motifs like Aeneas's journey into the underworld and back and the old mariner's journey to the polar regions and back) The boy went to Araby hoping that his dream would be fulfilled there and that he would be able to come back with a gorgeous gift for his beloved. But what he experienced there was enough to fill him with disenchantment. He came back empty-handed but with a self-awareness that filled him with anguish and anger. Thus, his journey to Araby may be regarded as his quest for beauty that ended in frustration. On a larger level it symbolizes man's universal search for the ideal that is universally frustrated. His journey may symbolize man's quest for self-realization through insight into the human condition or man's wandering to learn his identity and place in the world.

If the theme of 'Araby' is escape from drab surroundings with the help of love, or the boy's frustrated quest for beauty amidst drab surroundings or conflict between dream and reality, there is no doubt that the above images help to convey the theme of the story in a fine way.

# CHAPTER SIX

# Vanka

Vanka

Anton Chekhov

Translated from Russian by Constance Garnett

Vanka Zhukov, a boy of nine, who had been for three months apprenticed to Alyahin the shoemaker, was sitting up on Christmas Eve. Waiting till his master and mistress and their workmen had gone to the midnight service, he took out of his master's cupboard a bottle of ink and a pen with a rusty nib, and, spreading out a crumpled sheet of paper in front of him, began writing. Before forming the first letter he several times looked round fearfully at the door and the windows, stole a glance at the dark ikon, on both sides of which stretched shelves full of lasts, and heaved a broken sigh. The paper lay on the bench while he knelt before it.

"Dear grandfather, Konstantin Makaritch," he wrote, "I am writing you a letter. I wish you a happy Christmas, and all blessings from God Almighty. I have neither father nor mother, you are the only one left me."

Vanka raised his eyes to the dark ikon on which the light of his candle was reflected, and vividly recalled his grandfather, Konstantin Makaritch, who was night watchman to a family called Zhivarev. He was a thin but extraordinarily nimble and lively little old man of sixty-five, with an everlastingly laughing face and drunken eyes. By day he slept in the servants' kitchen, or made jokes with the cooks; at night, wrapped in an ample sheepskin, he walked round the grounds and tapped with his little mallet. Old Kashtanka and Eel, so-called on account of his dark colour and his long body like a weasel's, followed him with hanging heads. This Eel was exceptionally polite and affectionate, and looked with equal kindness on strangers and his own masters, but had not a very good reputation. Under his politeness and meekness was hidden the most Jesuitical cunning. No one knew better how to creep up on occasion and snap at one's legs, to slip into the store-room, or steal a hen from a peasant. His hind legs had been nearly pulled off more than once, twice he had been hanged, every week he was thrashed till he was half dead, but he always revived.

At this moment grandfather was, no doubt, standing at the gate, screwing up his eyes at the red windows of the church, stamping with his high felt boots, and joking with the servants. His little mallet was hanging on his belt. He was clasping his hands, shrugging with the cold, and, with an aged chuckle, pinching first the housemaid, then the cook.

"How about a pinch of snuff?" he was saying, offering the women his snuff-box.

The women would take a sniff and sneeze. Grandfather would be indescribably delighted, go off into a merry chuckle, and cry:

"Tear it off, it has frozen on!"

They give the dogs a sniff of snuff too. Kashtanka sneezes, wriggles her head, and walks away offended. Eel does not sneeze, from politeness, but wags his tail. And the weather is glorious. The air is still, fresh, and transparent. The night is dark, but one can see the whole village with its white roofs and coils of smoke coming from the chimneys, the trees silvered with hoar frost, the snowdrifts. The whole sky spangled with gay twinkling stars, and the Milky Way is as distinct as though it had been washed and rubbed with snow for a

holiday. . . .

Vanka sighed, dipped his pen, and went on writing:

"And yesterday I had a wigging. The master pulled me out into the yard by my hair, and whacked me with a boot-stretcher because I accidentally fell asleep while I was rocking their brat in the cradle. And a week ago the mistress told me to clean a herring, and I began from the tail end, and she took the herring and thrust its head in my face. The workmen laugh at me and send me to the tavern for vodka, and tell me to steal the master's cucumbers for them, and the master beats me with anything that comes to hand. And there is nothing to eat. In the morning they give me bread, for dinner, porridge, and in the evening, bread again; but as for tea, or soup, the master and mistress gobble it all up themselves. And I am put to sleep in the passage, and when their wretched brat cries I get no sleep at all, but have to rock the cradle. Dear grandfather, show the divine mercy, take me away from here, home to the village. It's more than I can bear. I bow down to your feet, and will pray to God for you for ever, take me away from here or I shall die."

Vanka's mouth worked, he rubbed his eyes with his black fist, and gave a sob.

"I will powder your snuff for you," he went on. "I will pray for you, and if I do anything you can thrash me like Sidor's goat. And if you think I've no job, then I will beg the steward for Christ's sake to let me clean his boots, or I'll go for a shepherd-boy instead of Fedka. Dear grandfather, it is more than I can bear, it's simply no life at all. I wanted to run away to the village, but I have no boots, and I am afraid of the frost. When I grow up big I will take care of you for this, and not let anyone annoy you, and when you die I will pray for the rest of your soul, just as for my mammy's.

Moscow is a big town. It's all gentlemen's houses, and there are lots of horses, but there are no sheep, and the dogs are not spiteful. The lads here don't go out with the star, and they don't let anyone go into the choir, and once I saw in a shop window fishing-hooks for sale, fitted ready with the line and for all sorts of fish, awfully good ones, there was even one hook that would hold a forty-pound sheat-fish. And I have seen shops where there are guns of all sorts, after the pattern of the master's guns at home, so that I shouldn't wonder if they are a hundred roubles each...... And in the butchers' shops there are grouse and woodcocks and fish and hares, but the shopmen don't say where they shoot them.

"Dear grandfather, when they have the Christmas tree at the big house, get me a gilt walnut, and put it away in the green trunk. Ask the young lady Olga Ignatyevna, say it's for Vanka."

Vanka gave a tremulous sigh, and again stared at the window. He remembered how his grandfather always went into the forest to get the Christmas tree for his master's family, and took his grandson with him. It was a merry time! Grandfather made a noise in his throat, the forest crackled with the frost, and looking at them Vanka chortled too. Before chopping down the Christmas tree, grandfather would smoke a pipe, slowly take a pinch of snuff, and laugh at frozen Vanka. The young fir trees, covered with hoar frost, stood motionless,

waiting to see which of them was to die. Wherever one looked, a hare flew like an arrow over the snowdrifts. . . . Grandfather could not refrain from shouting: "Hold him, hold him . . . hold him! Ah, the bob-tailed devil!"

When he had cut down the Christmas tree, grandfather used to drag it to the big house, and there set to work to decorate it. The young lady, who was Vanka's favourite, Olga

Ignatyevna, was the busiest of all. When Vanka's mother Pelageya was alive, and a servant in the big house, Olga Ignatyevna used to give him goodies, and having nothing better to do, taught him to read and write, to count up to a hundred, and even to dance a quadrille.

When Pelageya died, Vanka had been transferred to the servants' kitchen to be with his grandfather, and from the kitchen to the shoemaker's in Moscow.

"Do come, dear grandfather," Vanka went on with his letter. "For Christ's sake, I beg you, take me away. Have pity on an unhappy orphan like me; here everyone knocks me about, and I am fearfully hungry; I can't tell you what misery it is, I am always crying. And the other day the master hit me on the head with a last, so that I fell down. My life is wretched, worse than any dog's. I send greetings to Alyona, one-eyed Yegorka, and the coachman,

and don't give my concertina to anyone. I remain, your grandson, Ivan Zhukov. Dear grandfather, do come."

Vanka folded the sheet of writing-paper twice, and put it into an envelope he had bought the day before for a kopeck. After thinking a little, he dipped the pen and wrote the address:

To grandfather in the village.

Then he scratched his head, thought a little, and added: Konstantin Makaritch. Glad that he had not been prevented from writing, he put on his cap and, without putting on his little greatcoat, ran out into the street as he was in his shirt. . . .

The shopmen at the butcher's, whom he had questioned the day before, told him that letters were put in post-boxes, and from the boxes were carried about all over the earth in mailcarts with drunken drivers and ringing bells. Vanka ran to the nearest post-box, and thrust the precious letter in the slit. . . .

An hour later, lulled by sweet hopes, he was sound asleep.... He dreamed of the stove. On

the stove was sitting his grandfather, swinging his bare legs, and reading the letter to the cooks. . . .

By the stove was Eel, wagging his tail.

## *Vanka Summary Pointwise:-*

1.Vanka Zhukov is 9 years old. He is apprenticed to Alyakhin, a shoemaker. Vanka did not go to bed on Christmas Eve. When his master, master's wife, and the other senior apprentices went to Church, Vanka took a pen and a crumpled sheet of paper. Before starting to write he looked around the room, the door and window as if he was afraid. He looked at the lasts on the shelves and gave a sigh. Then he knelt on the floor and started writing.

2."Dear Grandad Konstantin Makarich, I am writing a letter to you. I send you Christmas greetings and I hope God will send you his blessings. I have no father and Mummie and you are all I have left."

3.Vanka saw his grandfather in his mind. His grandfather was a night watchman on the estate of a rich family. He was a small, lean old man about 65. But he was lively and agile. He had a smiling face but his eyes were bleary with drink. During daytime he slept in the dark kitchen or spent time joking with the cook and the kitchen maids. In the night he wore a sheepskin coat and walked around the estate making sounds with his rattle. With him there used to be two dogs. One was old Kashtanka. The other was Eel. Eel had black coat and a long weasel-like body. Eel was respectful and always tried to get people's affection. He looked at friends and strangers in the same manner. He did not give confidence to anyone. His respectful and obedient nature hid his hatred and vengeance. He could go quietly and bite somebody's foot, creep into the icehouse and steal a peasant's chicken. His back legs had been cut many times, twice he had been hung up, and every week he was beaten up very badly. But he survived all.

4.Grandad was perhaps standing at the gate looking at the bright red light coming from the church windows, or chatting with the servants. His rattle would be tied to his belt. He would be laughing and pinching a maid or one of the cooks. He would show his snuff box and ask the women to take a nip. The women would take some snuff and put into their nostrils. They would sneeze. Grandad would be shouting and laughing with joy, saying, "Good for frozen noses."

5.Even the dogs were given snuff. Kashtanka would sneeze, shake her head and walk away, feeling angry. But Eel very politely would wag his tail. The weather was good. The air was still and fresh. It was a dark night. But the whole village could be seen' clearly because the houses had white roofs. Smoke rose from the chimneys. Trees were covered with frost. Snow was falling. The sky was filled with twinkling stars. The Milky Way was shining as if polished with snow.

Vanka continued with his letter: "Yesterday I got a lot of beating. The master took me by the hair and dragged me into the yard. He beat me badly with the stirrup-strap (the belt used to connect the foot rest of the rider to the saddle). I had gone to sleep while rocking his baby. One day last week, the mistress told me to clean a herring. I began from the tail. She took it and rubbed its head on my face. Other apprentices make fun of me. They send me to buy vodka and make me steal the master's cucumbers.

6.I don't get enough to eat. They give me bread in the morning, gruel for dinner and again bread for supper. I never get tea or cabbage soup. They take it all themselves. They make me sleep in the passage. When their baby cries, I don't get any sleep at all. I have to rock it. Dear Grandad, for the Lord's sake, take me away from this place. Take me home to the village. I can't suffer it any longer. I beg you. I always pray for you. Do take me away or I will die...."

7.Vanka's lips trembled. He rubbed his eyes. He sobbed. Vanka continued: "I will grind your snuff for you. I will pray for you. You can beat me as hard as you like if I do mischief. If you think I have nothing to do, I will clean the boots or go as a shepherd instead of Fedya. I wanted to run away to the village but I have no boots and I was afraid of the frost. When I grow up to be a man I will look after you and I will not let anyone hurt you. When you die, I will pray for your soul like I do for my Mummie."

8."Moscow is such a big town. There are many gentlemen's houses and many horses there. There are no sheep. The dogs there are not at all fierce. The boys go about with a sta,r at Christmas. They don't let you sing in church. Once I saw them selling fishing hooks of different sizes. I saw one hook that could hold a catfish weighing 30 pounds. I have seen shops selling guns like the one my master has. The guns might cost 100 roubles each. In the butcher's shop we can buy grouse, woodcock (both mean different kinds of 'kattukozhi') and hares. The shopkeepers don't say how they got them."

9."Dear Grandad, when they have a Christmas tree at the big house, take a fine nut for me and put it away in the green chest. Ask Miss Olga Ignatyevna and tell her it is for Vanka."

10. Vanka sighed. He looked at the window glass. He remembered his grandfather going to get a Christmas tree for his employers. He had taken Vanka with him. How happy Vanka was then! Grandfather would laugh. The frost covered trees would laugh and Vanka also laughed. Before cutting the tree, grandfather would smoke his pipe, take a long pinch of snuff. He would laugh at the shivering Vanka. The young firtrees, covered with frost, stood without moving. They were waiting to see which one would be cut. Suddenly a hare would appear. Grandfather would shout: 'Stop it, stop it.'

11. Grandfatherwould drag the tree to the big house. They all would decorate it. Miss Olga Ignatyevna, Vanka's favourite, was the busiest of all. Pelageya was Ninka's mother. She is dead. When she was working in the big house, Olga Ignatyevna used to give Vanka sweets. As her pastime, she also taught Vanka to read, write and count to a hundred. She even tried to teach him to dance. When his mother died, Vanka was sent to the back kitchen to his grandmother. From there he was sent to Moscow, to Alyakhin.

12. Vanka continued writing. "Come to me dear grandad. Take me from here. Feel pity for me. They always beat me and I am always hungry and miserable. I send my love to Alyona, one eyed-Yegor and the coachman. Don't give my concertina to anyone. I remain your grandson Ivan Zhukov. DearGrandad do come."

13. He folded the sheet and put into an envelope. He wrote the address: To Grandfather in the village. After some thought he added: To Konstantin Makarich'.

14. He was happy that nobody saw him writing. He put his cap and ran out into the street. He did not wear his coat. The men at the butcher's had told him that letters are put into letter-boxes. Then they are sent all over the world in mail coaches with 3 horses and drunken drivers and jingling bells. Vanka dropped his letter in the letter box.

15. An hour later he fell asleep. He dreamed of a stove. His grandfather was sitting on the stove-ledge, with his bare feet dangling. He was reading the letter to the cooks. Eel was walking backwards and forwards, wagging his tail.

## *Major Characters in the Story Vanka*

### Vanka

Vanka is the central character in the story Vanka by Anton Chekhov. He is a nine year old orphan. He was living in a village with his mother and grandfather. After his mother's death, he was sent to Moscow to apprentice under a shoe-maker named Alyakhin. At a very tender age he became a child labourer. He was deprived of all his child rights. He did not get his primary education other than what he learned from his play-mate Olga. Vanka has to suffer a lot at Alyakhin's house. It has been only three months since he reached Moscow. But his sufferings are so severe and beyond description that made him write a letter pleading his grandpa to come and save him as quickly as possible. Vanka is very much afraid of his master, mistress and other senior apprentices. When he wrote the secret letter, he was watchful not to be seen by others. He is very nostalgic about his village life, especially of the Christmas time when he used to spend with his mother, grandpa and Olga. Vanka's child-like innocence is very visible in his letter. Even when he wrote about his miserable life, which was worse than that of a dog, he did not forget to write about the wonderful sights of the big town of Moscow. In a little village boy's eyes, shops selling fishing-hooks, guns and even butchery are sights of surprise. The boy is very innocent and he does not know even the basics of sending a letter. He posted the letter without proper address and postage stamp. Then the innocent boy spends days in the dreams of his grandpa's arrival, his sole saviour!

**Konstantin Makarich**

Konstantin Makarich is the grandfather of Vanka, the protagonist in the story Vanka. He is a night watchman on the estate of the Zhivarev family. He is a small, lean, old man about sixty-five years of age. He is remarkably lively and agile with a smiling face and eyes bleary with drink. He is a fun-loving man. In the day time either he sleeps in the back kitchen or spends time cracking jokes with the cooks and other kitchen maids. In the night he does his watchman duty walking round and round the estate, sounding his rattle, wearing a large sheepskin coat and felt boots. He has two dogs named Kashtanka and Eel. He will always be in the company of his beloved dogs. He has the habit of snuffing tobacco and he will offer the snuff to kitchen maids and even to his dogs. He enjoys seeing them sneeze, breaking out into jolly laughter. This grandfather is the only relative of Vanka now remaining in this world for him. When we read about Vanka's miserable plight at Alyakhin's house, we might ask ourselves why this man has sent the boy to such a cruel person. But we cannot blame the old, innocent and illiterate man. We are sure that while sending Vanka to Moscow, he must have in his mind only the thought that his grandchild should learn a trade and earn a living!

## *Vanka Short Questions and Answers*

**1.What were the specialties of the dog Eel?**

Eel had black coat and a long weasel-like body. He was respectful and always tried to get people's affection. He looked at friends and strangers in the same manner. He did not give confidence to anyone. His respectful and obedient nature hid his hatred and vengeance. He could go quietly and bite somebody's foot, creep into the icehouse and steal a peasant's chicken. His back legs had been cut many times, twice he had been hung up, and every week he was beaten up very badly. But he survived all.

**2.Is there a shift in the setting of the story in paragraphs 3 and 4? Where do the events take place?**

There is a shift. The events in paragraphs 3, 4 and 5 take place in the estate where Vanka's grandfather worked.

**3. How does grandfather create an atmosphere of fun and laugher?**

Grandfather creates an atmosphere of fun and laugher by playfully pinching one of the maids or cook and making them take snuff. He also gave snuff to the dogs. The women would sneeze and then the grandfather would say "Good for frozen noses".

**4.Pick out words and phrases used to describe the night.**

Dark night; trees were silver with rime; sky sprinkled with gaily twinkling stars; the Milky Way looked newly scrubbed and polished with snow.

**4.What sort of life did vanka lead at the shoemaker's place?**

Vanka led a very miserable life there. He did not get enough food to eat. He had to rock the shoemaker's baby in the night and this prevented him from getting enough sleep. He was badly beaten by Alyakhin. Senior boys ridiculed him.

**5.What, according to Vanka, would happen to him if his grandfather did not take him back home? Why did he think so?**

If his grandfather did not take him back home, he would die. He thought so because it was impossible for him to continue with his cruel master Alyakhin, who made him work hard, starved him, made him rock his baby in the night and beat him up cruelly.

**6.Why could not Vanka run away from the home of the shoemaker?**

Vanka could not run away from the home of the shoemaker because he had no shoes or boots. He was afraid of frostbite.

**7.Vanka is working for a shoemaker, but he does not have boots. What do you understand from this?**

This means although he works with a shoemaker he can't have shoes of his own. This is the case with many workers. A worker in a five-star hotel will not enjoy the same food or facilities that he helps to give to the guests. It is like 'Water, water everywhere, not a drop to drink!"

**8.What promises does Vanka make to his grandfather so that he would take him back home?**

Vanka makes a lot of promises to his grandfather so that he would take him back home. He would grind his snuff. He would pray for him. He could even beat him as hard as he liked if he did mischief. He would clean the boots or go as a shepherd instead of Fedya. When he grows up to be a man he would look after him and he will not let anyone hurt him. When he dies, he would pray for his soul like he does for his Mummie.

**9.What beautiful memories of Christmas do Vanka Cherish?**

Vanka remembers his grandfather going to get a Christmas tree for his employers. He had taken Vanka with him. How happy Vanka was then! Grandfather would laugh. The frost-covered trees would laugh and Vanka also laughed. Before cutting the tree, grandfather would smoke his pipe, take a long pinch of snuff. He would laugh at the shivering Vanka. The young firtrees, covered with frost, stood without moving. They were waiting to see which one would be cut. Suddenly a hare would appear. Grandfather would shout: 'Stop it, stop it.' Grandfather would drag the tree to the big house. They all would decorate it.

**10.Who was Vanka's favorite? Why did he like her?**

Miss Olga Ignatyevna was Vanka's favorite. She used to give Vanka sweets. She also taught him to read, write, count and also to dance.

**11.How did Vanka reach Moscow?**

When he became an orphan, after the death of his mother Pelageya, he was sent to his grandfather. His grandfather apprenticed him to the shoemaker Alyakhin in Moscow.

**12."I have such a miserable life worse than a dog's. " What made Vanka say so?**

Vanka said so for so many reasons. He did not get enough to eat. He could not sleep properly as he had to rock Alyakhin's baby in the night. He was laughed at by the senior apprentices and above all he was often beaten by Alyakhin.

**13.Do you think Vanka's letter will reach his grandfather? Why?**

It won't reach his grandfather. He just wrote the name of his grandfather and simply the village'. Which village? Where? Nobody would know.

**14.What did Vanka dream about in his sleep?**

He dreamed of a stove. His grandfather was sitting on the stove-ledge, with his bare feet dangling. He was reading the letter to the cooks. Eel was walking backwards and forwards, wagging his tail.

**15.Does the reference to the Eel have any significance in the story? How?**

The Eel in spite of his reverential manner and docility had spite and malice in his heart. So did the grandfather to the gentry he worked for. If he got a chance he too would bite them, as did Eel when he got a chance.

**16.According to Vanka, what kind of a person is Konstantin Makarich? It was Makarich who had sent Vanka away, when Vanka's mother Pelageya died. Do you justify Makarich's decision to send Vanka away to Moscow? Why?**

Vanka thinks Makarich is a good person. That is why he writes him a letter when he finds his life is miserable in Moscow. Makarich is a happy-go-lucky man having fun with the maids, the cook and the dogs. Some people might find fault with Makarich for sending the boy to Moscow. But we should know that he is an orphan with no education. He has to learn a trade to make a living. So Makarich's sending Vanka to Moocow is justified. But unfortunately, Alyakhin turned out to be a cruel man.

**17.How is Moscow, the big town, contrasted with the village where Vanka lived?**

Moscow is a big city. There are huge houses of rich men. They have horses. Children sold fishing hooks and lines there showing you could catch fish. There were shops there selling all kinds of guns. People hunted birds. Life was busy in the city. In the village, life was easy-going. There were a lot of sheep and dogs. The boys played with stars at Christmas and they sang songs in the church.

## *Some more Short Questions and Answers:*

**Q: Who is Vanka and what is his situation?**

A: Vanka is a nine-year-old orphan apprenticed to a shoemaker in Moscow. He is miserable, overworked, and abused by his master and the mistress, feeling lonely and desperate for affection.

**Q: Why does Vanka write a letter to his grandfather?**

A: Vanka writes to his grandfather to ask for help, comfort, and to be taken away from his harsh life in Moscow. He hopes his grandfather will rescue him from suffering.

**Q: How does Vanka describe his master and mistress in the letter?**

A: Vanka portrays them as cruel and harsh. He explains how he is beaten, overworked, and mistreated, highlighting his feelings of helplessness and the injustice he faces daily.

**Q: What memories does Vanka share with his grandfather?**

A: Vanka recalls the warmth of his village home, the love of his grandfather, and the simpler, happier times before coming to Moscow, emphasizing the contrast with his current suffering.

**Q: How does the story end and what is its tone?**

A: The story ends ambiguously with Vanka mailing the letter, unaware if it will reach his grandfather. The tone is sad and poignant, emphasizing the innocence and helplessness of childhood.

**Q: Where does Vanka live while working as an apprentice?**

A: Vanka lives in Moscow with his cruel master and mistress. He sleeps in the workshop, often on the floor, enduring cold, hunger, and neglect, far from the warmth of his grandfather's home in the village.

**Q: How does Vanka feel about Christmas?**

A: Vanka feels lonely and sad during Christmas. While others celebrate, he suffers from mistreatment, longing for love and care. The holiday reminds him of the joy he once knew at his grandfather's home.

**Q: What does Vanka ask his grandfather to do?**

A: He pleads with his grandfather to take him away from Moscow, send money, and protect him from his abusive master. He desperately wants to escape the harsh conditions of the workshop.

**Q: How does Chekhov show Vanka's innocence?**

A: Through Vanka's simple, honest letter and his naïve hope that his grandfather can save him, Chekhov highlights the purity of childhood and the contrast between innocence and the cruelty around him.

**Q: Why is Vanka afraid while writing the letter?**

A: Vanka worries the letter might be lost or intercepted and fears that no one will listen to him. His fear reflects his vulnerability and the precariousness of his lonely, powerless situation.

**Q: How is the city life contrasted with Vanka's village memories?**

A: The harsh, noisy, and uncaring life of Moscow is contrasted with Vanka's warm, happy memories of the village, where he felt loved and safe, emphasizing the cruelty and alienation he now endures.

**Q: What does the letter reveal about Vanka's emotions?**

A: The letter reveals fear, loneliness, and desperation. It shows his longing for care and protection, as well as a child's hope that someone he trusts will rescue him from suffering.

**Q: How does Chekhov create sympathy for Vanka?**

A: Chekhov uses Vanka's first-person perspective, his tender memories, and descriptions of abuse, allowing readers to feel his pain, helplessness, and innocence, evoking deep emotional sympathy.

**Q: What is the significance of the ending?**

A: The ending is open and tragic; Vanka posts the letter, hoping for rescue, but the outcome is uncertain. It emphasizes the vulnerability of children and the indifference of the world around them.

**Q: How does Vanka describe the work he has to do?**

A: Vanka explains that he must work long hours making shoes, often in pain and hunger. His tasks are physically exhausting, showing both the cruelty of his master and the harsh reality of child labor.

## *Some long Questions and Answers*

**1.What does the letter Vanka writes to his grandfather reveal about his character and his situation?**

Vanka's letter to his grandfather is a powerful window into both his personal character and the harsh realities of his life. Through this letter, Chekhov skillfully exposes Vanka's innocence, longing for love, and the severe hardships he endures as an apprentice. The letter begins with a childlike address, demonstrating his trust and deep affection for his grandfather, whom he remembers as a source of warmth and care. The simplicity of his language and the earnestness of his tone highlight Vanka's naivety and his inability to fully grasp the adult complexities surrounding his situation. He does not embellish or manipulate the truth; instead, he recounts events as he experiences them, which reflects a purity of heart that contrasts sharply with the cruelty he faces in the adult world. This honesty and transparency also suggest that Vanka still clings to a moral framework where telling the truth and appealing to family love are natural responses to suffering.

At the same time, the letter lays bare the depth of Vanka's suffering. He describes his life as an apprentice in Moscow, enduring grueling labor, insufficient food, and harsh treatment from his master. These depictions are not exaggerated or dramatic; they are straightforward statements of fact, which makes his plight all the more poignant. Chekhov uses this narrative strategy to emphasize the oppressive conditions faced by many children in 19th-century Russia, particularly those from poor families sent to work in cities far from home. Vanka's recounting of his physical discomfort—the cold, the exhaustion, and the occasional punishment—evokes a vivid sense of empathy from the reader. By presenting his struggles in this unembellished way, Chekhov underscores the cruelty of societal indifference and the vulnerability of children in the absence of protective adults.

Vanka's letter also reveals his deep emotional longing and desire for human connection. He reminisces about his grandfather with nostalgia, recalling the kindness and attention he once received. This contrast between past affection and present neglect enhances the emotional impact of the story, highlighting how isolation and neglect can shape a child's perspective. The letter becomes more than a simple plea for help; it is a testament to Vanka's hope and faith that love and compassion still exist in the world. He believes that by writing honestly and directly to his grandfather, someone who truly cares for him, he might escape his misery, which shows his reliance on trust and emotional bonds rather than manipulation or cunning.

Furthermore, the letter demonstrates Vanka's limited understanding of the world. He does not consider practical obstacles, such as whether the letter will reach his grandfather or if his grandfather has the means to intervene. This naïveté reinforces his vulnerability and innocence, making the reader keenly aware of the dangers children like Vanka face. Yet, it also underscores his bravery; despite knowing he is powerless in many ways, he still acts, choosing to express himself and hope for rescue. In this way, Chekhov crafts a character who embodies resilience, hope, and purity amid suffering.

In conclusion, Vanka's letter is a microcosm of the story's central themes: the innocence of childhood, the cruelty of societal neglect, and the enduring hope for love and connection. Through his candid words, readers witness both the harsh realities of Vanka's life and the enduring humanity within him, making the letter a profoundly moving and revealing element of Chekhov's narrative.

**2.How does Chekhov use the setting in "Vanka" to highlight the contrast between Vanka's past and present life?**

In "Vanka", Chekhov uses the story's settings to emphasize the stark contrast between the warmth and security of Vanka's early life in the village and the harsh, oppressive conditions of his current existence in Moscow. The settings are not mere backdrops; they are integral to the story, reflecting Vanka's emotional state and underscoring key themes such as innocence, neglect, and the loss of childhood. Chekhov begins by establishing Vanka's present reality in the cramped workshop of a shoemaker's shop, which immediately conveys discomfort and confinement. The physical space is small, dark, and cold, mirroring the emotional and psychological oppression he experiences under the care of his master. Every detail—from the laborious work to the inadequate food and the lack of warmth—serves to heighten the sense of vulnerability and suffering. Chekhov's attention to these details immerses the reader in the relentless hardships of Vanka's day-to-day life, emphasizing that his childhood has been effectively stolen by the demands of adult society.

This urban setting in Moscow functions as a symbol of alienation and neglect. The city, bustling and impersonal, is inhospitable to a child, offering no comfort, guidance, or affection. The shoemaker's shop, rather than being a place of learning or protection, is depicted as a site of punishment and relentless toil. Chekhov deliberately contrasts this with Vanka's memories of the village, creating a duality that heightens the emotional resonance of the story. The village, in Vanka's recollection, is imbued with warmth, care, and familial love, particularly associated with his grandfather. It is a pastoral setting, open and nurturing, where Vanka experiences safety, affection, and a sense of belonging. The vividness of these memories makes the present misery more acute, as the reader can see what Vanka has lost: not only comfort and freedom but also the emotional security that comes with being genuinely loved and protected.

Chekhov also uses the letter as a literary device to bridge these two contrasting settings. While writing from the bleak, confining workshop, Vanka mentally transports himself to the village, describing in detail the things he longs for—the grandfather's hands, the warmth of the home, and the simple pleasures of rural life. This contrast underscores both his nostalgia and his helplessness, as he is physically trapped in one world while emotionally yearning for another. The settings, therefore, reflect his internal struggle: the oppressive workshop represents reality and suffering, while the village represents memory, hope, and the ideal of love and safety. Through this juxtaposition, Chekhov conveys a profound sense of loss, highlighting how displacement and hardship can intensify the innocence and vulnerability of childhood.

Additionally, the geographical and social distances between Moscow and the village emphasize the theme of isolation. Vanka's hope that his letter will reach his grandfather relies on faith in a connection that is physically distant and socially mediated. The setting reinforces the tension between helplessness and hope, as the urban environment is depicted as cold and uncaring, while the rural environment exists in memory as a symbol of human kindness and familial support. In this way, Chekhov's use of setting is not merely descriptive but deeply psychological, shaping the reader's understanding of Vanka's suffering and his longing for rescue.

In conclusion, Chekhov's contrasting settings in "Vanka" serve to highlight the emotional and physical hardships of the protagonist's life while illuminating the innocence, nostalgia, and yearning that define his character. The oppressive city and the warm, remembered village together create a poignant reflection on childhood lost and the human need for love, safety, and belonging.

**3.How is the character of Vanka portrayed in Chekhov's story, and what does he reveal about childhood and society?**

Vanka Zhukov, the protagonist of Anton Chekhov's "Vanka", is portrayed as an innocent, vulnerable, and deeply emotional child whose character serves as the heart of the story and a lens through which Chekhov critiques societal neglect. Through Vanka, Chekhov highlights the plight of children forced into harsh labor, the resilience of the human spirit, and the enduring need for love and care. Vanka is nine years old, an orphan sent to Moscow to work as an apprentice for a shoemaker, a situation that exposes him to relentless labor, abuse, and deprivation. Chekhov's portrayal of Vanka is multilayered, combining external suffering with an inner world rich in longing, moral sensitivity, and imagination.

One of the most striking aspects of Vanka's character is his innocence. He approaches the world with a pure, untainted perspective, expressing his feelings honestly and without manipulation. This is most evident in the letter he writes to his grandfather, which serves as the story's centerpiece. In the letter, Vanka recounts the cruel treatment he receives from his master and the neglect of his current environment. Despite the severity of his suffering, Vanka's tone remains candid and straightforward, revealing a child who has not yet been corrupted by cynicism or deceit. His innocence is further highlighted by his unawareness of practical realities: he believes that simply sending a letter will result in immediate rescue, demonstrating both trust in his grandfather and a limited understanding of the adult world. This naivety underscores the vulnerability of children like Vanka and makes the reader acutely aware of the dangers faced by those who lack protection and guidance.

At the same time, Vanka's character is defined by resilience and hope. Although he experiences daily abuse, cold, and hunger, he continues to dream of a better life and seeks comfort in his memories of his grandfather and the village. These recollections provide him with emotional sustenance, revealing his capacity for longing, imagination, and emotional depth. Chekhov uses Vanka's hope as a stark contrast to the harshness of his surroundings, emphasizing the story's central tension between the innocence of childhood and the cruelty of an uncaring society. His hope is fragile yet persistent, reflecting the universal human desire for love and belonging.

Vanka also embodies sensitivity and moral awareness. Despite his own suffering, he notices the unfairness of the world and experiences empathy for others in his letters, reflecting a natural sense of justice. This moral clarity, combined with emotional openness, makes Vanka a fully human character, not merely a victim. Chekhov's attention to these inner qualities allows readers to connect deeply with Vanka and experience the poignancy of his situation.

Furthermore, Vanka's character illustrates broader social commentary. He represents countless children in 19th-century Russia subjected to exploitation and neglect. Through his story, Chekhov critiques a society that allows such suffering while highlighting the enduring innocence, emotional depth, and hope that can survive even in the most oppressive circumstances.

In conclusion, Vanka's character is a remarkable blend of vulnerability, innocence, moral sensitivity, and resilience. Through him, Chekhov explores themes of childhood suffering, societal neglect, and the longing for love and protection. Vanka's portrayal elicits empathy, highlights social injustice, and reminds readers of the fragile yet enduring spirit of children in adversity. He is not just a character; he is a symbol of innocence confronting a harsh, indifferent world, making "Vanka" a timeless study of human vulnerability and hope.

**4. How is the grandfather depicted in "Vanka," and what does his character reveal about love, family, and Vanka's longing?**

In Anton Chekhov's "Vanka", the grandfather, though never appearing directly in the narrative, plays a central role in shaping the emotional world of the protagonist and conveying the story's themes of love, family, and childhood longing. Chekhov develops the grandfather primarily through Vanka's letter, memories, and appeals, allowing readers to understand him as both a real figure and a symbolic embodiment of care and protection. Though physically absent, his presence dominates the story, highlighting the stark contrast between the warmth of familial love and the harsh cruelty of the external world Vanka now inhabits.

The grandfather is depicted as a figure of unwavering kindness and affection, someone who provided Vanka with comfort, guidance, and moral support during his early childhood in the village. In Vanka's memory, the grandfather is attentive, nurturing, and protective—a stark contrast to the shoemaker and his wife, who are cruel and indifferent. Chekhov emphasizes these qualities through the child's recollections of simple, intimate details: the grandfather's hands, his guidance in daily life, and the comfort he offered when Vanka felt scared or alone. These memories reveal not only the grandfather's warmth but also the intensity of the emotional bond he shares with Vanka. In this way, Chekhov portrays the grandfather as a symbol of familial love, highlighting how such bonds shape a child's sense of security, self-worth, and hope.

The grandfather's characterization also serves to underscore Vanka's current suffering and isolation. By comparing the harshness of Moscow, the shoemaker's cruelty, and the cold indifference of the city with the warmth and care of his grandfather, Chekhov intensifies the reader's awareness of the child's vulnerability. The grandfather becomes a point of reference for everything Vanka has lost: safety, affection, and a sense of belonging. This juxtaposition deepens the emotional impact of the story and allows Chekhov to explore the devastating consequences of neglect and exploitation, particularly in the lives of children who are separated from protective, loving adults.

Moreover, the grandfather functions as a beacon of hope and a moral compass in Vanka's world. The letter Vanka writes is an appeal for rescue, reflecting both desperation and enduring trust. Despite his suffering, Vanka believes in the grandfather's goodness and ability to act on his behalf, demonstrating a child's faith in familial love and moral responsibility. Chekhov uses this dynamic to highlight the universal human longing for protection and care, particularly in moments of vulnerability. The grandfather's absence is therefore a powerful narrative tool: it magnifies Vanka's loneliness while simultaneously representing the ideal of loving guidance that children instinctively seek.

The grandfather is also symbolic of the simplicity and warmth of rural life, contrasting sharply with the cruelty and impersonality of the city. Through this symbolic role, Chekhov comments on societal neglect: the story suggests that in an industrialized, urbanized environment, the natural bonds of family and care can be disrupted, leaving children vulnerable. The grandfather embodies what is morally and emotionally right—a standard against which the injustices Vanka suffers are measured.

In conclusion, the grandfather in "Vanka" is both a literal and symbolic figure of love, protection, and moral guidance. Though absent from the immediate narrative, he shapes Vanka's emotional life, representing the warmth, care, and family bonds that the child craves. Through the grandfather, Chekhov underscores themes of childhood vulnerability, social neglect, and the enduring human need for affection and security. His character is essential not only for understanding Vanka's longing but also for grasping the story's deeper critique of a society that allows children to suffer in the absence of love.

**5.How is the shoemaker portrayed in "Vanka," and what does his character reveal about cruelty and societal neglect?**

In Anton Chekhov's "Vanka", the shoemaker is a central figure representing the cruelty and neglect that define Vanka's harsh urban existence. Unlike the grandfather, who embodies warmth and care, the shoemaker is depicted as an oppressive, morally indifferent adult whose treatment of Vanka underscores the story's themes of child suffering, social injustice, and the failure of adult responsibility. Chekhov develops the shoemaker through Vanka's perspective, highlighting the contrast between the child's innocence and the adult's callousness, and using this contrast to critique the broader societal conditions that allow such exploitation.

The shoemaker's character is established primarily through Vanka's description in the letter, emphasizing his cruelty, harshness, and lack of empathy. Vanka recounts that the shoemaker punishes him physically, demanding long hours of labor and showing no concern for his well-being. This portrayal immediately conveys the power imbalance between adult and child and situates the shoemaker as a figure of authority that enforces oppression rather than protection. Chekhov's choice to reveal the shoemaker's character indirectly—through Vanka's suffering and fear—intensifies the reader's sense of injustice, as the child is powerless to resist the adult's control. The shoemaker is not merely an individual villain but also a symbol of systemic neglect, reflecting societal indifference to the welfare of vulnerable children in 19th-century Russia.

The shoemaker's cruelty extends beyond physical punishment. He is emotionally indifferent, treating Vanka as a tool for labor rather than a human being with needs, feelings, or rights. Chekhov emphasizes this aspect of his character to highlight the dehumanizing nature of child labor: Vanka's emotional and psychological suffering is amplified by the lack of care and affection. The shoemaker's neglect mirrors a broader societal failure, suggesting that children like Vanka are vulnerable not only to direct abuse but also to the apathy of those who hold power over them. In this sense, the shoemaker embodies the social forces that perpetuate child exploitation, making him a vehicle for Chekhov's social critique.

Despite being a negative figure, the shoemaker is essential to the story's emotional impact. His harshness provides the contrast necessary to appreciate Vanka's innocence, vulnerability, and moral sensitivity. Chekhov's careful juxtaposition of the shoemaker's cruelty and the grandfather's warmth intensifies the reader's empathy for Vanka while underscoring the stark dichotomy between love and neglect. The shoemaker's presence demonstrates how external circumstances can shape a child's life, highlighting the fragility of childhood in an unforgiving society.

Additionally, the shoemaker represents the broader urban environment that Chekhov portrays as cold, impersonal, and indifferent. Unlike the village, where Vanka experienced care and guidance from his grandfather, the city—embodied in the shoemaker and his household—offers exploitation, harsh labor, and emotional neglect. Through this characterization, Chekhov emphasizes that cruelty is not simply a matter of individual personality but also a reflection of systemic societal issues that fail to protect the young and powerless.

In conclusion, the shoemaker in "Vanka" is a symbol of cruelty, neglect, and societal indifference. Through Vanka's eyes, Chekhov portrays him as physically and emotionally oppressive, highlighting the suffering of children subjected to labor and abuse. The shoemaker's character contrasts sharply with the warmth of Vanka's grandfather, emphasizing themes of vulnerability, injustice, and the enduring human need for care. By depicting the shoemaker as both an individual and a representation of societal failure, Chekhov crafts a critique of a world in which innocence is exploited and childhood is endangered.

# CHAPTER SEVEN

# THE HUNGRY STONES

**THE HUNGRY STONES**
**Rabindranath Tagore**

My kinsman and myself were returning to Calcutta from our Puja trip when we met the man in a train. From his dress and bearing we took him at first for an up-country Mahomedan, but we were puzzled as we heard him talk. He discoursed upon all subjects so confidently that you might think the Disposer of All Things consulted him at all times in all that He did. Hitherto we had been perfectly happy, as we did not know that secret and unheard-of forces were at work, that the Russians had advanced close to us, that the English had deep and secret policies, that confusion among the native chiefs had come to a head. But our newly-acquired friend said with a sly smile: "There happen more things in heaven and earth, Horatio, than are reported in your newspapers." As we had never stirred out of our homes before, the demeanour of the man struck us dumb with wonder. Be the topic ever so trivial, he would quote science, or comment on the Vedas, or repeat quatrains from some Persian poet; and as we had no pretence to a knowledge of science or the Vedas or Persian, our admiration for him went on increasing, and my kinsman, a theosophist, was firmly convinced that our fellow-passenger must have been supernaturally inspired by some strange "magnetism" or "occult power," by an "astral body" or something of that kind. He listened to the tritest saying that fell from the lips of our extraordinary companion with devotional rapture, and secretly took down notes of his conversation. I fancy that the extraordinary man saw this, and was a little pleased with it.

When the train reached the junction, we assembled in the waiting room for the connection. It was then 10 P.M., and as the train, we heard, was likely to be very late, owing to something wrong in the lines, I spread my bed on the table and was about to lie down for a comfortable doze, when the extraordinary person deliberately set about spinning the following yarn. Of course, I could get no sleep that night.

When, owing to a disagreement about some questions of administrative policy, I threw up my post at Junagarh, and entered the service of the Nizam of Hydria, they appointed me at once, as a strong young man, collector of cotton duties at Barich.

Barich is a lovely place. The Susta "chatters over stony ways and babbles on the pebbles," tripping, like a skilful dancing girl, in through the woods below the lonely hills. A flight of 150 steps rises from the river, and above that flight, on the river's brim and at the foot of the hills, there stands a solitary marble palace. Around it there is no habitation of man—the village and the cotton mart of Barich being far off.

About 250 years ago the Emperor Mahmud Shah II. had built this lonely palace for his pleasure and luxury. In his days jets of rose-water spurted from its fountains, and on the cold marble floors of its spray-cooled rooms young Persian damsels would sit, their hair dishevelled before bathing, and, splashing their soft naked feet in the clear water of the reservoirs, would sing, to the tune of the guitar, the ghazals of their vineyards.

The fountains play no longer; the songs have ceased; no longer do snow-white feet step gracefully on the snowy marble. It is but the vast and solitary quarters of cess-collectors like us, men oppressed with solitude and deprived of the society of women. Now, Karim Khan, the old clerk of my office, warned me repeatedly not to take up my abode there. "Pass the day there, if you like," said he, "but never stay the night." I passed it off with a light laugh. The servants said that they would work till dark and go away at night. I gave my ready assent. The house had such a bad name that even thieves would not venture near it after dark.

At first the solitude of the deserted palace weighed upon me like a nightmare. I would stay out, and work hard as long as possible, then return home at night jaded and tired, go to bed and fall asleep.

Before a week had passed, the place began to exert a weird fascination upon me. It is difficult to describe or to induce people to believe; but I felt as if the whole house was like a living organism slowly and imperceptibly digesting me by the action of some stupefying gastric juice.

Perhaps the process had begun as soon as I set my foot in the house, but I distinctly remember the day on which I first was conscious of it.

It was the beginning of summer, and the market being dull I had no work to do. A little before sunset I was sitting in an arm-chair near the water's edge below the steps. The Susta had shrunk and sunk low; a broad patch of sand on the other side glowed with the hues of evening; on this side the pebbles at the bottom of the clear shallow waters were glistening. There was not a breath of wind anywhere, and the still air was laden with an oppressive scent from the spicy shrubs growing on the hills close by.

As the sun sank behind the hill-tops a long dark curtain fell upon the stage of day, and the intervening hills cut short the time in which light and shade mingle at sunset. I thought of going out for a ride, and was about to get up when I heard a footfall on the steps behind. I looked back, but there was no one.

As I sat down again, thinking it to be an illusion, I heard many footfalls, as if a large number of persons were rushing down the steps. A strange thrill of delight, slightly tinged with fear, passed through my frame, and though there was not a figure before my eyes, methought I saw a bevy of joyous maidens coming down the steps to bathe in the Susta in that summer evening. Not a sound was in the valley, in the river, or in the palace, to break the silence, but I distinctly heard the maidens' gay and mirthful laugh, like the gurgle of a spring gushing forth in a hundred cascades, as they ran past me, in quick playful pursuit of each other, towards the river, without noticing me at all. As they were invisible to me, so I was, as it were, invisible to them. The river was perfectly calm, but I felt that its still, shallow, and clear waters were stirred suddenly by the splash of many an arm jingling with bracelets, that the girls laughed and dashed and spattered water at one another, that the feet of the fair swimmers tossed the tiny waves up in showers of pearl.

I felt a thrill at my heart—I cannot say whether the excitement was due to fear or delight or curiosity. I had a strong desire to see them more clearly, but naught was visible before me; I thought I could catch all that they said if I only strained my ears; but however hard I strained them, I heard nothing but the chirping of the cicadas in the woods. It seemed as if a dark curtain of 250 years was hanging before me, and I would fain lift a corner of it tremblingly and peer through, though the assembly on the other side was completely enveloped in darkness.

The oppressive closeness of the evening was broken by a sudden gust of wind, and the still surface of the Suista rippled and curled like the hair of a nymph, and from the woods wrapt in the evening gloom there came forth a simultaneous murmur, as though they were awakening from a black dream. Call it reality or dream, the momentary glimpse of that invisible mirage reflected from a far-off world, 250 years old, vanished in a flash. The mystic forms that brushed past me with their quick unbodied steps, and loud, voiceless laughter, and threw themselves into the river, did not go back wringing their dripping robes as they went. Like fragrance wafted away by the wind they were dispersed by a single breath of the spring.

Then I was filled with a lively fear that it was the Muse that had taken advantage of my solitude and possessed me—the witch had evidently come to ruin a poor devil like myself making a living by collecting cotton duties. I decided to have a good dinner—it is the empty stomach that all sorts of incurable diseases find an easy prey. I sent for my cook and gave orders for a rich, sumptuous moghlai dinner, redolent of spices and ghi.

Next morning the whole affair appeared a queer fantasy. With a light heart I put on a sola hat like the sahebs, and drove out to my work. I was to have written my quarterly report that day, and expected to return late; but before it was dark I was strangely drawn to my house—by what I could not say—I felt they were all waiting, and that I should delay no longer. Leaving my report unfinished I rose, put on my sola hat, and startling the dark, shady, desolate path with the rattle of my carriage, I reached the vast silent palace standing on the gloomy skirts of the hills.

On the first floor the stairs led to a very spacious hall, its roof stretching wide over ornamental arches resting on three rows of massive pillars, and groaning day and night under the weight of its own intense solitude. The day had just closed, and the lamps had not yet been lighted. As I pushed the door open a great bustle seemed to follow within, as if a throng of people had broken up in confusion, and rushed out through the doors and windows and corridors and verandas and rooms, to make its hurried escape.

As I saw no one I stood bewildered, my hair on end in a kind of ecstatic delight, and a faint scent of attar and unguents almost effected by age lingered in my nostrils. Standing in the darkness of that vast desolate hall between the rows of those ancient pillars, I could hear the gurgle of fountains plashing on the marble floor, a strange tune on the guitar, the jingle of ornaments and the tinkle of anklets, the clang of bells tolling the hours, the distant note of nahabat, the din of the crystal pendants of chandeliers shaken by the breeze, the song of bulbuls from the cages in the corridors, the cackle of storks in the gardens, all creating round me a strange unearthly music.

Then I came under such a spell that this intangible, inaccessible, unearthly vision appeared to be the only reality in the world—and all else a mere dream. That I, that is to say, Srijut So-and-so, the eldest son of So-and-so of blessed memory, should be drawing a monthly salary of Rs. 450 by the discharge of my duties as collector of cotton duties, and driving in my dog-cart to my office every day in a short coat and soia hat, appeared to me to be such an astonishingly ludicrous illusion that I burst into a horse-laugh, as I stood in the gloom of that vast silent hall.

At that moment my servant entered with a lighted kerosene lamp in his hand. I do not know whether he thought me mad, but it came back to me at once that I was in very deed Srijut So-and-so, son of So-and-so of blessed memory, and that, while our poets, great and small, alone could say whether inside of or outside the earth there was a region where unseen fountains perpetually played and fairy guitars, struck by invisible fingers, sent forth an eternal harmony, this at any rate was certain, that I collected duties at the cotton market at Banch, and earned thereby Rs. 450 per mensem as my salary. I laughed in great glee at my curious illusion, as I sat over the newspaper at my camp-table, lighted by the kerosene lamp.

After I had finished my paper and eaten my moghlai dinner, I put out the lamp, and lay down on my bed in a small side-room. Through the open window a radiant star, high above the Avalli hills skirted by the darkness of their woods, was gazing intently from millions and millions of miles away in the sky at Mr. Collector lying on a humble camp-bedstead. I wondered and felt amused at the idea, and do not knew when I fell asleep or how long I slept; but I suddenly awoke with a start, though I heard no sound and saw no intruder—only the steady bright star on the hilltop had set, and the dim light of the new moon was stealthily entering the room through the open window, as if ashamed of its intrusion.

I saw nobody, but felt as if some one was gently pushing me. As I awoke she said not a word, but beckoned me with her five fingers bedecked with rings to follow her cautiously. I got up noiselessly, and, though not a soul save myself was there in the countless apartments of that deserted palace with its slumbering sounds and waiting echoes, I feared at every step lest any one should wake up. Most of the rooms of the palace were always kept closed, and I had never entered them.

I followed breathless and with silent steps my invisible guide—I cannot now say where. What endless dark and narrow passages, what long corridors, what silent and solemn audience-chambers and close secret cells I crossed!

Though I could not see my fair guide, her form was not invisible to my mind's eye,—an Arab girl, her arms, hard and smooth as marble, visible through her loose sleeves, a thin veil falling on her face from the fringe of her cap, and a curved dagger at her waist! Methought that one of the thousand and one Arabian Nights had been wafted to me from the world of romance, and that at the dead of night I was wending my way through the dark narrow alleys of slumbering Bagdad to a trysting-place fraught with peril.

At last my fair guide stopped abruptly before a deep blue screen, and seemed to point to something below. There was nothing there, but a sudden dread froze the blood in my heart-methought I saw there on the floor at the foot of the screen a terrible negro eunuch dressed in rich brocade, sitting and dozing with outstretched legs, with a naked sword on his lap. My fair guide lightly tripped over his legs and held up a fringe of the screen. I could catch a glimpse of a part of the room spread with a Persian carpet—some one was sitting inside on a bed—I could not see her, but only caught a glimpse of two exquisite feet in gold-embroidered slippers, hanging out from loose saffron-coloured paijamas and placed idly on the orange-coloured velvet carpet. On one side there was a bluish crystal tray on which a few apples, pears, oranges, and bunches of grapes in plenty, two small cups and a gold-tinted decanter were evidently waiting the guest. A fragrant intoxicating vapour, issuing from a strange sort of incense that burned within, almost overpowered my senses.

As with trembling heart I made an attempt to step across the outstretched legs of the eunuch, he woke up suddenly with a start, and the sword fell from his lap with a sharp clang on the marble floor. A terrific scream made me jump, and I saw I was sitting on that camp-bedstead of mine sweating heavily; and the crescent moon looked pale in the morning light like a weary sleepless patient at dawn; and our crazy Meher Ali was crying out, as is his daily custom, "Stand back! Stand back!!" while he went along the lonely road.

Such was the abrupt close of one of my Arabian Nights; but there were yet a thousand nights left.

Then followed a great discord between my days and nights. During the day I would go to my work worn and tired, cursing the bewitching night and her empty dreams, but as night came my daily life with its bonds and shackles of work would appear a petty, false, ludicrous vanity.

After nightfall I was caught and overwhelmed in the snare of a strange intoxication, I would then be transformed into some unknown personage of a bygone age, playing my part in unwritten history; and my short English coat and tight breeches did not suit me in the least. With a red velvet cap on my head, loose paijamas, an embroidered vest, a long flowing silk gown, and coloured handkerchiefs scented with attar, I would complete my elaborate toilet, sit on a high-cushioned chair, and replace my cigarette with a many-coiled narghileh filled with rose-water, as if in eager expectation of a strange meeting with the beloved one.

I have no power to describe the marvellous incidents that unfolded themselves, as the gloom of the night deepened. I felt as if in the curious apartments of that vast edifice the fragments of a beautiful story, which I could follow for some distance, but of which I could never see the end, flew about in a sudden gust of the vernal breeze. And all the same I would wander from room to room in pursuit of them the whole night long.

Amid the eddy of these dream-fragments, amid the smell of henna and the twanging of the guitar, amid the waves of air charged with fragrant spray, I would catch like a flash of lightning the momentary glimpse of a fair damsel. She it was who had saffron-coloured paijamas, white ruddy soft feet in gold-embroidered slippers with curved toes, a close-fitting bodice wrought with gold, a red cap, from which a golden frill fell on her snowy brow and cheeks.

She had maddened me. In pursuit of her I wandered from room to room, from path to path among the bewildering maze of alleys in the enchanted dreamland of the nether world of sleep.

Sometimes in the evening, while arraying myself carefully as a prince of the blood-royal before a large mirror, with a candle burning on either side, I would see a sudden reflection of the Persian beauty by the side of my own. A swift turn of her neck, a quick eager glance of intense passion and pain glowing in her large dark eyes, just a suspicion of speech on her dainty red lips, her figure, fair and slim crowned with youth like a blossoming creeper, quickly uplifted in her graceful tilting gait, a dazzling flash of pain and craving and ecstasy, a smile and a glance and a blaze of jewels and silk, and she melted away. A wild glist of wind, laden with all the fragrance of hills and woods, would put out my light, and I would fling aside my dress and lie down on my bed, my eyes closed and my body thrilling with delight, and there around me in the breeze, amid all the perfume of the woods and hills, floated through the silent gloom many a caress and many a kiss and many a tender touch of hands, and gentle murmurs in my ears, and fragrant breaths on my brow; or a sweetly-perfumed kerchief was wafted again and again on my cheeks. Then slowly a mysterious serpent would twist her stupefying coils about me; and heaving a heavy sigh, I would lapse into insensibility, and then into a profound slumber.

One evening I decided to go out on my horse—I do not know who implored me to stay-but I would listen to no entreaties that day. My English hat and coat were resting on a rack, and I was about to take them down when a sudden whirlwind, crested with the sands of the Susta and the dead leaves of the Avalli hills, caught them up, and whirled them round and round, while a loud peal of merry laughter rose higher and higher, striking all the chords of mirth till it died away in the land of sunset.

I could not go out for my ride, and the next day I gave up my queer English coat and hat for good.

That day again at dead of night I heard the stifled heart-breaking sobs of some one—as if below the bed, below the floor, below the stony foundation of that gigantic palace, from the depths of a dark damp grave, a voice piteously cried and implored me: "Oh, rescue me! Break through these doors of hard illusion, deathlike slumber and fruitless dreams, place by your side on the saddle, press me to your heart, and, riding through hills and woods and across the river, take me to the warm radiance of your sunny rooms above!"

Who am I? Oh, how can I rescue thee? What drowning beauty, what incarnate passion shall I drag to the shore from this wild eddy of dreams? O lovely ethereal apparition! Where didst thou flourish and when? By what cool spring, under the shade of what date-groves, wast thou born—in the lap of what homeless wanderer in the desert? What Bedouin snatched thee from thy mother's arms, an opening bud plucked from a wild creeper, placed thee on a horse swift as lightning, crossed the burning sands, and took thee to the slave-market of what royal city? And there, what officer of the Badshah, seeing the glory of thy bashful blossoming youth, paid for thee in gold, placed thee in a golden palanquin, and offered thee as a present for the seraglio of his master? And O, the history of that place! The music of the sareng, the jingle of anklets, the occasional flash of daggers and the glowing wine of Shiraz poison, and the piercing flashing glance! What infinite grandeur, what endless servitude!

The slave-girls to thy right and left waved the chamar as diamonds flashed from their bracelets; the Badshah, the king of kings, fell on his knees at thy snowy feet in bejewelled shoes, and outside the terrible Abyssinian eunuch, looking like a messenger of death, but clothed like an angel, stood with a naked sword in his hand! Then, O, thou flower of the desert, swept away by the blood-stained dazzling ocean of grandeur, with its foam of jealousy, its rocks and shoals of intrigue, on what shore of cruel death wast thou cast, or in what other land more splendid and more cruel?

Suddenly at this moment that crazy Meher Ali screamed out: "Stand back! Stand back!! All is false! All is false!!" I opened my eyes and saw that it was already light. My chaprasi came and handed me my letters, and the cook waited with a salam for my orders.

I said; "No, I can stay here no longer." That very day I packed up, and moved to my office. Old Karim Khan smiled a little as he saw me. I felt nettled, but said nothing, and fell to my work.

As evening approached I grew absent-minded; I felt as if I had an appointment to keep; and the work of examining the cotton accounts seemed wholly useless; even the Nizamat of the Nizam did not appear to be of much worth. Whatever belonged to the present, whatever was moving and acting and working for bread seemed trivial, meaningless, and contemptible.

I threw my pen down, closed my ledgers, got into my dog-cart, and drove away. I noticed that it stopped of itself at the gate of the marble palace just at the hour of twilight. With quick steps I climbed the stairs, and entered the room.

A heavy silence was reigning within. The dark rooms were looking sullen as if they had taken offence. My heart was full of contrition, but there was no one to whom I could lay it bare, or of whom I could ask forgiveness. I wandered about the dark rooms with a vacant mind. I wished I had a guitar to which I could sing to the unknown: "O fire, the poor moth that made a vain effort to fly away has come back to thee! Forgive it but this once, burn its wings and consume it in thy flame!"

Suddenly two tear-drops fell from overhead on my brow. Dark masses of clouds overcast the top of the Avalli hills that day. The gloomy woods and the sooty waters of the Susta were waiting in terrible suspense and in an ominous calm. Suddenly land, water, and sky shivered, and a wild tempest-blast rushed howling through the distant pathless woods, showing its lightning-teeth like a raving maniac who had broken his chains. The desolate halls of the palace banged their doors, and moaned in the bitterness of anguish.

The servants were all in the office, and there was no one to light the lamps. The night was cloudy and moonless. In the dense gloom within I could distinctly feel that a woman was lying on her face on the carpet below the bed—clasping and tearing her long dishevelled hair with desperate fingers. Blood was tricking down her fair brow, and she was now laughing a hard, harsh, mirthless laugh, now bursting into violent wringing sobs, now rending her bodice and striking at her bare bosom, as the wind roared in through the open window, and the rain poured in torrents and soaked her through and through.

All night there was no cessation of the storm or of the passionate cry. I wandered from room to room in the dark, with unavailing sorrow. Whom could I console when no one was by? Whose was this intense agony of sorrow? Whence arose this inconsolable grief?

And the mad man cried out: "Stand back! Stand back!! All is false! All is false!!"

I saw that the day had dawned, and Meher Ali was going round and round the palace with his usual cry in that dreadful weather. Suddenly it came to me that perhaps he also had once lived in that house, and that, though he had gone mad, he came there every day, and went round and round, fascinated by the weird spell cast by the marble demon.

Despite the storm and rain I ran to him and asked: "Ho, Meher Ali, what is false?"

The man answered nothing, but pushing me aside went round and round with his frantic cry, like a bird flying fascinated about the jaws of a snake, and made a desperate effort to warn himself by repeating: "Stand back! Stand back!! All is false! All is false!!"

I ran like a mad man through the pelting rain to my office, and asked Karim Khan: "Tell me the meaning of all this!"

What I gathered from that old man was this: That at one time countless unrequited passions and unsatisfied longings and lurid flames of wild blazing pleasure raged within that palace, and that the curse of all the heart-aches and blasted hopes had made its every stone thirsty and hungry, eager to swallow up like a famished ogress any living man who might chance to approach. Not one of those who lived there for three consecutive nights could escape these cruel jaws, save Meher Ali, who had escaped at the cost of his reason.

I asked: "Is there no means whatever of my release?" The old man said: "There is only one means, and that is very difficult. I will tell you what it is, but first you must hear the history of a young Persian girl who once lived in that pleasure-dome. A stranger or a more bitterly heart-rending tragedy was never enacted on this earth."

Just at this moment the coolies announced that the train was coming. So soon? We hurriedly packed up our luggage, as the tram steamed in. An English gentleman, apparently just aroused from slumber, was looking out of a first-class carriage endeavouring to read the name of the station. As soon as he caught sight of our fellow-passenger, he cried, "Hallo," and took him into his own compartment. As we got into a second-class carriage, we had no chance of finding out who the man was nor what was the end of his story.

I said; "The man evidently took us for fools and imposed upon us out of fun. The story is pure fabrication from start to finish." The discussion that followed ended in a lifelong rupture between my theosophist kinsman and myself.

**Rabindranath Tagore and Short Story:**

"**Hungry Stones**" (Bengali: *Kshudhita Pashan or Khudito Pashan*) is a Bengali short story written by Rabindranath Tagore in 1895. As a key figure in the modernization of Bengali literature, Rabindranath Tagore wrote in every literary form that existed at the time: poetry, drama, prose, memoir, philosophy, musical lyrics. But he didn't write in every form all of the time, and the vast majority of his short stories were written at the end of the 19th century. As the introduction to this Penguin collection of Tagore's stories states, the vast majority of Tagore's short stories were written in the 1890s, and this collection almost exclusively focuses on short fiction from that period.

Tagore wrote short fiction during this period mainly because that's what there was a demand for at the time. Readers of Bengali fiction at the time first and foremost read Bengali-language literature publications. It wasn't an uncommon practice for Bengali writers to serialize novels in these periodicals, much like Charles Dickens would serialize his novels in the British literary press.

Given the demands of his readership, Tagore embraced the short story form, and these works bear many of his hallmarks. Their subject matter is concerned with everyday lives of all sorts of people, and there's equal attention and reverence paid to characters from all works of life. As was the case in his political beliefs and religious practice, Tagore's stories valued individual humans themselves over the class or caste distinctions that might define them, and the sympathy or antipathy he generates for his characters has to do with the character's own ethical merits or peculiarities—not any sort of class or ethnic identity. Tagore's stories, while focused on a wide swath of characters, do tend to employ a few common tropes and themes. We see a number of tribulations caused by the need to acquire a bridal dowry, as well as the evolving discussion of male and female domestic roles within a marriage. There are also a number of supernatural tales with run the gamut from all-out ghost stories to otherwise realist shorts that touch on superstition.

**Summary and Analysis:**

**Summary:**

The story opens with a man and his theosophist relative boarding a train on a return trip home to Calcutta from their puja holiday. They sit near a man who they first mistake for a Muslim from Northern India on account of his style of dress, but who they quickly realize is a Bengali Babu. They are struck by his eloquence and worldliness, and can't tear themselves away from listening to him talk. He keeps them up all night telling them a story.

The storyteller recounts a time when he took a job in the Indian Hyderabad region, collecting a cotton tax in the town of Barich. He describes the town as the most romantic place, cut through by the river Shusta. On the outskirts of the town is a towering white palace built by Shah Mahmud II, impressive to look at but long abandoned. Local townspeople tell the storyteller not to live in the temple, and it has such a bad reputation that even the thieves stay away from it.

It's easy for the storyteller to heed the locals' warnings while he is busy with his job, but as the pace of the cotton market slows down, he can't help but succumb to its hard-to-place allure. He visits the temple one night and is drawn into a vision in which the temple's festivities from 250 years ago come to life, with flowing decorations, bathing women, and a royal scene. A gust of wind shakes him from his trance.

He's drawn back for dozens of subsequent nights, referring to these as his *One Thousand and One Nights.* During the day he lives his tedious life as a tax collector, but at night he goes to the temple and disappears into these elaborate hallucinations of lust for beautiful women and boundless material pleasures. In his waking life, he totally forgets his dream life in the temple, and in his dream life in the temple, his existence as a functionary seems just as much a fantasy.

One night a spirit cries to the storyteller, asking him to help her escape from the temple, and he is consumed by an urge to help her out. It's now that the storyteller starts to wonder what the local madman means when he hollers "Keep away! Keep away! All is false! All is false!" The storyteller asks a friend at his office, Karim Khan about it, and Khan tells him that the palace used to be a site of extravagant lust, and now it's haunted by spirits who want to consume the soul of whoever enters it. The only man who has spent more than three nights there and made it out is that very mad man, Meher Ali.

Just as the storyteller is about to tell the original pair introduced in the story—the man that boards the train and his theosophist relative—how he managed to escape the clutches of the temple, the pair gets off the train at their destination. The man and his theosophist relative begin to argue over whether the storyteller's tale was true, and their argument ends in an irreconcilable split between the two men.

**Analysis:**

"The Hungry Stones" is one of the several stories in Tagore's oeuvre that depicts functionaries of the Indian government, which Tagore uses to draw a tension between the modernizing Indian state and the types of Indian lives that fall outside the hegemony of that British colonial order. Here, we have the tale of a tax-collector who sheds his tight-fitting Western garb—a jacket and trousers—to assume the baggy pajamas of the royal court from 250 years ago that he's drawn deeper into during his sleeping hours.

While Tagore makes it clear at the end of the story that this royal court's extravagance makes it a deadly trap for those who succumb to the temptation to try and indulge their lustiest desires, this supernatural explanation falls a bit short of what we may suspect the appeal of this older Indian court truly is. Under current British colonial rule, our storyteller is a functionary, but perhaps under Shah Mahmud II's he would have been able to indulge in all manner of earthly pleasures instead. Tagore draws a keen parable of Indian yearning for a kind of past that represents something radically different than its colonized present in the late 1800s.

This story also illustrates Tagore's sense of humor when it comes to the conventions of the narrative form. For one, the storyteller references *One Thousand and One Arabian Nights*, a collection of folk tales often framed as stories within stories much like "The Hungry Stones" itself. Speaking of Tagore's narrative playfulness, he seems to have fun weaving a shaggy dog tale that lacks any real climax. Just as the story is getting really good—just as the storyteller is about to tell us how he escaped the Shah's temple with (presumably) his sanity intact—the people who we are listening to the story must get off the train. Our pleasure as readers mirrors the storyteller's pleasure in the fantasies: tempted, but never truly fulfilled.

**Short questions and answers:**

1. **Who is the protagonist of "The Hungry Stones"?**

    Ans: Mydeen, a young tax collector.

    **2. What is the legend of the "hungry stones"?**

    Ans: The legend states that the stones are possessed by the spirits of merchants who were wrongly punished by the king.

3. **What is the significance of the deserted station?**

    Ans: The deserted station serves as a symbol of isolation and foreboding.

4. **What is the role of the stranger in the story?**

    Ans: The stranger serves as a warning to Mydeen about the dangers of the village.

5. **What is the theme of the story?**

    Ans:The theme of the story is the power of superstition and the supernatural.

6. **What is the significance of the "hungry stones"?**

    Ans: The "hungry stones" symbolize the destructive power of greed and revenge.

7. **What is the fate of Mydeen?**

    Ans: Mydeen disappears, and his fate is left unknown.

8. **What is the author's message?**

Ans: The author's message is that there are forces in the world that are beyond human understanding and control.

9. **What is the significance of the village?**

Ans: The village serves as a symbol of isolation and superstition.

10. **What is the genre of the story?**

Ans: The genre of the story is supernatural fiction/horror.

**2marks Questions and Answers:**

**1. What is the central theme of The Hungry Stones?**

The story explores themes of illusion, memory, and the supernatural. It shows how the past can overpower the present, especially in a place filled with history. The palace symbolizes how human emotions and desires linger, blurring the line between reality and imagination.

**2. Who is the narrator of the story?**

The narrator is a tax collector who recounts his strange experiences while staying in a deserted palace. He is educated and rational, yet gradually becomes influenced by the mysterious atmosphere of the place, making his account both believable and haunting.

**3. What is special about the palace in the story?**

The palace is believed to be haunted by the past, especially by spirits of Mughal-era inhabitants. It seems alive with memories, drawing people into its illusionary world. The building symbolizes history's grip, where emotions and past lives continue to echo.

**4. How does the palace affect the narrator?**

The narrator becomes enchanted by the palace and starts experiencing visions of a royal past filled with music, dance, and beauty. He feels emotionally connected to these illusions, losing touch with reality and becoming deeply absorbed in the imagined world.

**5. Who warns the narrator about the palace?**

A fellow traveler warns the narrator about staying in the palace, suggesting it is dangerous due to supernatural forces. However, the narrator ignores the warning, driven by curiosity and fascination, which ultimately leads him into a strange and dreamlike experience.

**6. What role does imagination play in the story?**

Imagination plays a crucial role, as it shapes the narrator's experiences. It is unclear whether the events are real or imagined, emphasizing how the human mind can create vivid realities. The story suggests that imagination can be both enchanting and dangerous.

**7. What is the significance of the title The Hungry Stones?**

The title suggests that the stones of the palace are "hungry" for human emotions and experiences. They absorb and replay the past, trapping visitors in their spell. It symbolizes how places can retain memories and influence those who come near them.

**8. What is the ending of the story?**

The narrator eventually leaves the palace, but the experience leaves a lasting impact on him. The story ends ambiguously, leaving readers unsure whether the events were supernatural or psychological, reinforcing the mysterious and haunting nature of the tale.

**9. What kind of place surrounds the palace?**

The palace is surrounded by a lonely and quiet area near a river. There are rocky hills and very few people living nearby. The place feels isolated and mysterious, which adds to the strange and supernatural atmosphere of the story.

**10. What time period do the narrator's visions belong to?**

The narrator's visions seem to belong to the Mughal period. He sees scenes of royal life, including kings, courtiers, and beautiful women. These images suggest that the palace was once full of luxury, pleasure, and grand celebrations.

**11. What kind of sounds does the narrator hear?**

The narrator hears soft music, footsteps, and the sound of flowing water. These sounds seem to come from another time and create a magical atmosphere. They make the narrator feel that the palace is alive with memories of its past.

**12. Why does the narrator ignore the warning?**

The narrator ignores the warning because he is curious and does not believe in ghosts. He thinks the stories are exaggerated and wants to experience the place himself. His confidence and interest in adventure led him to stay in the palace.

**13. What kind of people lived in the palace earlier?**

The palace was once inhabited by rich and powerful people, likely from the Mughal court. They lived a life of luxury, with music, dance, and entertainment. Their presence seems to remain in the palace through the narrator's strange visions.

**14. How does the palace influence the narrator's mind?**

The palace slowly controls the narrator's thoughts and imagination. He becomes deeply involved in the visions and begins to feel that they are real. This influence weakens his connection with the present and draws him into the past.

**15. What is the mood of the story?**

The mood of the story is mysterious and slightly frightening. It creates a sense of wonder and suspense. The strange events, quiet surroundings, and unclear reality make the reader feel both curious and uneasy.

**16. Is the story completely supernatural?**

The story is not completely supernatural. It leaves room for doubt, as the events could be caused by the narrator's imagination. This mix of reality and fantasy makes the story more interesting and open to different interpretations.

Questions and Answers:

**1. Analyze the theme of superstition in "The Hungry Stones". How does the author use the legend of the "hungry stones" to explore the power of superstition in shaping human behavior?**

**Answer**

In "The Hungry Stones", Tagore explores the theme of superstition through the legend of the "hungry stones". The author shows how superstition can control people's lives, leading them to commit terrible acts. The legend of the "hungry stones" is used to explain the strange occurrences in the village, and the villagers' belief in the legend is what gives it power. The author suggests that superstition can be a powerful tool for social control, and that it can be used to justify violence and oppression. Through the character of Mydeen, Tagore also shows how superstition can be used to manipulate and exploit individuals.

**2. Discuss the symbolism of the "hungry stones" in the story. What do they represent, and how do they relate to the themes of the story?**

**Answer**

The "hungry stones" are a symbol of the destructive power of greed and revenge. They represent the darker aspects of human nature, and the ways in which people can be consumed by their own desires and ambitions. The "hungry stones" are also a symbol of the supernatural forces that lie beyond human understanding. They represent the unknown, and the ways in which it can be both fascinating and terrifying. Through the symbolism of the "hungry stones", Tagore explores the themes of superstition, greed, and the supernatural.

**3. Analyze the character of Mydeen in "The Hungry Stones". What are his strengths and weaknesses, and how does he relate to the themes of the story?**

**Answer**

Mydeen is the protagonist of "The Hungry Stones", and he is a complex and nuanced character. His strengths include his curiosity and his determination to uncover the truth about the "hungry stones". However, his weaknesses include his skepticism and his lack of understanding of the supernatural forces that are at work in the village. Through Mydeen's character, Tagore explores the theme of superstition and the ways in which it can be both fascinating and terrifying. Mydeen's experiences in the village serve as a catalyst for the events of the story, and his character helps to illustrate the dangers of underestimating the power of superstition.

**4. Discuss the setting of "The Hungry Stones" and its significance to the story. How does the author use the setting to create a sense of atmosphere and mood?**

**Answer**

The setting of "The Hungry Stones" is a remote village in India, and it plays a crucial role in the story. The author uses the setting to create a sense of atmosphere and mood, and to explore the themes of superstition and the supernatural. The village is portrayed as a place of mystery and intrigue, where the boundaries between reality and the supernatural are blurred. The author's use of descriptive language helps to create a sense of foreboding and tension, and to draw the reader into the world of the story. The setting also serves to isolate the characters and to heighten the sense of drama and suspense.

**5. Analyze the ending of "The Hungry Stones" and its significance to the story. What message do you think the author is trying to convey through the ending?**

**Answer**

The ending of "The Hungry Stones" is ambiguous and open to interpretation. Mydeen disappears, and the villagers return to their normal lives. However, the reader is left with the sense that the "hungry stones" are still out there, waiting for their next victim. The ending suggests that the supernatural forces that are at work in the village are beyond human understanding and control. The author may be trying to convey the message that there are forces in the world that are beyond our comprehension, and that we must be careful not to underestimate their power. The ending also serves to underscore the theme of superstition and the ways in which it can be both fascinating and terrifying.

**6. Discuss the role of the stranger in "The Hungry Stones". What significance does he hold in the story, and how does he relate to the themes of the story?**

**Answer**

The stranger in "The Hungry Stones" plays a crucial role in the story. He is the one who tells Mydeen about the legend of the "hungry stones" and warns him about the dangers of the village. The stranger's significance lies in the fact that he is the only one who seems to understand the true nature of the village and the supernatural forces that are at work there. He serves as a foil to Mydeen, who is skeptical and dismissive of the legend. Through the stranger's character, Tagore explores the theme of superstition and the ways in which it can be both fascinating and terrifying.

**7. Analyze the use of imagery and symbolism in "The Hungry Stones". How does the author use these literary devices to create a sense of atmosphere and mood?**

**Answer**

Tagore's use of imagery and symbolism in "The Hungry Stones" is masterful. He uses vivid and evocative language to create a sense of atmosphere and mood that draws the reader into the world of the story. The image of the "hungry stones" themselves is a powerful symbol of the supernatural forces that are at work in the village. The author also uses imagery and symbolism to create a sense of foreboding and tension, such as the description of the deserted station and the hidden chamber. Through his use of imagery and symbolism, Tagore creates a sense of atmosphere and mood that is both haunting and unforgettable.

**8. Discuss the theme of isolation in "The Hungry Stones". How does the author use the setting and characters to explore this theme?**

**Answer**

The theme of isolation is a powerful one in "The Hungry Stones". Tagore uses the setting and characters to explore this theme in a way that is both subtle and profound. The village itself is isolated and remote, cut off from the rest of the world. Mydeen, the protagonist, is also isolated, both physically and emotionally. He is a stranger in the village, and his skepticism and dismissiveness of the legend serve to further isolate him from the villagers. Through the theme of isolation, Tagore explores the idea that we are all alone in the world, and that our experiences and perceptions are unique to us.

**9. Analyze the character of Mydeen's servant in "The Hungry Stones". What role does he play in the story, and what significance does he hold?**

**Answer**

Mydeen's servant plays a significant role in "The Hungry Stones". He is the one who first tells Mydeen about the strange occurrences in the village, and he serves as a source of information and guidance for Mydeen throughout the story. The servant's significance lies in the fact that he is the only one who seems to understand the true nature of the village and the supernatural forces that are at work there. He serves as a foil to Mydeen, who is skeptical and dismissive of the legend. Through the servant's character, Tagore explores the theme of superstition and the ways in which it can be both fascinating and terrifying.

**10. Discuss the significance of the title "The Hungry Stones". What does it reveal about the story, and what themes does it relate to?**

**Answer**

The title "The Hungry Stones" is significant because it reveals the central theme of the story: the supernatural forces that are at work in the village. The "hungry stones" themselves are a symbol of the destructive power of greed and revenge. The title also relates to the theme of superstition, which is a powerful force in the story. The use of the word "hungry" also implies a sense of longing and desire, which is reflected in the characters' experiences throughout the story. Overall, the title "The Hungry Stones" is a powerful and evocative one that sets the tone for the rest of the story.

**Some More Questions to Look at :-**

**1. Who is the narrator of the story, and what is his relationship with his kinsman?**

The narrator is a government servant who tells the story of his kinsman, a young man who took up a post under the Nizam of Hyderabad. The narrator's exact relationship to his kinsman is not explicitly defined, but he seems to be an elder relative or a mentor figure.

**2 Describe the initial impression the narrator and his kinsman have of the man they meet on the train. What qualities make him stand out?**

The man they meet on the train, known as Srijut, impresses them with his sophisticated and commanding presence. He exudes confidence and has an air of mystery about him, which captivates the narrator and his kinsman.

**3. What was the narrator's occupation and why did he leave his previous job to work for the Nizam of Hydria?**

The narrator's kinsman was a government servant who took up a new position with the Nizam of Hyderabad for better prospects and possibly a more prestigious role. The change is driven by career advancement opportunities.

**4. Describe the setting of the marble palace in Barich. What historical details are provided about its construction and original use?**

The marble palace in Barich is depicted as a grand, yet eerie structure built by a Mughal emperor for leisure and pleasure. The palace was a site of opulent parties and luxurious living, now fallen into disrepair and rumored to be haunted.

**5. Why does Karim Khan, the old clerk, warn the narrator about staying in the palace at night?**

Karim Khan warns the narrator because the palace is believed to be haunted by the spirits of its past occupants. He shares stories of inexplicable and frightening events experienced by those who previously stayed there, suggesting a malevolent supernatural presence.

**6 What strange experiences does the narrator begin to have in the palace? How does he describe these occurrences?**

The narrator begins to have vivid visions and auditory hallucinations of the past, seeing grand parties, hearing music, and feeling the presence of people who once inhabited the palace. These occurrences are so realistic that they make him question his own sanity.

**7. How does the narrator's perception of reality change during his star palace?**

The narrator's perception of reality becomes increasingly distorted. live more in the past he sees in his visions than in the present, maki for him to distinguish between what is real and what is a hallucination.

**8. Who does the narrator believe is guiding him through the palace at night, and what scenes does he witness?**

The narrator believes that an unseen spirit or force is guiding him through the palace. He witnesses scenes of royal banquets, dances, and other activities from the Mughal era, experiencing them as if he were actually present in those times.

**9. What role does the character Meher Ali play in the story?**

Meher Ali is a local madman who serves as a warning figure in the story. His repeated cries of "Stop! Don't go there!" suggest he has had his own terrifying experiences with the palace, reinforcing its ominous reputation and the dangers of the supernatural.

**10. What specific warnings does Karim Khan give the narrator about the palace, and how does the narrator initially react to these warnings?**

Karim Khan warns the narrator about the palace's haunted nature, sharing stories of previous tenants who encountered terrifying supernatural events. The narrator initially dismisses these warnings, considering them to be superstitions or exaggerations.

**11. Detail the historical context of the marble palace as described in the story. Who built it and for what purpose?**

The marble palace was constructed by a Mughal emperor as a pleasure retreat. It was designed to be a place of extravagant leisure, filled with lavish decorations, beautiful gardens, and spaces for entertainment and relaxation.

**12. What changes occur in the narrator's behavior and routine as he spends more time in the palace?**

As the narrator spends more time in the palace, he becomes more withdrawn and preoccupied with his visions. He starts to spend his nights wandering through the palace, captivated by the scenes from the past, which leads to his increasing isolation from reality.

**13. Describe the interactions between the narrator and the figure he believes to be guiding him through the palace.**

The interactions are subtle and mysterious. The narrator feels the presence of the guide, who leads him to various parts of the palace where he witnesses different scenes. The guide's identity remains ambiguous, adding to the story's supernatural allure.

**14. What significant events or visions does the narrator experience during his nighttime wanderings in the palace?**

The narrator experiences grand feasts, musical performances, and intimate. moments of the past inhabitants. These visions are rich in detail, making him feel

**LONG QUESTIONS AND ANSWERS**

**1. Discuss the theme of illusion vs reality in "The Hungry Stones."**

The theme of illusion versus reality forms the backbone of "The Hungry Stones." Through the narrator's experiences, Tagore explores how fragile human perception can be and how easily it can be shaped by imagination, environment, and desire.

At the beginning of the story, the narrator is presented as a rational and practical individual. As a tax collector, he represents logic, order, and modern thinking. He dismisses local superstitions about the haunted palace and confidently chooses to stay there. However, this sense of certainty gradually begins to weaken once he becomes exposed to the palace's mysterious atmosphere.

As night falls, thc narrator starts experiencing strange and vivid sensations. He hears music, footsteps, and voices, and he sees images of dancers, courtiers, and a beautiful woman from the Mughal era. These experiences are described in such rich detail that they appear real not only to the narrator but also to the reader. This creates a powerful sense of ambiguity—are these supernatural events, or are they merely illusions produced by the narrator's mind?

Tagore deliberately avoids giving a definite answer. Instead, he keeps the boundary between illusion and reality blurred throughout the story. This ambiguity is crucial because it reflects the narrator's psychological state. As he spends more time in the palace, his ability to distinguish between what is real and what is imagined gradually diminishes. He becomes emotionally involved in the dream-like world of the past, particularly in his fascination with the mysterious woman.

The palace itself plays a key role in strengthening this theme. Its silence, isolation, and historical richness create the perfect environment for imagination to flourish. The narrator, cut off from the outside world, becomes more vulnerable to these influences. His mind begins to recreate or accept the illusions as reality.

Through this theme, Tagore presents a deeper message about human nature. People often seek escape from their mundane lives, and in doing so, they may become trapped in illusions. The narrator's experience serves as a warning about the dangers of losing oneself in fantasy. When imagination overpowers reason, it can lead to confusion, obsession, and even loss of identity.

Thus, "The Hungry Stones" masterfully portrays the interplay between illusion and reality, showing that the line between them is often thin and easily crossed. The story reminds readers to remain grounded in reality while acknowledging the powerful influence of imagination.

**2. Describe the role of the palace in the story.**

In "The Hungry Stones," the palace is far more than just a physical setting; it is the central force that shapes the narrative and influences the characters. Rabindranath Tagore presents the palace as a mysterious and almost living entity, filled with the echoes of its past.

Historically, the palace belonged to Mughal rulers and was once a place of immense luxury, pleasure, and cultural richness. Even though it is now abandoned, it seems to retain the memories of its glorious past. This makes the palace a powerful symbol of history that refuses to fade away. The narrator's decision to stay there, despite warnings, sets the stage for the unfolding of supernatural or psychological events.

One of the most striking aspects of the palace is its transformation at night. During the day, it appears silent and lifeless, but at night, it seems to awaken. The narrator hears music, sees dancers and courtiers, and feels as though he has been transported into another era. This transformation gives the palace a dual nature—both real and illusory.

The palace also plays a crucial role in influencing the narrator's mind. Its isolation and eerie silence create a sense of detachment from reality. In such an environment, the narrator's imagination becomes more active, making him more susceptible to visions and hallucinations. Gradually, he becomes emotionally and psychologically absorbed in the world the palace presents to him.

Moreover, the palace symbolizes danger and entrapment. It is described as having "hungry stones," suggesting that it consumes those who become fascinated by it. The narrator's growing obsession with the palace and its visions shows how it feeds upon his thoughts and identity. He risks losing himself completely in its illusions.

The palace also represents the theme of the power of the past. It acts as a bridge between past and present, showing how history can influence and even dominate the living. The narrator becomes a medium through which the past seems to relive itself.

Thus, the palace functions as a setting, a symbol, and a character all at once. It is central to the story's themes of illusion, memory, and psychological influence, making it one of the most important elements in the narrative.

### 3. Give a character sketch of the narrator.

The narrator of "The Hungry Stones" is a well-developed character whose transformation reflects the central themes of the story. Rabindranath Tagore uses him to explore the conflict between reason and imagination.

At the beginning, the narrator is introduced as a rational and educated tax collector. He represents modern, logical thinking and does not believe in supernatural stories. His confidence in his own reasoning is evident when he ignores the warnings about the haunted palace and decides to stay there.

This shows his self-assurance and curiosity.

Curiosity is one of his most defining traits. It drives him to explore the unknown and experience something beyond his ordinary life. However, this curiosity also becomes his weakness, as it leads him into a situation where he loses control over his perceptions.

As the story progresses, the narrator undergoes a significant psychological transformation. He begins to experience strange visions and sensations, which gradually weaken his rational mindset. His logical thinking gives way to imagination, and he starts accepting the unreal as real.

The narrator is also emotionally sensitive and romantic. He is deeply affected by the beauty and charm of the visions he sees, particularly the image of a mysterious woman. This emotional vulnerability makes him more susceptible to the palace's influence.

Another important aspect of his character is his internal conflict. He struggles between his rational understanding of the world and his fascination with the supernatural experiences. This conflict highlights the central theme of illusion versus reality.

By the end of the story, the narrator appears almost obsessed and detached from reality. He becomes so deeply involved in the palace's world that he risks losing his identity. However, he is eventually rescued, suggesting that he regains some control over his mind.

Thus, the narrator represents the complexity of human nature. He shows how even a rational person can be influenced by imagination and desire, emphasizing the importance of maintaining a balance between reason and emotion.

**4. Explain the significance of the title "The Hungry Stones."**

The title "The Hungry Stones" is deeply symbolic and plays a crucial role in conveying the meaning of the story. Rabindranath Tagore uses this striking phrase to capture the mysterious and psychological nature of the narrative.

On a literal level, the "stones" refer to the palace where the narrator stays. These stones are part of an ancient structure that has witnessed a rich and luxurious past during the Mughal era. However, the addition of the word "hungry" gives these stones a living quality, suggesting that they possess a strange and supernatural power.

The "hunger" of the stones is not physical but psychological. The palace seems to consume the thoughts, emotions, and imagination of those who enter it. The narrator becomes a victim of this process as he becomes increasingly fascinated by the visions of the past. The palace draws him in and gradually takes control of his mind.

The title also highlights the theme of the power of the past. The palace is filled with memories of its former glory, and it "feeds" on the living by recreating those memories. This suggests that the past is never truly dead and can have a strong influence on the present.

Another important aspect of the title is its connection to illusion and entrapment. The palace creates a dream-like world that traps the narrator, making it difficult for him to return to reality. The "hungry stones" symbolize this consuming and imprisoning nature.

Furthermore, the title serves as a warning. It suggests that certain places or experiences can have a dangerous effect on the human mind. The narrator's near loss of identity shows how powerful this influence can be.

Thus, the title is highly effective in summarizing the main ideas of the story. It reflects the mystery, psychological depth, and thematic richness of the narrative, making it both memorable and meaningful.

# CHAPTER EIGHT

# Terms related to Narratology

## *Terms related to Narratology*

### *1.Author*

In literature, the author is the individual who conceives, creates, and shapes a literary work. The author is the originator of the ideas, language, narrative structure, and stylistic choices that define a text. While often identified as the person whose name appears on the cover of a book, in literary theory, the term carries a broader significance, encompassing both the creative and interpretive dimensions of writing. The author is the architect of meaning, the mind behind characters, plots, and settings, and the mediator between imagination and expression.

An author's role is multifaceted. First, they are the creator of content—the one who invents characters, constructs plots, and imagines worlds. For instance, J.K. Rowling created the fictional universe of *Harry Potter*, complete with magical rules, institutions, and characters. Second, the author functions as a stylistic designer, choosing diction, sentence structure, tone, and rhetorical devices that give the work its distinctive voice. The stylistic fingerprint of Ernest Hemingway, known for terse sentences and understated narration, is as influential as the story itself.

Authors also bear cultural and historical significance, as their work often reflects the society, time period, and personal experiences in which it was created. Chinua Achebe, for example, drew from the cultural and political realities of colonial and postcolonial Nigeria to explore themes of identity, conflict, and tradition in *Things Fall Apart*. Similarly, Jane Austen depicted the social norms and gender dynamics of early 19th-century England, blending satire with keen social observation.

While the author originates a work, literary theory distinguishes the author from the narrator or characters. The narrator's voice and perspective may differ significantly from the author's beliefs or intentions. This distinction is central in modern critical theory. Roland Barthes' essay "The Death of the Author" argues that a literary text should be interpreted independently of the author's biography or intention. From this perspective, meaning resides not in the author but in the interplay between text and reader. Nevertheless, understanding the author's background, context, and worldview can enrich comprehension and reveal subtler layers of meaning.

Authors may also serve as agents of ideology and philosophy, consciously or unconsciously embedding moral, political, or philosophical ideas within their narratives. Through choices in plot, character, and theme, they communicate perspectives on human nature, society, and ethics. Moreover, the author's decisions regarding form—poetry, prose, drama, or experimental structures—affect how readers experience and interpret the work.

In conclusion, the author in literature is both the originator of a text and the guiding creative force that shapes its narrative, style, and thematic resonance. While literary theory sometimes separates the author from textual interpretation, acknowledging the author's influence provides valuable insights into the historical, cultural, and personal dimensions of a literary work. The author is simultaneously a creator, a designer of style, and a lens through which readers can engage with the world of the text, making them an indispensable figure in literary studies.

## *2.Story*

In literature, a story is a sequence of events, real or imagined, that unfolds over time and is recounted or narrated for an audience. It represents the backbone of a literary work, providing the framework through which themes, characters, and conflicts are explored. While often used interchangeably with "plot," the story refers specifically to the raw chain of events—what happens in the narrative—without consideration of how those events are organized or presented.

A story typically comprises several fundamental elements. First, it requires characters, who act, experience, and interact within the narrative.

These characters can be human, animal, supernatural, or even symbolic embodiments of abstract ideas. Second, a story unfolds within a setting, encompassing both spatial and temporal dimensions. The setting situates the narrative in a specific place and time, providing context for characters' actions and societal influences. Third, a story involves events connected by causality: actions lead to consequences, conflicts arise, and resolutions or outcomes follow. The story is thus the chronological sequence of happenings, distinct from the plot, which may rearrange events for thematic, emotional, or narrative effect.

Stories serve multiple purposes in literature. They can entertain, engaging readers with suspense, humor, or adventure. They can educate, conveying moral lessons, philosophical insights, or historical knowledge. They can also preserve culture, transmitting myths, folklore, and collective memory across generations. For example, the epic stories in The Odyssey combine myth, history, and cultural ideals to teach values like heroism, loyalty, and perseverance. In modern literature, stories often delve into psychological realism, exploring inner conflicts and the complexities of human experience, as seen in Crime and Punishment.

The structure of a story can vary. Some narratives follow a straightforward chronological sequence, presenting events in the order they occur. Others may employ flashbacks, foreshadowing, or parallel storylines, creating a non-linear experience. Despite variations, stories maintain a causal chain where one event influences another, ensuring coherence and intelligibility.

Stories also interact with themes and motifs, which give them depth beyond the mere sequence of events. A story about a journey, for instance, may explore themes of self-discovery, freedom, or societal oppression, while a tale of conflict may examine moral choices, justice, or human nature. The narrative voice—who tells the story and from what perspective—further shapes the story's interpretation and emotional impact, linking it closely to the narrator and point of view.

In essence, the story is the fundamental "what happens" of literature. It provides the continuity, causality, and temporal framework that allow characters, settings, and themes to function effectively. While the plot, characterization, and stylistic devices organize and present the story, the story itself remains the essential sequence of events that defines the literary work. Understanding the story enables readers to grasp the skeleton of a narrative, the underlying sequence of experiences, and the foundation upon which all other literary elements are built.

# *3.Setting*

In literature, the setting refers to the time and place in which a story occurs, along with the social, cultural, and environmental conditions that shape the narrative. It provides the backdrop against which characters act and events unfold, influencing both the mood of the story and the behavior of the characters. Setting is more than a physical location; it encompasses historical period, societal norms, weather, architecture, and even symbolic or psychological dimensions.

**Components of Setting:**

1. Time – This includes the historical period, era, or specific moment in which a story takes place. It could be as broad as the Middle Ages in The Name of the Rose or as specific as a single night in The Tell-Tale Heart. Time shapes the plot, dictates technological and social possibilities, and influences characters' attitudes and choices.

2. Place – Physical locations such as cities, countries, buildings, or natural landscapes. For example, the moors in Wuthering Heights reflect the wild and turbulent emotions of the characters, while the confined spaces of 1984's dystopian London reinforce the novel's atmosphere of oppression.

3. Social Environment – Includes cultural norms, class structures, religion, politics, and economic conditions. In Pride and Prejudice, the social setting of early 19th-century England dictates courtship, marriage, and social mobility, shaping both plot and character decisions.

4. Atmosphere and Mood – The setting creates an emotional or psychological effect, often enhancing suspense, tension, or romance. A dark forest or stormy night may evoke fear or foreboding, while a sunny garden may symbolize innocence or hope.

**Types of Setting:**

- Historical Setting – Situates the story in a particular historical era, affecting events, social norms, and characters. Example: A Tale of Two Cities is set during the French Revolution.

- Geographical Setting – Focuses on physical landscapes and locations, which can symbolize themes or reflect character states. Example: The Australian Outback in Picnic at Hanging Rock conveys isolation and mystery.
- Cultural Setting – Highlights social customs, values, and beliefs influencing characters. Example: The caste system in India shapes social interactions in Untouchable.
- Symbolic or Psychological Setting – Places reflect inner states or thematic concerns. Example: the decaying mansion in *The Fall of the House of Usher* represents mental decay and doom.

**Functions of Setting:**

1. Contextualizes the Narrative – Time and place help readers understand the plausibility of events and the actions of characters.
2. Shapes Character Behavior – Characters respond to physical, social, and historical pressures imposed by the setting.
3. Enhances Mood and Atmosphere – Setting contributes to tone, suspense, and emotional resonance.
4. Supports Themes and Symbols – Physical and social environments often embody thematic elements or symbolism.

In conclusion, the setting is not merely a backdrop but an active force in literature. It situates the narrative in a specific context, shapes characters' actions and choices, establishes mood, and reinforces themes. By carefully analyzing the setting, readers gain insight into both the world of the story and the deeper messages the author conveys. A vivid, well-integrated setting makes a narrative immersive, believable, and meaningful.

# 4.Character

In literature, a character is an individual, animal, or personified entity that participates in the events of a narrative. Characters are central to storytelling because they drive the plot, embody themes, and allow readers to connect emotionally with the text. Through their actions, choices, and interactions, characters make abstract ideas concrete and create meaning in the story.

**Types of Characters:**

1. Protagonist – The main character around whom the story revolves. The protagonist typically faces conflicts, challenges, or dilemmas that drive the narrative forward. Example: Elizabeth Bennet is the protagonist whose intelligence, wit, and moral judgment shape the story's events.
2. Antagonist – The character or force that opposes the protagonist, creating conflict and tension. Example: Iago manipulates events and other characters to thwart Othello's goals.
3. Round Characters – Complex, multi-dimensional characters with a variety of traits, motivations, and emotions. They are realistic and capable of change. Example: Hamlet is psychologically complex, struggling with indecision, morality, and revenge.
4. Flat Characters – One-dimensional characters who exhibit a single trait or serve a specific function, often to support main characters or illustrate a theme. Example: The housekeeper in Frankenstein provides limited insight into the narrative and is mostly functional.
5. Dynamic Characters – Characters who undergo significant internal change, growth, or transformation over the course of the narrative. Example: Ebenezer Scrooge evolves from miserly and selfish to generous and compassionate.
6. Static Characters – Characters who remain largely unchanged, providing stability or contrast. Example: Sherlock Holmes in Sherlock Holmes is consistent in logic, intellect, and personality throughout the stories.
7. Stock Characters – Stereotypical or conventional figures representing common traits, roles, or social types. Examples include the "mad scientist," the "damsel in distress," or the "wise mentor."

**Characterization:**

Authors reveal characters through direct characterization, where traits are explicitly described, or indirect characterization, where traits are inferred from dialogue, actions, thoughts, appearance, or the reactions of other characters. For instance, Jay Gatsby is portrayed indirectly through his lavish parties, enigmatic behavior, and Nick Carraway's observations, creating layers of mystery and aspiration.

**Functions of Characters in Literature:**

1. Driving the Plot – Characters' decisions, conflicts, and actions propel the narrative forward.

2. Expressing Themes – Characters often embody ideas or societal issues. For example, in *To Kill a Mockingbird*, Atticus Finch represents justice and moral integrity.

3. Creating Emotional Engagement – Readers connect with characters through empathy, admiration, or dislike, deepening investment in the story.

4. Symbolic Roles – Characters can symbolize abstract concepts, such as innocence, corruption, or freedom.

In conclusion, characters are the lifeblood of literature. They give narratives meaning, shape plots, and embody themes, while providing readers with psychological, emotional, and moral points of connection. A well-crafted character—whether round, dynamic, or symbolic—transforms the story from a sequence of events into a meaningful human experience. Through character study, readers gain insight into both the narrative and the universal truths literature seeks to explore.

# 5.Plot

In literature, plot refers to the structured sequence of events in a narrative, arranged to create meaning, tension, and engagement for the reader. While a story is the raw chronological sequence of events—"what happens"—the plot is how those events are organized and presented, emphasizing causality, conflict, and resolution. The plot is the architecture of the narrative, shaping how the audience experiences the story.

**Elements of Plot:**

1. Exposition – The beginning of the story, which introduces characters, setting, and basic background information. Example: In Romeo and Juliet, the feud between the Montagues and Capulets is established, along with the social and historical context of Verona.

2. Rising Action – The series of events and conflicts that build tension and complicate the protagonist's situation. These events often reveal character traits and deepen thematic concerns. Example: The secret meetings and growing love between Romeo and Juliet intensify suspense.

3. Climax – The turning point or moment of greatest tension, where the main conflict reaches its peak. Example: Romeo kills Tybalt in *Romeo*

*and Juliet*, dramatically altering the story's trajectory.

4. Falling Action – Events that unfold after the climax, showing the consequences of the protagonist's decisions and the unraveling of conflicts.
5. Resolution / Denouement – The conclusion, where conflicts are resolved, loose ends tied, and the story reaches closure. Example: The tragic deaths of Romeo and Juliet bring resolution to their families' feud.

**Types of Plot Structures:**

- Linear Plot – Events occur in chronological order. Example: The Old Man and the Sea follows a straightforward timeline.
- Non-linear Plot – Events are presented out of order, often using flashbacks, dreams, or multiple perspectives. Example: One Hundred Years of Solitude employs non-linear chronology to enhance thematic depth.
- Circular / Cyclical Plot – The story ends where it begins, emphasizing repetition or inevitability. Example: Many myths and folktales feature cyclical structures.
- Episodic Plot – Consists of loosely connected episodes or adventures, typical in picaresque novels. Example: *Don Quixote* is structured around individual quests rather than a single linear arc.

**Plot vs. Story:**
The story is the chronological "what happened," while the plot is the deliberate arrangement of events, often designed to highlight themes, build suspense, or develop character. Authors manipulate plot through devices such as foreshadowing, flashbacks, suspense, and pacing to control readers' emotional and intellectual responses.

**Functions of Plot in Literature:**

1. Organizes the Narrative – Provides structure and coherence, ensuring that events make sense causally.
2. Drives Character Development – Conflicts and challenges force characters to act, change, or reveal their true selves.
3. Enhances Themes – Plot can underscore central ideas, such as justice, revenge, or transformation.

4. Engages the Reader – A well-crafted plot maintains interest through tension, surprise, and emotional resonance.

In conclusion, the plot is the engine of a literary work. It arranges events to create meaning, tension, and thematic resonance. By shaping how readers experience the story, the plot transforms a mere sequence of events into a structured, compelling narrative that conveys both entertainment and insight into human nature.

# 6.Narrator

In literature, a narrator is the voice or entity that tells the story to the reader. Unlike the author, who exists outside the text, the narrator exists within the narrative framework and shapes how events, characters, and settings are perceived. The narrator acts as an intermediary between the story and the audience, controlling the flow of information, revealing or withholding knowledge, and influencing the reader's interpretation.

**Functions of the Narrator:**

1. Conveying the Story – The narrator presents the sequence of events, guiding readers through the plot.
2. Shaping Perception – The narrator influences how characters and events are understood, whether objectively or subjectively.
3. Establishing Tone and Style – Through word choice, perspective, and personality, the narrator sets the mood and voice of the narrative.
4. Controlling Knowledge – The narrator determines what readers know, when they know it, and how much insight they gain into characters' thoughts and motivations.

**Types of Narrators:**

1. First-Person Narrator – Uses "I" or "we," providing a personal and subjective perspective. This narrator often shares thoughts, emotions, and interpretations but may be limited or biased.

   ◦ Example: The Catcher in the Rye is told by Holden Caulfield, whose personal biases, emotional turmoil, and limited understanding shape the story.

1. Second-Person Narrator – Uses "you," directly addressing the reader as a character. This is rare and often experimental, creating immersion and immediacy.

   ◦ Example: Bright Lights, Big City uses second-person narration to immerse the reader in the protagonist's experiences.

3. Third-Person Narrator – Uses "he," "she," or "they," and can vary in scope and knowledge.

   ◦ Omniscient – All-knowing, able to reveal multiple characters' thoughts, histories, and motives.

     ▪ Example: War and Peace presents the thoughts, feelings, and actions of numerous characters.

   ◦ Limited – Focuses closely on one character's perspective, revealing their thoughts and experiences while remaining external to others.

     ▪ Example: Harry Potter and the Sorcerer's Stone mainly follows Harry's perspective.

   ◦ Objective / Dramatic – Reports only observable actions and dialogue, without access to inner thoughts. This narrator is like a camera recording events.

     ▪ Example: Many short stories by Ernest Hemingway employ this "iceberg" style.

4. Unreliable Narrator – A narrator whose credibility is compromised due to bias, limited understanding, or intentional deceit. This creates ambiguity and invites readers to question the narrative.

   ◦ Example: The Tell-Tale Heart, where the narrator's madness distorts the story.

**Narrator vs. Author:**
It is crucial to distinguish the narrator from the author. The narrator may

express opinions, judgments, or biases that differ from those of the author. For instance, the satirical or ironic tone may come from the narrator, while the author uses this voice to convey commentary.

**Conclusion:**

The narrator is a pivotal element in literature, guiding readers through the narrative, shaping perception, and controlling access to information. By choosing a particular type of narrator—first-person, third-person limited or omniscient, objective, or unreliable—authors manipulate perspective, tone, and meaning. The narrator not only recounts events but also frames the reader's experience, transforming a simple sequence of events into a crafted literary work.

## 7.Points of View (POV)

In literature, point of view (POV) refers to the perspective from which a story is narrated. It determines who sees, experiences, and interprets the events of the narrative, shaping readers' understanding of characters, plot, and themes. The choice of POV affects intimacy, reliability, and the amount of information available to the audience, making it a crucial tool for authors in crafting meaning and emotional impact.

**Types of Point of View:**

1. First-Person POV – The story is told by a character using pronouns like "I" or "we." This perspective allows readers to experience events directly through the narrator's eyes, offering insight into their thoughts, feelings, and biases. However, it is inherently limited because readers only know what the narrator knows and may be subject to their personal interpretation.

   ◦ Example: The Catcher in the Rye is told by Holden Caulfield, whose subjective perspective colors the narrative with adolescent angst, cynicism, and emotional vulnerability.

2. Second-Person POV – Uses "you" to address the reader directly, effectively making them a character in the story. This POV is rare and often experimental, creating immediacy and immersive engagement.

- Example: Bright Lights, Big City immerses the reader in the protagonist's experiences by addressing them as "you," making them feel like part of the narrative.

3.  Third-Person POV – The story is told using "he," "she," or "they." It can vary in scope and knowledge:

    - Omniscient POV – The narrator knows everything: the thoughts, feelings, histories, and motives of all characters. This allows broad thematic exploration and multiple perspectives.

        - Example: War and Peace employs an omniscient narrator to explore the inner lives of numerous characters across historical events.

    - Limited POV – Focuses closely on a single character, revealing only their thoughts and perceptions. Other characters are seen externally.

        - Example: Harry Potter and the Sorcerer's Stone primarily follows Harry's perspective.

    - Objective / Dramatic POV – The narrator reports only observable actions and dialogue, without access to inner thoughts. This creates a detached, "camera-like" perspective.

        - Example: Many of Ernest Hemingway's short stories use this style, leaving interpretation to the reader.

4.  Multiple or Shifting POV – Some narratives use more than one POV, alternating between characters or narrative levels to show different perspectives. This can add complexity, tension, or irony.

    - Example: As I Lay Dying features multiple first-person narrators, providing fragmented and contrasting views of the same events.

**Functions of POV in Literature:**

1. Controls Reader Knowledge – POV determines how much information is revealed and when, creating suspense, surprise, or dramatic irony.
2. Shapes Reader Empathy – First-person and limited POVs foster intimacy, while omniscient POV allows broader understanding of multiple characters.
3. Influences Tone and Style – A narrator's personality and perspective affect the voice, mood, and thematic emphasis of the story.
4. Guides Interpretation – POV frames how readers perceive events, judge characters, and understand themes, shaping meaning throughout the text.

**Conclusion:**

Point of view is a foundational narrative element, determining who narrates the story, how events are filtered, and how readers engage with characters and plot. By selecting first-person, second-person, third-person limited or omniscient, or multiple POVs, authors control intimacy, reliability, and interpretation, making POV central to the art and craft of storytelling.

# 8.Chronotope

In literary theory, the term chronotope was introduced by Mikhail Bakhtin and refers to the intrinsic connection between time ("chrono") and space ("topos") in a narrative. Unlike mere setting, which identifies where and when a story occurs, the chronotope examines how time and space interact to shape the story's events, characters, and meaning. It emphasizes that narrative structures are inseparable from temporal and spatial dimensions, and that these dimensions influence how events unfold and how readers perceive them.

**Understanding the Concept:**

The chronotope is not simply the backdrop of a story; it is the narrative logic linking action to context. By analyzing chronotopes, critics can see how a story's temporal and spatial organization affects plot, character development, and thematic resonance. Time may be linear, circular, fragmented, or accelerated, while space may be confined, expansive, symbolic, or socially defined. The interaction of these elements creates a framework within which the narrative operates.

**Types of Chronotope:**

1. Adventure or Road Chronotope – Emphasizes movement across space and often depicts a journey through different locations over time. This chronotope is central to picaresque novels, epics, and travel narratives.

   ◦ Example: The Odyssey features Odysseus's long journey across various lands, where time and distance are integral to his adventures and character growth.

2. Threshold or Liminal Space Chronotope – Occurs in places of transition or decision-making, such as doorways, crossroads, or borders, where time and space intersect to create tension. Characters at these thresholds often face moral, emotional, or existential choices.

   ◦ Example: In Hamlet, the castle of Elsinore serves as a liminal space where political intrigue and personal dilemmas converge.

3. Historical Chronotope – Embeds the narrative in a specific historical period, where the conditions of time and place directly shape events, character behavior, and social dynamics.

   ◦ Example: War and Peace situates characters' personal stories within the Napoleonic Wars, showing how historical events influence individual lives.

4. Domestic or Home Chronotope – Focuses on enclosed spaces such as homes, villages, or estates, linking personal time with social and familial structures.

   ◦ Example: The Bennet family estate in Pride and Prejudice reflects social hierarchy, marital expectations, and character relationships.

5. Symbolic or Psychological Chronotope – The narrative space and temporal progression reflect internal states, dreams, or subjective experiences rather than literal geography.

   ◦ Example: The decaying mansion in The Fall of the House of Usher mirrors the characters' mental decline and impending doom.

**Functions of Chronotope in Literature:**

1. Shapes Plot and Conflict – The way time and space interact can heighten tension, influence pacing, and structure the story's events.
2. Develops Characters – Characters' actions and decisions are often determined or constrained by temporal and spatial contexts.
3. Supports Themes – Chronotopes can reinforce motifs, such as journey, confinement, historical inevitability, or psychological states.
4. Influences Reader Perception – By structuring narrative time and space, authors guide readers' understanding, emotional response, and interpretation of events.

**Conclusion:**

The chronotope is a critical tool for analyzing literature because it reveals how time and space function together to create meaning. By studying the chronotope, readers and critics gain insight into the narrative structure, character development, and thematic depth of a work. It demonstrates that literature is not merely a series of events but a complex temporal-spatial web that shapes human experience within the story.

**This table is designed to be thorough and easy to study:**

Term

Definition

Types

Examples

Functions in Literature

Author

The individual who creates a literary work, shaping ideas, style, narrative, and meaning.

N/A (focuses on creative role)

J.K. Rowling, Jane Austen, Chinua Achebe

Originates the work; shapes narrative, style, and themes; reflects personal, cultural, and historical context; mediates meaning for the reader.

Story

The chronological sequence of events in a narrative ("what happens"), independent of how it is told.

Linear, non-linear, episodic, cyclical

The Odyssey, Crime and Punishment

Provides the skeleton of the narrative; conveys events and experiences; underpins plot, character development, and thematic expression.

Setting

The time, place, and social environment in which a story occurs. Includes historical period, cultural context, and atmosphere.

Historical, geographical, cultural, symbolic/psychological

Wuthering Heights, Pride and Prejudice, 1984

Provides context; shapes character behavior; establishes mood and atmosphere; reinforces themes; situates narrative in space-time.

Character

A person, animal, or entity in a story whose actions and decisions drive the narrative and express themes.

Protagonist, antagonist, round, flat, dynamic, static, stock

Elizabeth Bennet, Ebenezer Scrooge, Iago

Drives plot; embodies themes; engages readers emotionally; allows exploration of human experience; can symbolize abstract ideas.

Plot

The structured arrangement of events in a narrative, showing causality, conflict, and resolution ("how it happens").

Linear, non-linear, cyclical, episodic

Romeo and Juliet, One Hundred Years of Solitude, The Old Man and the Sea

Organizes narrative; drives character development; enhances themes; maintains reader engagement; creates tension, suspense, and resolution.

Narrator

The voice that tells the story, guiding readers' understanding of events, characters, and themes.

First-person, second-person, third-person omniscient, third-person limited, objective/dramatic, unreliable

The Catcher in the Rye, Bright Lights, Big City, The Tell-Tale Heart

Conveys narrative; shapes perception; establishes tone; controls information; influences reliability and interpretation.

Point of View (POV)

The perspective from which a story is told, determining what readers know and how they interpret events.

First-person, second-person, third-person limited, third-person omniscient, objective, multiple/shifting

As I Lay Dying, Harry Potter and the Sorcerer's Stone, The Catcher in the Rye

Controls knowledge; shapes empathy; influences tone; frames interpretation; affects intimacy and reliability of narrative.

Chronotope

The intrinsic connection between time and space in a narrative, shaping events, characters, and meaning.

Adventure/road, threshold/liminal, historical, domestic/home, symbolic/psychological

The Odyssey, War and Peace, The Fall of the House of Usher

Integrates temporal and spatial dimensions; structures plot; shapes characters; reinforces themes; guides reader perception; links narrative events to context.

Here's a visual diagram linking all eight literary terms to show their relationships and how they interact in a narrative:

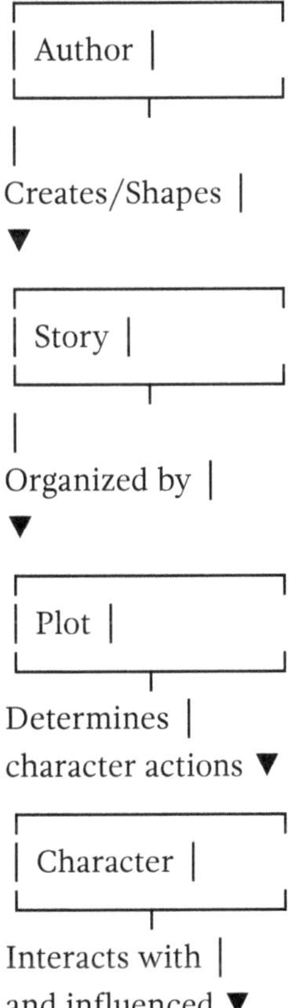

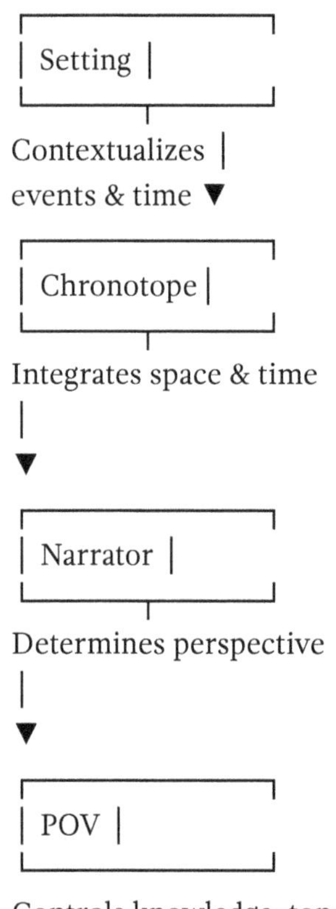


*How to read this diagram:*

1. Author → Story → Plot: The author creates the story (the raw sequence of events) and organizes it into a plot (structured events with conflict and resolution).
2. Plot → Character → Setting → Chronotope: The plot drives characters' actions, who interact with and are influenced by the setting. The chronotope links the temporal and spatial dimensions, giving meaning to events.
3. Chronotope → Narrator → POV: The narrative framework (time + space) is presented through a narrator, whose point of view controls how readers perceive events, characters, and themes.

Here's a color-coded, fully labeled visual study chart of the eight literary terms, including examples for each.

```
┌────────────────┐
│ Author │
│ (Creator of │
│ story & style)│
│ Examples: │
│ J.K. Rowling │
│ Jane Austen │
│ Chinua Achebe │
└───────┬────────┘
│
▼
┌────────────────┐
│ Story │
│ (Chronological│
│ sequence of │
│ events) │
│ Examples: │
│ The Odyssey │
│ Crime and │
│ Punishment │
└───────┬────────┘
│
▼
┌────────────────┐
│ Plot │
│ (Organized │
│ sequence; │
│ conflict & │
│ resolution) │
│ Examples: │
│ Romeo & Juliet│
│ The Old Man & │
│ the Sea │
└───────┬────────┘
```

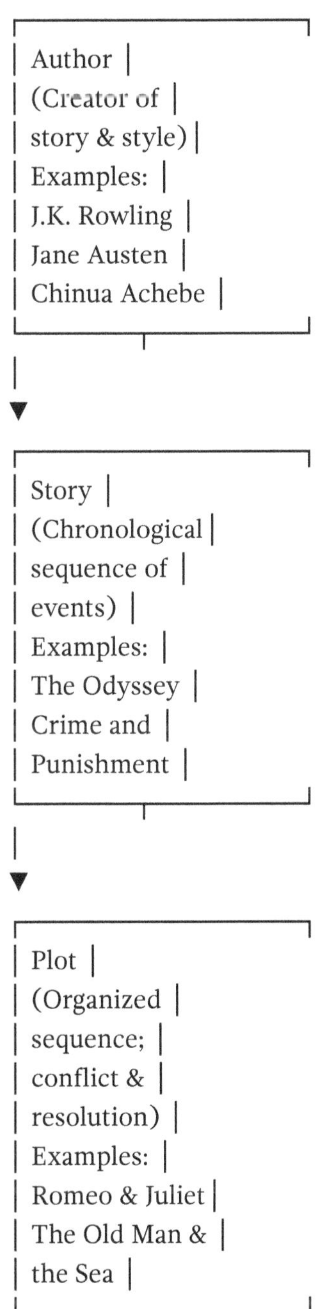

```
      |
      ▼
  ┌──────────────────┐
  │ Character        │
  │ (Agents of       │
  │ action;          │
  │ theme carriers)  │
  │ Examples:        │
  │ Elizabeth Bennet │
  │ Ebenezer Scrooge │
  │ Iago             │
  └────────┬─────────┘
      |
      ▼
  ┌──────────────────┐
  │ Setting          │
  │ (Time, Place,    │
  │ Social Context   │
  │ Atmosphere)      │
  │ Examples:        │
  │ Wuthering Heights│
  │ Pride & Prejudice│
  │ 1984             │
  └────────┬─────────┘
      |
      ▼
  ┌──────────────────┐
  │ Chronotope       │
  │ (Time + Space    │
  │ Interaction)     │
  │ Examples:        │
  │ The Odyssey      │
  │ War & Peace      │
  │ House of Usher   │
  └────────┬─────────┘
      |
```

▼

| Narrator |
| (Voice telling |
| the story) |
| Examples: |
| Holden Caulfield |
| Bright Lights, |
| Big City |
| The Tell-Tale |
| Heart |

|

▼

| POV |
| (Perspective; |
| knowledge & |
| interpretation) |
| Examples: |
| First-person |
| Third-person |
| Omniscient & |
| Limited |

## *How to Use This Chart:*

1. Follow the flow top to bottom: Author → Story → Plot → Character → Setting → Chronotope → Narrator → POV.
2. Color coding (if drawing by hand or digitally):

    - Author/Story/Plot: Creative & structural layer
    - Character/Setting/Chronotope: World-building & thematic layer
    - Narrator/POV: Perception & reader-experience layer

3. Examples in each box help anchor abstract concepts to real literature, improving recall.